COMMERCIAL GOODWILL

This is a volume in the
Arno Press collection

DIMENSIONS OF ACCOUNTING THEORY AND PRACTICE

Advisory Editor
Richard P. Brief

See last pages of this volume
for a complete list of titles

COMMERCIAL GOODWILL

ITS HISTORY, VALUE, AND TREATMENT IN ACCOUNTS

P. D. LEAKE

ARNO PRESS
A New York Times Company
New York • 1980

Editorial Supervision: Brian Quinn

Reprint Edition 1980 by Arno Press Inc.

DIMENSIONS OF ACCOUNTING THEORY AND PRACTICE
ISBN for complete set: 0-405-13475-4
See last pages of this volume for titles.

Manufactured in the United States of America

Library of Congress Cataloging in Publication Data

Leake, Percy Dewe.
Commercial goodwill.

(Dimensions of accounting theory and practice)
Reprint of the 1921 ed. published by I. Pitman, London.
1. Good-will (in business, etc.)--Accounting--History. I. Title. II. Series.
HF5681.G6L4 1980 657'.7 80-1507
ISBN 0-405-13532-7

COMMERCIAL GOODWILL

COMMERCIAL GOODWILL

ITS HISTORY, VALUE, AND TREATMENT IN ACCOUNTS

BY

P. D. LEAKE

FELLOW OF THE INSTITUTE OF CHARTERED ACCOUNTANTS IN ENGLAND AND WALES; FELLOW OF THE INSTITUTE OF DIRECTORS; FELLOW OF THE ROYAL STATISTICAL SOCIETY

AUTHOR OF

"*Depreciation and Wasting Assets and their Treatment in Computing Annual Profit and Loss*"; "*The Question of Depreciation, and the Measurement of Expired Outlay on Productive Plant: a Plea for the Study and Use of Better Methods*"; "*Leake's Register of Industrial Plant for the Measurement of Depreciation, with Introductory Notes*"; "*The Need of Present Accounting for Past Unexpired Capital Outlay*"; "*Can the Annual Assessment of Industrial Profit and Loss be Raised to an Exact Science?*"; "*The Use and Mis-use of the Sinking Fund,*" *etc., etc.*

LONDON

SIR ISAAC PITMAN & SONS, LTD.

PARKER STREET, KINGSWAY, W.C.2

BATH, MELBOURNE, TORONTO, NEW YORK

1921

Printed by
Sir Isaac Pitman & Sons, Ltd.
Bath, England

PREFACE

COMMERCIAL goodwill is legal property, and consists wholly of rights which may or may not have present exchangeable value. In its true economic meaning the term "commercial goodwill" covers a vast field of rights growing out of all kinds of past effort in seeking profit, increase of value, or other advantage which may be capable of future profitable development. These rights are legally protected under various names, both by statute law and by common law, for the use and benefit of the owner. Commercial goodwill may include any or all such property as business connection associated with names, persons and places of business, trade marks, patents and designs, copyright, and the right to exercise monopolies. The exchangeable value of goodwill is based on anticipation, and the character of the anticipation always is that the owner of any of these rights will earn future profit, increase of value, or other advantage in excess of the normal reward of any capital and human effort (which includes labour) needed to carry on the undertaking. Goodwill is generally assumed to possess present exchangeable value, and it often possesses great present exchangeable value.

The question whether or not these rights, growing out of past effort in profit-seeking, possess present exchangeable value, does not concern the legislature. The law extends its protection impartially to all such rights as a matter of equity, and on grounds of public policy, sometimes by statute as in (*a*) trade marks which are protected by the Trade Marks Act, 1905, (*b*) patents and designs, which are protected by the Patents and Designs Acts, 1907 and 1919, and (*c*) copyright, which is protected by the Copyright Act, 1911, and (*d*) other rights, less easy to define—which are protected by common law under the name of goodwill. Thus, although there is no Goodwill Act, a person who has acquired a business connection, either by his own industry and ability or by purchase from another man, and whether it be profitable or not, has a common law right. This right operates to prevent the connection being interfered with by the improper use of information or influence possessed by other persons formerly employed in the business. And a person who in his business uses any name or mark—other than a registered trade mark which is specially protected by the Trade Marks Act, 1905—has a common law right to prevent other persons from using the same so as to deceive the public into thinking that the business carried on by them, or the goods sold by them, are his.

It is clear that the word "goodwill" covers a more restricted area in its ordinary legal meaning than in its commercial meaning, because some of the rights having this common characteristic of growing out of past effort in profit-seeking are protected in law by separate statutes under names other than goodwill. For this reason the area covered by goodwill in law appears not to extend to those rights which are protected by separate statutes. Legal goodwill is confined to the connection of an established undertaking associated with names, persons and places of business, and also to unregistered marks. It is equally clear that the area covered by commercial goodwill is much wider including, by custom, and in fact, all rights growing out of past effort in profit-seeking. That this is so is obvious, and it often happens that a purchaser buys for a lump sum under the name of goodwill that which includes all these various rights commonly expected to be capable of earning in the future " extra-normal " or " super "-profit. Thus, although some of these allied rights receive separate statutory protection in law, their values cannot usually be ascertained and treated separately in commercial practice, and it is necessary always to bear this in mind when considering the nature and value of goodwill.

Certain legal aspects of commercial goodwill are stated in Chapter I, and grateful acknowledgment is made of indebtedness in this respect to standard legal works, and particularly to *The Laws of England*, by Lord Halsbury and other lawyers, published by Messrs. Butterworth & Co.

Particular attention is invited to the new definition of commercial goodwill which will be found in Chapter I; and to the demonstration, contained in Chapter II, of the fact that the value of commercial goodwill is equal to the present value of future super-profit. Practical illustrations of the method of computing the value of commercial goodwill of private undertakings and of public companies will be found in Chapters III and IV. It is shown in Chapter V that the cost of purchased goodwill should be gradually written off on the lines of some definite and regular scheme, and that the common practice adopted by companies of issuing permanent share capital to represent purchased goodwill is wrong in principle. It is suggested that all such capital should be issued in a redeemable form. In Chapter VII the interesting question is discussed—"To what extent is the value of goodwill included in plant valuations?" and Chapter VIII is devoted to a consideration of the question—"Whether, and if so to what extent, the value of commercial goodwill enters into and forms part of valuations of national capital, as computed from time to time by economists?"

It should be noted that the subject matter and illustrations contained in Chapter V are not directly concerned with the methods of computing the value of commercial goodwill. They are concerned rather with the consideration and development of suitable schemes for the gradual writing off of the cost of goodwill, where this is already included in the value of assets as stated in the accounts of a profit-seeking undertaking. Such value may either appear as a separate item, or be included in the accounts together with other items.

P. D. LEAKE.

LONDON.

CONTENTS

PAGE

PREFACE v

CHAPTER I

THE HISTORY AND NATURE OF GOODWILL. . 1

Origin of Commercial Goodwill.—Ancient use of the term " Goodwill."—Earliest reported legal decision.—Usual form of definition of goodwill criticized.—Definition of commercial goodwill.—Meanings of " trade " and "business."--General freedom of trade.--Restraint of trade by custom.—Restraint of trade by Statute —Restraint of trade by agreement; public policy.—Nature of agreements in restraint of trade.—Meaning of monopoly.—Letters patent, an ancient prerogative of the Crown.—Statute of Monopolies.—Meaning of " patent."—Patents and Designs Acts, 1907 and 1919; meaning of Invention.—Nature of Patent.—Authors' work compared with inventors' work.—Rights of the Crown.—Designs.—Trade names and trade marks.—Trade Marks Act, 1905.—Registration of trade names.—Place-name as trade mark.—Surname as trade mark.—Surname as trade name.—Copyright.—Legal goodwill.—Personal and local goodwill in its restricted legal meaning.—Position of vendor of legal goodwill.—Alienation of commercial goodwill for debt.—Transfer of legal goodwill.—Use of name of old firm.—Ownership of goodwill on dissolution of partnership.—Canvassing old customers of partnership.

CHAPTER II

THE VALUE OF GOODWILL 19

Basis of value of goodwill.—Definition of super-profit.—Necessary to look forward, not backward.—The past is no sure guide to the future.—Exchangeable value depends upon future super-profit.—Special value to competing traders of an established connection.—Special value of an established connection to a qualified purchaser commencing business.—Personal value of an undertaking to the individual owner.—Super-profit theory of value.—Only purchased goodwill is recorded in accounts.—Money can always obtain a normal annual interest or wage.—Payment for goodwill is payment for future super-profit.—Varying degrees of uncertainty attaching to factors to be regarded in valuing goodwill.—The vendor of goodwill is entitled only to the fair present value of the future

PAGE

annual super-profit.—Super-profit can never exist permanently.—Difference between the value of an annuity and the sum of the annual payments.—10 per cent. annuity of £100 for three years.—Method of computing annuity value.—20 per cent. annuity of £100 for three years.—20 per cent. diminishing annuity for three years commencing with £100.—Illustration of effect of interest on value of goodwill.—Further illustration of effect of interest.—Super-profit arising out of varying conditions. —Super-profit dependent upon personal connection.—Super-profit dependent upon impersonal connection.—Super-profit from new or unexplored source.—Deduction of income tax from super-profit.

CHAPTER III

PRIVATE UNDERTAKINGS AND GOODWILL . . 37

Meaning of " private undertakings."—Professional practices.—Trades and businesses.—Valuing goodwill of private undertakings.—Goodwill of professional practice ; retirement of partner.—Decease of partner.—Private partnership converted into limited company with additional partners.—Private limited company. Death of one or two partners ; valuation of shares.—Disadvantages of old method of valuing goodwill.

CHAPTER IV

PUBLIC COMPANIES AND GOODWILL . . . 55

Meaning of " public companies."—Value of established connection.—Value of new undertaking.—Market quotation of shares at a premium, its causes and meaning discussed.—Balance sheet values.—Issue of shares at a premium.—Undistributed profit and premiums on new shares distributed as dividend ; deduction of income tax.—Rule for ascertaining total value placed upon goodwill of undertaking issuing shares at a premium.—Industrial and commercial concerns.—Test of Stock Exchange values ; a great retail business.—Test of value of shares of an insurance company.

CHAPTER V

THE ACCOUNTING VALUE OF PURCHASED GOODWILL AND ITS RECORD AND TREATMENT IN ACCOUNTS 77

Fallacy of treating purchased goodwill as having permanent value.—Spasmodic writing-off is unsatisfactory. —Why should cost of purchased goodwill be written off ? —Comparison between goodwill purchased and goodwill created.—Cost of purchased goodwill is a fixed and

PAGE

definite quantity.—Usual rough-and-ready method of computing value of goodwill.—Rate of interest required, in view of risk, a determining factor of value.—Interest required not often less than 10 per cent. per annum.—Reason that accounting value of purchased goodwill must diminish.—Permanent share capital should not be issued to pay for purchased goodwill.—Purchased goodwill may be written off in thirty-one years by applying only 5 per cent. of amount equal to expected super-profit.—Illustration of plan for writing off the cost of purchased goodwill.—Other plans illustrated.—Plans modified when annual profits prove to be less than expected.—Plan involving a stricter policy.—Case of private partnership; more drastic plan.—Need for adoption of sounder and more adequate rules of finance.—Balance sheet note of present value of goodwill computed on reasoned basis.—Securities issued against cost of goodwill should be in a redeemable form.

CHAPTER VI

ANNUAL INCOME TAX AND PURCHASED GOODWILL 93

The two classes of wasting assets.—Inherently wasting assets.—Fundamental difference between annuity and lease.—Wasting assets other than inherently wasting assets.—Income tax must be levied on profits in the year they actually arise.—Transfer from owner to owner of rights to future profits.—Different case where vendor is outside United Kingdom.

CHAPTER VII

PUBLIC COMPANY PROSPECTUS AND OTHER PITFALLS 104

Public company prospectuses.—Mills, factories, etc., valued "as going-concern."—Object of a valuation.—"Then-value" of plant.—To what extent is the value of goodwill included in plant valuations?—Illustration of goodwill included in plant valuation.—Three distinct bases of plant valuation.—Need of a register of wasting assets.—Periods of currency inflation.—Ordinary shares issued as fully paid.—Founders' shares.—Ordinary shares 1s. nominal value.—Preferred shares ranking between debentures and deferred shares.—Shares "no par value."

CHAPTER VIII

COMMERCIAL GOODWILL AND NATIONAL CAPITAL 125

Is value of goodwill included in valuations of national capital?—Stamp's valuation of British national capital.—Nothing exists except materials and commodities.—

PAGE

Meaning of present exchangeable value.—All exchange is barter. Meaning of barter power.—Usual method of valuing national capital. — British income tax statistics.—Multiplier applied to annual income of capital.—Method of estimating annual income of capital. —Method is subject to serious limitations and difficulties.—New valuation of British national capital.—Existing things which represent British national capital. —Lands, houses, and farmers' capital.—Industrial capital.—Location of industrial capital.—Household furniture, works of art, wearing-apparel, etc.—Details of Government and local property.—Treatment of Government and local property, and Government and local debts.—Analysis of new valuation.—National capital consists of materials and commodities, with one exception.—Extent and location of capital used in industry or production.—Extent of capital used for purposes of leisure or consumption.—Government and local property. Foreign, Indian, and colonial securities. Cash.—Pre-war absence of the factor of inflation.—Valuations of national capital include the value of commercial goodwill. —Valuations of national capital are dependent upon the future maintenance of industry.—Difficulties of making future valuations of national capital.—Any valuations of national capital in the near future must be useless.

APPENDICES 143

INDEX 251

COMMERCIAL GOODWILL

CHAPTER I

THE HISTORY AND NATURE OF GOODWILL

Origin of commercial goodwill

COMMERCIAL goodwill is a form of legal property which has gradually grown up and developed with the development of trade and business. In its earliest and simplest form, apart from monopolies which are referred to later, goodwill was the good reputation of the individual as an honest and efficient worker. The good reputation of the individual is obviously of great importance to him, and upon it depends the reputation of his particular trade or business by means of which he earns his living. With the development of trade and business commercial goodwill has emerged from its early obscurity, and has rapidly increased in importance, until it now represents a division of legal property of vast extent, and of no little complication.

Ancient use of the term "goodwill"

The word "Goodwill" has been in commercial use for centuries, as is shown by the following references to old writers—

1571, Wills and Inv. N.C. (Surtees, 1835), 352: "I gyue to John Stephen . . . my whole interest and good will of my Quarrell" (i.e., quarry). 1766, Goldsmith, Vic. W.I.V.: "Having given a hundred pounds for my predecessor's goodwill." 1786, Lounger, No. 79: "On her marriage with the knight she had sold the good-will of her shop and warehouse." 1836, Marryat, *Japhet,* 7: "The shop, fixtures, stock-in-trade, and goodwill, were all the property of our ancient antagonist." 1863, Fawcett, *Political Economy,* IV. ii. (1876), 536: "A solicitor can either sell the goodwill of his business, or leave it to his children."

Earliest reported legal decision

The earliest reported legal decision on goodwill seems to be *Crutwell* v. *Lye* (1810, 17 Ves., 335), in the course of which Lord Eldon said—"The Goodwill which has been the subject of sale is nothing more than the probability that the old customers will resort to the old place." The class of business under discussion was that of a country wagoner. It was not the name or the personality of the driver, but the place whence he starts and the probability that those who take their goods there will find a carriage for them, which form the value of such a business.

Usual form of definition of goodwill criticized

A usual form of definition of goodwill which, however, is now quite inadequate, is thus—

> GOODWILL.—The privilege, granted by the seller of a business to the purchaser, of trading as his recognized successor; the possession of a ready-formed "connection" of customers, considered as an element in the saleable value of a business, additional to the value of the plant, stock-in-trade, book debts, etc.

This definition is altogether too narrow in restricting the application of the term "goodwill" to an existing business, or to a ready-formed "connection" of customers.

Definition of commercial goodwill

Commercial goodwill is the right which grows out of all kinds of past effort in seeking profit, increase of value, or other advantage. This right is legally protected under various names, both by statute law, and by common law, for the use and benefit of the owner. Thus trade marks are now protected by the Trade Marks Act, 1905, patents and designs by the Patents and Designs Acts, 1907 and 1919, copyrights by the Copyright Act, 1911, and any right outside such statutes is protected by common law under the name of goodwill, and is referred to in this work as "legal goodwill" or "goodwill in its restricted legal meaning."

Meanings of "trade" and "business"

It will be convenient now to consider the meanings of the words "trade" and "business." "Trade" means the exchanging of goods for goods, or goods for money, including all transactions whether manual or mercantile entered into in the course of seeking profits, as distinguished from the liberal arts or learned professions or from agriculture. The word is one of very general application, and was once used in a much wider sense; it must always be considered in relation to its context. The word "business" has now a wider meaning than the word "trade." Lindley, L. J., said, in *Rolls* v. *Miller* (1884, 27 Ch.D. 71, C.A.) "business means almost anything which is an occupation as distinguished from a pleasure—anything which is an occupation or duty which requires attention is a business." 1860, Ld. Denman in All Year Round, 5th May, 83, "Every trade . . . . is a business, but every business is not a trade. To answer that description it must be conducted by buying and selling, which the business of keeping a lunatic asylum is not."

General freedom of trade

An individual is entitled under the common law to exercise any lawful trade as and where he wills. The law has always regarded jealously any interference with trade even at the risk of interfering with freedom of contract between one individual and another, because it is public policy to oppose all restraints upon liberty of individual action which may be injurious to the general freedom of trade, and so to the interests of the State. Thus, since the date of Magna Charta, it has always been against the policy of the law for any person or group of persons to be allowed to monopolize the carrying on of any known trade in the Kingdom, and the Crown cannot generally grant such a monopoly without statutory authority.

Restraint of trade by custom

Certain cities, towns, and boroughs, however, possessed, by custom, power vested in the corporation or in companies or guilds of traders, to restrict trade within certain areas or by certain persons, and by-laws regulating such customs were held to be valid. But in 1835 the Municipal Corporations Act abolished all such customs and by-laws, except in the City of London, and any person may now keep any shop and follow any trade or handicraft in any borough. The City of London was not a borough within the Act, but the old customs and by-laws, though not actually abolished within the City of London by the Municipal Corporations Act, have apparently become obsolete.

Restraint of trade by statute

Certain trades, such as the slave trade, have been prohibited by law. And Parliament has imposed restrictions on the exercise of some trades and professions with the object of maintaining a proper standard of competence in, and suitable control over, those engaged in them, or with the object of protecting employees and the public, or for the better regulation of public order, public health, and public safety, or for revenue purposes. Trades and professions in regard to which restrictions exist include, for instance, the medical and legal professions, moneylenders and pawnbrokers, hawkers, pedlars, etc., and certain restrictions are imposed on the manufacture and sale of intoxicating liquors, drugs, poisons, explosives, guns, coal, bread, and so on. The Old Metal Dealers Act, 1861, imposes restrictions with a view to diminishing facilities for the disposal of stolen goods, and the Merchant Shipping Act of 1894, and the Public Health Acts Amendment Act, 1907, provide other examples of restraint of trade by statute.

Restraint of trade by agreement; public policy

If a person voluntarily enters into an agreement not to carry on his trade he may be restrained at law from breaking that agreement. The general principle of law that a person is entitled to exercise any lawful trade as and where he wills must in such case be applied with due regard to the fact that it is public policy that a person of full age and understanding shall have the utmost freedom of contract, and that he shall be able to give effective possession of his business to a competent successor. Again, it is clearly sound public policy to afford to an employer an unrestricted choice of assistants, and the opportunity to instruct them in the secrets of his trade, without fear of their becoming his competitors. There is no restraint upon freedom of contract unless such restraint is shown to be necessary in order to maintain freedom of trade. Apart from agreement, express or implied, to the contrary, either a retiring partner, or the vendor of a business, may start a competing business.

Nature of agreements in restraint of trade

Agreements in restraint of trade may be generally divided under the following heads—(1) between vendors and purchasers of businesses; (2) between employers and employed; (3) between partners and partners; (4) between traders and traders in regard to competition output, treatment of employees, etc.; and (5) between employers and employers in regard to common action towards those whom they employ. In order to make valid an agreement in restraint of trade it must be reasonable; it must be founded on good consideration; and it must not be too vague.

Meaning of monopoly

Sir E. Coke defines monopoly as an institution or allowance by the King by his grant, commission or otherwise, to any person or persons, bodies politic or corporate, of or for the sole buying, selling, making, working, or using anything. (3 Co. Inst. c. 85, 181.) At common law, however, it was not every monopoly that was valid. Where a man had by his own charge and industry or by his own wit and invention, brought any new trade into the realm, or any engine, tending to the furtherance of a trade, that was not used before, and that for the good of the realm, the King might grant him a monopoly patent for some reasonable time until the subjects might have learned the same, in consideration of the good that he brought by his invention to the commonwealth, otherwise not.

Letters patent, an ancient prerogative of the Crown

The granting of letters-patent is an ancient prerogative of the Crown, and this prerogative remains unaffected by the Patents and Designs Acts, 1907 and 1919. In the reign of Queen Elizabeth the use of this prerogative of the Crown had been extended far beyond its proper limits, being used to confer exclusive rights of buying and selling ordinary commodities, thus creating monopolies which her successor, King James, found himself obliged to remedy. Accordingly, by the first section of a statute passed in the twenty-first year of his reign (1623) and commonly called the Statute of Monopolies, it was declared and enacted that all such monopolies were unlawful and altogether contrary to the laws of this realm.

Statute of Monopolies

This Statute, which declares monopolies to be unlawful, makes certain exceptions and particularly one on which the modern law with respect to patents may be said to be founded. This exception is contained in Section 6 which reads as follows—

Provided also that any declaration before mentioned shall not extend to any letters-patent and grants of privilege for the term of fourteen years or under, hereafter to be made, of the sole working or making of any manner of new manufactures within this realm, to the true and first inventor or inventors of such manufactures, which others at the time of making such letters-patent and grants shall not use, so as also they be not contrary to the law or mischievous to the State, by raising prices of commodities at home, or hurt of trade, or generally inconvenient; the said fourteen years to be accounted from the date of the first letters-patent or grant of such privilege hereafter to be made; but the same shall be of such force as they should be if this Act had never been made, and of none other.

It will be observed that the granting of letters-patent is not expressly warranted by this Statute which merely reserves to such letters-patent as fall within the terms of the exception, such force as they would have had if the Statute of Monopolies had never been passed. The term limiting the duration of patents is increased from fourteen to sixteen years by Section 6 of the Patents and Designs Act, 1919.

Meaning of "patent"

The word "patent" is used somewhat loosely, and is often employed instead of the word "invention," sometimes to denote the grant contained in a patent, and sometimes the privilege which is the subject-matter of such grant. The word "patent" is derived from Latin "patens," and signifies an open record made by the Crown in Chancery and under the Great Seal, and patents, or more properly letters-patent, are made for very many purposes besides granting sole rights to use inventions. In "patent law" "patent" means letters-patent for an invention.

Patents and Designs Acts, 1907 and 1919. Meaning of Invention

The text of the Patents and Designs Acts, 1907 and 1919, will be found in the appendix. The law relating to the grant of letters-patent for an invention is now regulated by these Acts. Section 93 of the Act of 1907 provides that invention means any manner of new manufacture the subject of letters-patent and grant of privilege within Section 6 of the Statute of Monopolies, and includes an alleged invention. The term for which a patent is granted is now limited to sixteen years from the date of the patent, but the High Court may, under certain circumstances, extend this term.

Nature of patent

The nature of a patent at common law is that of a bargain between the inventor and the Crown, the consideration being the good resulting to the commonwealth from the invention. In view of this, therefore, the first inventor is the individual who first discloses his invention to the public, and not he who discovers in secrecy, and keeps secret his invention. If several persons discover the same thing at the same time, the person who first communicates it to the public under the protection of letters-patent is the true and first inventor. There may be many investigators working on the same subject at the same time, but the person entitled to the benefit of the patent is he who first comes to the Crown and takes out a patent. The important question is—did the public know of the invention at the time of the grant? If they did, then the patent is void, but if they did not, then assuming the patentee is the true inventor, he is also the true and first inventor. It will be seen from this, therefore, that a man may be the true and first inventor if he rediscovers a lost art.

Authors' work compared with inventors' work

After much controversy as to whether an individual is entitled to have reserved for his use and benefit the future profits which may arise out of his mental effort in the same way that profits arising out of his corporeal labour and industry are reserved, it was finally decided that an author has a natural right of property in his work. An inventor, however, is not, it is said, in the same position as an author. It has been pointed out that while an author creates his work, an inventor creates nothing, but only discovers what was already there. If Milton had not written *Paradise Lost* no one else would have written it, but if Watt had not discovered how to utilize high pressure steam, someone else would certainly have discovered it. It is clear that except by letters-patent, an inventor has no exclusive right of property in his invention.

Rights of the Crown

The Crown and its agents and servants have the right to use any invention patented in this country on such terms as may be agreed upon with the approval of the Treasury, or in default of agreement as may be settled by the court, referee or arbitrator after hearing all parties interested.

Designs

Section 49 of the Patents and Designs Act, 1907, provides that application may be made to the Comptroller General of Patents, Designs, and Trade Marks for the registration of any new or original design not previously published in the United Kingdom, and a certificate of registration is granted to a proprietor of a design when registered. When a design is registered, the registered proprietor of the design has, subject to the provisions of the Act, copyright in the design during five years from the date of registration. There is also a right of renewal for a second period of five years and the Comptroller may, subject to any rules under the Act, extend the period for a third term of five years. A Register of Designs is kept at the Patent Office.

Trade names and trade marks

In describing trade names and trade marks the *New English Dictionary* states—Trade name, (*a*) a descriptive or fancy name used to designate some proprietary article of trade ; (*b*) the name by which an article or substance is known to the trade ; (*c*) the name or style under which a business is carried on. 1900, Hopkins Law Unfair Trade, 29. Proper names are not trade marks, and . . . . there should not be such a thing as a technical trade name.

Trade marks. In Edmunds Patent Law (1897), 885, Letters Patent granted in 1571 to R. Mathews— "To make the said haftes called Turky haftes for knyves, and for his marke to have upon the blade and hafte of the same knyfes . . . . a halfe Moone."

Trade Marks Act, 1905

Particular marks or devices used by manufacturers to identify goods made by them are called trade marks, and a right may be acquired to the exclusive use of a trade mark. Since the year 1875 this right has been regulated ; first by a statute known as the Trades Mark Registration Act, 1875, 38 & 39 Vic., c. 91, but the statute now in force is the Trade Marks Act, 1905, 5 Edw. VII, c. 15, a copy of which is contained in the appendix. Before the year 1875 if a trade mark came, by use, to be recognized in trade as the mark of the goods of a particular manufacturer he acquired the exclusive right to use the trade mark in connection with goods of the same kind for the purpose of indicating their manufacture or place of manufacture. But since the 1875 Act took effect, a registration of a trade mark has been essential to the acquisition and enjoyment of an exclusive right to use it, or the nature of the right remains as before. The right is founded on the rule that no man is entitled to represent his goods as being the goods of another man.

Registration of trade names

The name of an individual or firm may be registered as a trade mark. But even if it has not been so registered the goods of a particular trader may come to be known in the market by his name, or by the name of his works, and when a name becomes well known in this way the trader acquires a right which entitles him to prevent any other person from using the same name in connection with the same kind of goods in a way likely to induce people to believe that the goods offered for sale by the latter person are the goods manufactured by the trader. A name so used is called a trade name. The right thus given by law to the exclusive use of a trade name is founded, as in the case of a trade mark, upon the rule that no man may represent his goods as being the goods of another man.

Place-name as trade mark

In *Brock & Co.* v. *Pain*, 28 R.P.C. 697, C.A. (1912), the plaintiffs, a firm of pyrotechnists, and their predecessors in business had for nearly fifty years—namely, since 1866 down to 1910—been making and selling fireworks under the description " Crystal Palace Fireworks " they having throughout that period the exclusive right of giving firework displays at the Crystal Palace. In 1891 they had registered as an old trade mark in connection with fireworks the words " Crystal Palace." They had also registered two other trade marks consisting of representations of the Crystal Palace. They used the term for all their goods of the firework class. It was not limited to the displays they gave at the Crystal Palace. Their goods were asked for as " Crystal Palace Fireworks," and were supplied under that name. The plaintiffs having ceased to hold the contract, the defendants another firm of pyrotechnists, obtained in the year 1910 the right to give firework displays at the Crystal Palace, and thereupon they sought to describe their fireworks as " Crystal Palace Fireworks," with the addition of their own name. Held, that the plaintiffs having for nearly fifty years applied the words "Crystal Palace" to their goods, it was irrelevant to consider whether they had still got the right to give displays of fireworks at the Crystal Palace; that the use of those words did not imply that they had; and that, therefore, they were entitled to a perpetual injunction to restrain the defendants.

Surname as trade mark

In *re Cadbury* (No. 2), 59 S.J. 161 (1914), it was held that although there is authority for saying that a surname is unsuitable for registration as a trade mark, and the Court has a discretion in such cases to refuse registration, yet the exercise of this discretion must not conflict with the meaning of the legislature. Where the name in everybody's mind refers to the goods of one firm, whether this has been brought about by the use of the name as a trade mark or the direct representation that the goods were made by that firm, such name is "distinctive" within the meaning of that word as used in Section 9, Sub-section 5, of the Trade Marks Act, 1905.

Surname as trade name

In *Brinsmead* v. *Brinsmead*, 29 T.L.R. 706, C.A. (1913), it was held that there being no evidence of dishonesty, the defendant Brinsmead could not be restrained at the instance of the plaintiffs from putting his own name on pianos made by him, although the fact of his doing so might bring him some advantage in connection with the sale of the pianos made by him in consequence of his surname being the same as that of the plaintiff firm.

Copyright

The text of the Copyright Act, 1911, will be found in the Appendix. In 1710 a Statute of Anne limited copyright in books to fourteen years from publication, with a reversionary second fourteen years' term to the author if still living. This Statute was repealed by the Copyright Act, 1842, which extended copyright in books to the life of the author and seven years from his death; and there were other Statutes relating to copyright in dramatic, musical and other works, but all these have been repealed by the Copyright Act, 1911, which now regulates copyright in every original literary, dramatic, musical, and artistic work, whether published or unpublished. The conditions which confer copyright are—(1) The work must be original; (2) In the case of a published work it must be first published within the area of copyright, and in the case of an unpublished work the author must at the date of making the work be a British subject or resident within the area of copyright. The term of copyright is the life of the author and a period of fifty years after his death, subject to certain conditions and restrictions set out in the Copyright Act, 1911.

The common law relating to goodwill in its restricted legal meaning has been frequently explained by the judges. In *Inland Revenue Commissioners* v. *Muller & Co.'s Margarine* (1901), A.C., Lord Macnaughten said—"What is goodwill? It is a thing very easy to describe, very difficult to define. It is the benefit and advantage of the good name, reputation, and connection of a business. It is the attractive force which brings in custom. It is the one thing which distinguishes an old-established business from a new business at its first start." This definition brings out clearly the strictly limited area covered by legal goodwill, which is shown, by inference, to exclude patent rights and copyrights, which rights need not, of course, appertain to an old-established business. A new business, formed to seek future profits out of the exploitation and development of either of these rights,

Legal goodwill

may evidently possess an important asset in the form of commercial goodwill. But such goodwill is specifically excluded from the above definition of legal goodwill. In the same case Lord Davy said—" The term 'goodwill' is nothing more than a summary of the rights accruing to the purchasers from their purchase of the business and property employed in it." And Lord Lindley said—" I understand the word to include whatever adds value to the business by reason of situation, name and reputation, connection, introduction to old customers, and agreed absence from competition, or any of these things."

Personal and local goodwill in its restricted legal meaning

In process of time, goodwill in its restricted legal meaning, viz., apart from patents and designs, trade marks and copyrights, came to be recognized as representing a species of property or rights of great importance, and a legal distinction was drawn between personal goodwill—which is the advantage of the good reputation and connection of the owner of a business—and local goodwill, which is attached to particular premises owing to the probability that old customers will continue to resort to those premises. Legal goodwill cannot be separated and dealt with apart from the business out of which it arises, but it may be dealt with as an entity separate from the particular premises in which the business is carried on. Where, however, goodwill is attached to premises in such a manner as to enhance their value, it is in law inseparable from them, and thus the price of such goodwill will belong to a mortgagee of the premises, and if the premises are freehold, the price does not form part of the legal personal estate of the owner.

Position of vendor of legal goodwill

The vendor of the legal goodwill of a business may, in the absence of an express agreement to the contrary, set up a competing business, unless he is estopped by conduct amounting to fraud which has influenced others to purchase the legal goodwill in the belief that the vendor will not continue the trade. A vendor may advertise the fact that he has been a partner in, or that he was founder of, or manager or employed in the old business, but he must not represent himself to be a successor to or to be carrying on a continuation of that old business, or use its trade marks. A vendor may not privately solicit any person who was a customer of the business prior to the sale, but he may advertise publicly his new business, and may deal with any persons who come to him unsolicited, and apparently even with any persons who, having been solicited, at first resisted such solicitation, but afterwards come to him without further solicitation and owing to their being dissatisfied with the old firm.

Alienation of commercial goodwill for debt

It seems there is not any direct process of execution available against patents, trade-marks, trade-names, copyrights, or legal goodwill, but in case of bankruptcy the benefit of letters-patent for an invention or of copyright passes to the trustee. Rights of this character appear to be things in action, so as to be excluded from the operation of the reputed ownership clauses of the bankruptcy law. A trustee in bankruptcy is expressly authorized to sell the goodwill of the bankrupt's business as part of his property; and in connection with such goodwill the trustee may dispose of all the advantages accruing from the bankrupt's exclusive right to use any trade-mark or trade-name.

Transfer of legal goodwill

The sale of a business implies the sale of its legal goodwill, even though this is not expressly mentioned.

An agreement by a partner to retire from a partnership is not, however, necessarily equivalent to an agreement to sell his share of the goodwill. A transfer of goodwill may be made without writing provided that the requirements of the Statute of Frauds as to contracts in writing are not transgressed. A transferee of legal goodwill has the exclusive right to carry on and to represent himself as carrying on the business transferred (*Walker* v. *Mottram* (1881), 19 Sch. D. 355, 363, C.A.); as against the transferor the transferee possesses the exclusive right to use the name under which the business has been carried on. (*Pomeroy (Mrs.) Ltd.* v. *Scalé* (1906), 22 T.L.R. 795; 23 T.L.R. 170). But the transferee must not use the old name so as to expose the transferor to a risk of personal liability by holding the transferor out as the owner of, or a partner in, the business.

Use of name of old firm

In a dissolution of partnership in which the assets are divided between the partners, each partner is entitled in the absence of agreement to the contrary to use the name of the old firm provided that in so doing he does not expose the other partner to risk either of litigation or responsibility. Unless, therefore, the use of the name of the old firm exposes the other partners to risk of liability—and this depends on the circumstances of the case—no injunction at law will be granted to restrain the use of the name of the old firm. *Banks* v. *Gibson* (1865), 34 Beav. 566. *Burchell* v. *Wilde* (1900), 1 Ch. 551, 564, C.A. The Court has refused to restrain a surviving partner who was executor and trustee of a deceased partner from carrying on a similar business, but a surviving partner may not carry on a rival business in such a way as to lead to the belief that it is the partnership business, and thus appropriate the goodwill. *Davies* v. *Hodgson* (1857), 25 Beav. 177, 182, 183.

Ownership of goodwill on dissolution of partnership

When on a dissolution of partnership the goodwill becomes the property of one of the partners, another partner may, for his own purpose, state that he was formerly a partner in the old firm, but he may not use the name of the firm in such a way as to suggest that he is carrying on the old business. *Hookham* v. *Pottage* (1872), 8 Ch. App. 91. A continuing partner who has purchased the assets but not specifically the goodwill may apparently be restrained from using the name of his former partner in the style of the firm. *Scott* v. *Rowland* (1872), 20 W.R. 508.

Canvassing old customers of partnership

Where two partners have agreed that, on a dissolution, the goodwill shall belong solely to one of them, the other partner may not do anything calculated to depreciate the value of the goodwill. He may, however, in the absence of contrary agreement, do business with the customers of the old firm, but he must not canvass them nor solicit them either to deal with him or not to deal with the purchasing partner. *Trego* v. *Hunt* (1896), A.C. 7. The restriction from canvassing, however, does not apply to a partner expelled under a power in the Articles (but he must not represent that the business he carries on is the business of the old firm), nor does it apply to a purchaser from the trustee in bankruptcy of a deceased partner. *Dawson* v. *Beeson* (1882), 22 Ch.D. 504, 507, C.A. When a partner, having sold his share of the business to his partners and undertaken not to compete with them, acts contrary to this undertaking, he will be restrained by injunction. *Turner* v. *Evans* (1852), 2 De G.M. & G. 740, C.A. But it has been held that the Court may refuse to restrain a vendor from breach of an agreement not to carry on, or to be interested in, any similar business in a case in which the vendor subsequently aided his wife to commence, or in commencing, a similar business with her separate capital. *Smith* v. *Hancock* (1894), 2 Ch. 377, C.A.

CHAPTER II

THE VALUE OF GOODWILL

HAVING now briefly considered the history and nature of goodwill we propose to examine the basis of its value. As already stated commercial goodwill is the right which grows out of all kinds of past effort in seeking profit, increase of value, or other advantage. It is important to bear in mind that this right exists altogether apart from the question of whether or not it has exchangeable value. The exchangeable value of the right depends upon the probability of earning future super-profit—the term " super-profit " meaning the amount by which revenue, increase of value, or other advantage received exceeds any and all economic expenditure incidental to its production.

Basis of value of goodwill

Definition of super-profit

In valuing goodwill it is necessary to endeavour to see into the future, and it is never possible to do this with very great success. In the case of established undertakings it is customary, owing to this difficulty, to value the goodwill as being equal to some number of years' purchase of past annual so-called profits, often, however, omitting from consideration in computing these profits such important factors of expense as expired capital outlay on wasting assets, personal remuneration for management, and a normal rate of interest on capital invested. In the case of new undertakings formed to purchase and work rights of various descriptions, including patent rights, the wildest estimates of the value of these rights—that is, the goodwill—are often made, based on some rough and ready calculation prepared by the vendor, and put forward

Necessary to look forward —not backward

in a prospectus, which perhaps contains the names of well-known men who have, without sufficient thought, been induced to become directors.

The past is no sure guide to the future

Owing to the difficulty of looking forward in valuing goodwill it has become customary to look backward and too readily to accept past events as an unerring guide to the future. But this cannot safely be done, and in seeking after better methods it is necessary to endeavour to isolate and separately examine, in the dim and uncertain light of future probability, each of the varying factors bearing upon the value of goodwill. Instead of looking too closely at past profits as a measure of the present value of goodwill, it will be well to consider the present value of an annuity equal in amount to the expected future annual profits. Whether the annuity is to be treated as constant in amount or as diminishing by equal sums over the term of years selected as suitable in each case must depend upon the particular circumstances.

Exchangeable value depends upon future super-profit

The exchangeable value of goodwill depends always on estimates of future probabilities. It does not depend upon the past, except to the extent that past events may be taken as a guide in estimating future probabilities. Thus, subject to certain exceptions mentioned below, goodwill may have no exchangeable value unless either (*a*) the future revenue expected to arise out of the undertaking consists wholly of super-profit (as would be the case if no economic expenditure is needed) or (*b*) the future revenue expected to arise is greater than all economic expenditure incidental to its production. The term "economic expenditure" includes any and all current expenses, expired capital outlay on wasting assets (depreciation) other than goodwill, personal remuneration sufficient to secure continued successful management (which may possibly need ability of a high order) and a rate of interest on capital invested which will attract and retain any necessary capital having regard to the degree of risk incidental to the character of the undertaking.

Special value to competing traders of an established connection

The exceptions referred to are of some importance. It frequently happens that a trader or a combination of traders may desire to buy up the business of a competitor in order to reduce competition which would otherwise have to be faced. For this reason it may be considered worth while to pay a large sum of money for the business of a competitor even though that business may not be earning super-profit and may be regarded as unlikely to earn super-profit in future years. This is perhaps the most important exception to the general rule stated above which governs the value of goodwill. There are, however, certain other exceptions.

Special value of an established connection to a qualified purchaser commencing business

In the case of a professional practice, or of a trading undertaking, needing special knowledge, skill, and ability to carry it on successfully, it is often worth the while of the qualified practitioner or trader to pay a sum of money for an established connection, although nothing which can be regarded as super-profit is expected to arise out of the purchased connection itself. The object of the qualified practitioner or trader is that he may at once become possessed of an established connection without which he would be unable to use his capabilities to the best advantage. The alternatives open to him may be either to attempt to build up a connection, *ab initio*, or to accept service as a paid assistant to another. In either case his earnings would be considerably less than he would expect if able at once to bring his special knowledge to bear upon an established connection. Thus the value of the goodwill of an undertaking required for use in combination with the personal knowledge, skill, and ability of the purchaser may be due to, and will vary with, the degree of opportunity for profitable use which the prospective purchaser thinks he possesses.

Personal value of an undertaking to the individual owner

The right, represented by commercial goodwill, though it may have no exchangeable value, may yet be highly prized by the individual owner. Owners of patent rights, copyrights, trade marks, trade names and trade connections of all kinds may often be ready to fight strenuously to protect their rights even though such rights may be quite unsaleable. It may, of course, be assumed that when a person seeks legal protection in defending rights connected with any kind of profit-seeking enterprise he thinks he will thereby gain some personal profit or advantage which he could not otherwise gain. This may not be a profit in money; it may consist partly, or even wholly, of the personal satisfaction the owner will feel at defeating a competitor who, he may think, has acted unfairly. The owner may set a high value upon this.

Super-profit theory of value

Having mentioned these special considerations as effecting the exchangeable value of the goodwill of certain classes of undertakings, which, however, are of comparatively minor importance, it is necessary to consider the theory of future "super-profit," as the basis for measuring the present value of goodwill. It has been pointed out that, apart from the exceptions referred to, the value of goodwill arises solely out of the inevitable and universal demand for super-profit, the meaning of which has been defined, and, therefore, without the reasonable probability of the earning of future super-profit, no present value in the form of goodwill can exist. An amount paid for the purchase of goodwill really represents a premium paid to secure an extra-profitable opening for the employment of capital. The transaction may be compared with the premium paid for the purchase of a lease of premises the annual value of which is greater than the annual rent which is payable.

Only purchased goodwill is recorded in accounts

It should be particularly noted that although the value of goodwill forms part of the present value of every profit-seeking undertaking expected to yield future super-profit, yet such value only takes recorded and visible form and becomes a practical financial question if and when the goodwill of the undertaking has been purchased, that is to say, transferred from one person to another for valuable consideration. It is probable, therefore, that the bulk of the value actually existing in the form of goodwill is not recorded in any financial books or accounts, and thus as to the greater part of the subject no question of the treatment of goodwill in accounts ever arises. The reason is, of course, that in the majority of profit-seeking undertakings, whether private or public, the goodwill has been created and developed by ability and effort exercised whilst in the hands of the present owners. It is important to bear this in mind, because it materially assists in arriving at a true understanding of the nature of this form of value which extends far beyond the limits of that comparatively small part which is recorded in financial books and accounts.

Money can always obtain a normal annual interest or wage

It has been said that the term "super-profit" means the amount by which future profits are expected to exceed a normal rate of interest on capital invested. For the sake of illustration it may be assumed that the annual wage or hire—viz., interest—of money for secure and easily convertible investment is 5 per cent., and when subjected to the risks incidental to industrial enterprise, 10 per cent. These rates may be too high or too low, but that is immaterial for the purpose of illustration if it be granted that money demands at least some minimum annual interest or wage, increasing with the degree of risk incidental to its employment. Easily marketable gilt-edged securities may yield 5 per cent. per annum, which is a reason for assuming 5 per cent. to be the minimum annual wage or hire of money.

Payment for goodwill is payment for future super-profit

There seems to be no doubt about the truth of the proposition, that before it is possible to justify value being put upon the goodwill of any undertaking it must be shown that the expected future annual profits exceed the normal annual wage or hire of the capital invested, having regard to the nature of the risk. This normal annual wage can obviously always be obtained by capital at any time without the payment of a premium because there are always opportunities free of charge for the employment of capital at normal rates of interest. The payment of a sum for goodwill can thus only be justified if the opportunity offered for the employment of capital is extra-normal.

Varying degrees of uncertainty attaching to factors to be regarded in valuing goodwill

The factors upon which estimates of the present value of goodwill may be based are more clearly defined in the case of some kinds of undertakings than of others. Generally speaking, the longer the period of years over which the future super-profit is expected to arise the greater the chances of error in estimating the present value of the goodwill. The reason is, of course, that the longer the period of realization the greater the likelihood that unforeseen conditions will arise in the meantime. It is comparatively easy to estimate the value of book debts, or of stock-in-trade, because such assets are likely to be turned into money within a short period of time. It is more difficult to estimate the value of material wasting assets such as buildings, plant and machinery, the useful life of which is uncertain, and which, owing to the progress of invention, may become obsolete before becoming worn out. The basis of exchangeable value of these last-mentioned assets is described in well known cases which have been before the Courts, as the " then-value," and is equal to the unexpired capital outlay (unexpired cost) adjusted in respect of subsequent fluctuations in the cost of material and labour as explained in Chapter VII. The class of assets most difficult of any to value is that represented by the various forms of goodwill owing to the peculiar uncertainty attaching to the factors which have to be taken into consideration.

The vendor of goodwill is entitled only to the fair present value of the future annual super-profit

In fixing the value or price to be paid for goodwill the vendor cannot reasonably expect to secure for himself more than the fair present value of the future annual super-profit. He must offer something attractive enough to induce an alert purchaser to buy so speculative a property. The vendor's position is infinitely superior to that of the purchaser, because he generally receives the consideration in cash or its equivalent, and thus absolutely secures his share, whereas the purchaser is in the position of having already paid away a share of each future year's estimated super-profit. For this reason the purchaser must make some annual provision out of super-profit earned to refund this share before he can safely enjoy the remainder. The question of the annual provision which should be made against the diminishing value of purchased goodwill is discussed in Chapter V.

Super-profit can never exist permanently

With regard to the degree of permanence in value of goodwill it is clear that, owing to the operation of economic laws, super-profit can never exist permanently, though it may sometimes continue to arise out of an undertaking for a great number of years. One principal reason for the temporary character of super-profit is the existence of competition. Commercial competition is universal and is constantly at work striving to secure a share in super-profit of all kinds wherever it arises, and whenever an undertaking is earning super-profit it will always tend to attract imitators. This operates to reduce, and will ultimately level, the earnings to a rate of profit not exceeding the normal rate of interest on the capital invested having regard to the nature of the risk. Another reason why super-profit is always of a temporary character is that the demand for any commodity or service may at any time slacken or cease, owing to all kinds of changing conditions including new inventions. On commonly accepted economic grounds, therefore, super-profit must never be treated as being in the nature of a perpetuity; it is essentially in the nature of an annuity extending over an unknown but limited period of years, and therefore the value of goodwill is not permanent.

Difference between the value of an annuity and the sum of the annual payments

It is necessary now to consider the difference between the value—viz., the present value—of the right to receive an annuity over a number of years and the sum of the future yearly amounts of that annuity. This difference in value arises from the fact that £100 due a year hence is worth less than £100 due now, because money can always earn an appropriate annual interest or wage, and, therefore, £100 due now will have increased a year hence by the amount of interest earned. The rate of this interest or wage depends upon the degree of risk incidental to the nature of the particular employment for which the money is required. If the rate is 10 per cent. per annum £100 due now will have increased to £110 a year hence. By the same process of reasoning £90·91 due now will have increased to £100 a year hence, and therefore the value of the right to receive £100 a year hence is £90·91; two years hence £82·65; and three years hence £75·13.

10 per cent. annuity of £100 for three years.

Thus allowing interest at 10 per cent. per annum the value of an annuity of £100 for three years is £248·69. This value is built up by adding together a number of units, each of which units represents the value of one future year's annuity, as under—

INSTALMENTS OF ANNUITY.

	1st Year.	2nd Year.	3rd Year.	Interest.	Amount.
	£	£	£	£	£
Present value of each £100 annual instalment . .	90·91	82·65	75·13	—	248·69
One year's interest at 10% for 1st year	9·09	8·26	7·52	24·87	
	£100	90·91	82·65		
One year's interest at 10% for 2nd year	—	9·09	8·26	17·35	
		£100	90·91		
One year's interest at 10% for 3rd year	—	—	9·09	9·09	
					51·31
			£100		£300

Method of computing annuity value

The value £248·69 plus the amount of the interest from the present date, with yearly rests, to the date when each instalment of £100 becomes due, amounting to £51·31 equals £300, being the sum of the three annual instalments. The value of each succeeding unit in this sum is less than the one before, because the time to elapse before that unit will be received is one year longer in each case. This longer time obviously entitles the purchaser to retain a larger sum for compound interest, accruing in the meantime on the purchase price.

20 per cent. annuity of £100 for three years

If the rate of interest is 20 per cent. per annum the value of an annuity of £100 for three years is £210·66 as under—

INSTALMENTS OF ANNUITY.

	1st Year.	2nd Year.	3rd Year.	Interest.	Amount.
	£	£	£	£	£
Present value of each £100 annual instalment . .	83·34	69·45	57·87	—	210·66
One year's interest at 20% for 1st year	16·66	13·89	11·58	42·13	
	£100	83·34	69·45		
One year's interest at 20% for 2nd year	—	16·66	13·89	30·55	
		£100	83·34		
One year's interest at 20% for 3rd year	—	—	16·66	16·66	
			£100		89·34
					£300

Again, allowing interest at 20 per cent. per annum, the value of an annuity for three years, commencing with £100 due at the end of the first year, and diminishing by equal annual sums, viz., to £66·67 due at the end of the second year, and to £33·33 due at the end of the third year, is £148·93 as under— 20 per cent. diminishing annuity for three years, commencing with £100

INSTALMENTS OF ANNUITY DIMINISHING BY EQUAL ANNUAL SUMS

	1st Year.	2nd Year.	3rd Year.	Interest.	Amount.
	£	£	£	£	£
Present value of each annual instalment, commencing with £100 and diminishing by equal annual sums .	83·34	46·30	19·29	—	148·93
One year's interest at 20% for 1st year	16·66	9·26	3·86	29·78	
	£100	55·56	23·15		
One year's interest at 20% for 2nd year	—	11·11	4·63	15·74	
		£66·67	27·78		
One year's interest at 20% for 3rd year	—	—		5·55	
					51·07
			£33·33		£200

As a further illustration of the effect of annual interest on the value of the right to receive amounts payable at a future time, it may be noted that, allowing interest at 5 per cent., 10 per cent., and 20 per cent. per annum respectively, the value of the Illustration of effect of interest on value of goodwill right to an annuity of £100 extending over a period of one hundred years is, with interest at 5 per cent. per annum, £1,985; with interest at 10 per cent. per annum, £1,000; and with interest at 20 per cent. per annum, £500. It will be observed from the following table that the bulk of the value, in each case, is represented by amounts which are receivable in the earlier decades of the period of one hundred years—

Table showing value (with proportion of value receivable in each decade) of annuity of £100 for 100 years—allowing interest at 5, 10, and 20 per cent. on value unexpired.

	5%	10%	20%
1st 10 years of the period . .	772·17	614·46	419·27
2nd 10 ,, ,, ,, . .	474·05	236·90	67·73
	1246·22	851·36	487·00
3rd 10 ,, ,, ,, . .	291·02	91·33	11·05
	1537·24	942·69	498·05
4th 10 ,, ,, ,, . .	178·66	35·21	1·85
	1715·90	977·90	499·90
5th 10 ,, ,, ,, . .	109·68	13·58	·21
	1825·58	991·48	
6th 10 ,, ,, ,, . .	67·34	5·24	—
	1892·92	996·72	
7th 10 ,, ,, ,, . .	41·34	2·02	—
	1934·26	998·74	
8th 10 ,, ,, ,, . .	25·38	·78	—
	1959·64	999·52	
9th 10 ,, ,, ,, . .	15·58	·30	—
	1975·22	999·82	
10th 10 ,, ,, ,, . .	9·57	·12	—
100 years.	1984·79	999·94	500·11

The above table brings out the fact that the instalments of an annuity receivable in the later decades of a period of 100 years have no practical present value if interest be allowed at any rate higher than about 5 per cent.

With the assistance of the ordinary mathematical interest tables it is possible to realize more clearly the effect of the interest factor, the importance of which is sometimes apt to be overlooked in considering the value of goodwill. Owing to the annual value of money, which at ordinary trade risk may be 10 per cent. per annum, that particular future instalment of an annuity of £100 which is not due until the lapse of ten years is worth now £39 only; that instalment not due until the lapse of twenty years £15 only; that instalment not due until the lapse of thirty years £8, and so on. Looking further down the table it will be seen that the present value of that particular future instalment of an annuity of £100 which is not due until the lapse of any period exceeding forty-eight years is worth less than £1. Therefore, if the price paid for goodwill does not exceed its value it is clear that substantially the whole of the benefit which has any considerable value is actually enjoyed by the purchaser within a period which cannot extend much beyond twenty years from the date of purchase, because that which is purchased is the right to receive an annuity over a number of years, and the annual payments of an annuity have comparatively little value unless they are receivable within a period of twenty or thirty years. Even if an annuity continues during one hundred years it will be seen from the tables that 85 per cent. of the present value is attributable to the annual payments to be received during the first twenty years of the period.

Further illustration of effect of interest

In computing the value of goodwill it is important to bear in mind that profit-seeking undertakings naturally fall into several classes, differing one from another in the sense that the future super-profit is

Super-profit arising out of varying conditions

expected to arise out of conditions clearly distinguishable and inherently different in character. In the case of each of these different classes of profit-seeking undertakings the method of computing the value of goodwill may vary. The several classes include the following—

(1) Where the future super-profit is expected to arise out of an established connection which is clearly dependent more or less upon the personal character, qualifications and skill of the creators. In this case, inasmuch as the influence of the creators will be withdrawn—or if retained for a longer or shorter period will presumably be remunerated at its full annual value—the connection, and therefore the super-profit, arising out of the creators' work already done, is likely to diminish rapidly year by year.

(2) Where the future super-profit is expected to arise out of an established connection which has set up a continuing public demand. Such demand may result from reputation and from acquired popular tastes, habits, and customs. It is seen in the demand which exists for various kinds of manufactured goods, many of which are known by a trade name, or trade mark, and in the customary business connection attached to such undertakings as banking, insurance, retail stores, and so on. In the case of many of these profit-seeking undertakings it seems difficult to place a limit in years to the period over which the super-profit may continue to arise, assuming always that the undertakings are managed with ordinary business skill.

(3) Where the future super-profit is expected to arise out of a new undertaking or out of an

unexplored source of possible profit such as, for instance, the manufacture of a patented invention, and the creation by advertising or other means of a public demand for the same.

Super-profit dependent upon personal connection

In the case of an established connection needing the continued attention of those possessing special personal qualifications as distinguished from ordinary business aptitude, for instance, the practice of a doctor or of a solicitor, the future annual super-profit, so far as it can be said to arise out of the already exercised personal qualifications and skill of the creator, must obviously tend to diminish rapidly in amount year by year. It is true that the amount of super-profit may still continue to arise undiminished in the future, but this will obviously depend upon the exercise of equally efficient personal effort by someone else in the future, and on his ability to attach to himself and to maintain the connection. The valuation of goodwill in such a case should, therefore, generally be based upon the present value of the estimated super-profit treated as an amount diminishing by equal sums over the number of years determined upon as being the appropriate period to be taken in the particular case. In undertakings of this kind the capital employed is, as a rule, small, and the risk is generally less than the risk attached to capital embarked in trade. The rate of interest may, therefore, be 5 per cent. per annum, or more or less. With interest at 5 per cent. per annum it will be found, on reference to the given tables, that the present value of each £100 of annual super-profit treated as diminishing by equal sums over a period of five years is £268, or treated as diminishing over a period of ten years the value is £456.

Super-profit dependent upon impersonal connection

The most valuable kind of goodwill attaches to an undertaking earning super-profit arising out of an established connection, which needs for its successful maintenance little more than ordinary business aptitude sufficient to insure good management. In the case of many old-established undertakings for the manufacture and sale of goods which have become favourably known throughout the world by a trade name or trade mark, it is, as has been said, difficult to place a limit to the period of years over which the super-profit may arise to the undertaking. The continuation and maintenance of the volume of super-profit will no doubt depend on the constant exercise of enterprise and good management, and upon its not being unexpectedly threatened by a change of public taste or custom. If, however, no unfavourable conditions should arise it may be said, in the case of some world-renowned profit-seeking undertakings, that the volume of profit seems likely to arise almost in perpetuity. It is important, therefore, always to bear in mind the fact that the value of goodwill based on super-profit, even if treated as a perpetual annuity, cannot exceed ten years' purchase of the annual super-profit if interest at the rate of 10 per cent. per annum be allowed on the purchase money, because on these terms the value of an annuity of £100 is practically ten times the annual super-profit. Interest at the rate of 10 per cent. per annum is not, generally speaking, an excessive rate of interest to be expected by those who embark their capital in the purchase of commercial goodwill.

Super-profit from new or unexplored source

The purchase of the right to future annual super-profit expected to arise out of a new undertaking, or out of an unexplored source, is a highly speculative venture. In cases of this kind, the amount of super-profit may be particularly likely to vary considerably as between one year and another. At the initiation of a new enterprise of this description it may be expected that during the first year or two annual super-profit may be either non-existent or small in amount. But as the enterprise develops the annual profits may increase rapidly. In valuing the goodwill of this class of undertaking the computation should be based on the present value of the expected future annual super-profit (average or otherwise) treated as an annuity over the period of years selected, and discounted at a rate of interest sufficiently high, in view of the degree of risk, to induce the alert purchaser to adventure his capital. In view of the very speculative nature of ventures of this kind the appropriate rate of interest may be 20 per cent. per annum, or more or less. On reference to the tables at the end of this volume it will be seen that the present value of an annuity of £100 over a period of five years taking interest at 20 per cent. per annum is £299—or three years' purchase; over a period of ten years, £419—or $4\frac{1}{5}$th years' purchase; and over a period of twenty years £487—or $4\frac{9}{10}$ths years' purchase.

In calling attention to these three different classes of profit-seeking undertakings, it is fully realized that in many cases it will be difficult to determine to which of these classes a particular undertaking most nearly belongs. It is, however, no doubt important to bear in mind the general distinctions which serve to mark these classes, as these differences will be found helpful in selecting the most equitable basis to be employed in computing the value of goodwill.

Deduction of income tax from super-profit

In estimating the value of goodwill an important factor always to be taken into consideration is the probable average rate of income tax during the period of years over which the estimated annual super-profit is calculated to arise. As an illustration of the importance of this factor, assume a case in which the super-profit, without deducting income tax, is estimated at £10,000 per annum to arise over a period of ten years. Allowing interest at 10 per cent. per annum the value of the goodwill is £61,446. But if income tax is deducted at an average rate of 5s. in the £, and the super-profit thus reduced to £7,500 per annum, the value of the goodwill is £46,085. The examples contained in the later chapters of the work illustrating the various methods of computing the value of goodwill, will omit the factor of income tax, but attention is called to its importance. The fact that the purchaser of goodwill takes upon himself the burden of future income tax on the whole of the future profits—a share of which he is paying to the vendor in advance—should always be fully allowed for in computing the value of the goodwill.

CHAPTER III

PRIVATE UNDERTAKINGS AND GOODWILL

THE term " private undertakings " includes all profit-seeking undertakings, which are in the main owned by the working proprietors or partners, whether carried on as private partnerships or registered under the Limited Liability Acts. Profit-seeking undertakings falling under the term " public companies," dealt with in the next chapter, are regulated by charter or statute. Public companies are generally registered under the Limited Liability Acts, and the proprietors are, for the most part, not concerned as actual workers in the business. Private undertakings include both professions, and all kinds of industrial and commercial business. They are often dependent upon the particular personal qualifications and skill of the owner, but on the other hand the connection may be, to a large extent, independent of the personality of the individual owner. In the latter case, the goodwill is obviously likely to be of more value than in the former case.

Meaning of " private undertakings "

The extent to which the future maintenance of the super-profit of private undertakings may be dependent upon the work of particular individuals varies greatly. Professions, such as those of barristers, solicitors, accountants, surgeons, doctors of medicine, architects, surveyors, dentists, and the like, all need the continuance of the exercise of personal skill in conjunction with special knowledge, although in many professions much of the detail work is properly deputed to clerks and other assistants and efficiently carried out by them.

Professional practices

4—(1790)

It is probable that there cannot be much value attaching to the personal practice of a barrister after his death or retirement, or to the personal practice of a specialist in surgery, and it would seem in such cases that the more eminent the practitioner the less is the practice likely to have a surviving value. But many professional practices need little more than the exercise of common ability by anyone possessing the special knowledge, and, where the practice is large, the connection is often more or less impersonal, so that a practice may have a very substantial value, based on expected future annual super-profit.

Trades and businesses

In other classes of private undertakings the personal knowledge, judgment and experience of the owner may be important. Trades and businesses such as those of manufacturers, contractors, merchants, stock-brokers, produce-brokers, ship-brokers, agents, publishers, and retailers, are often dependent in varying degrees—especially if they are small undertakings—upon the continued attention and influence of a particular person, who is sought after by customers and others, either because of his ability or because of his personal attraction and influence. In valuing the goodwill of comparatively small businesses, which are particularly apt to be personal, special care should be taken not to underrate the value of the personal services of a vendor. It should be remembered that a sale of goodwill owing to the death of the owner of the business is rather in the nature of a forced sale than otherwise, and the value may be less than when a willing seller meets a willing buyer.

Valuing goodwill of private undertakings

It is proposed now to consider the methods of calculating the value of the goodwill of private undertakings. In that class of undertakings in which the permanence of the super-profit depends to a greater or less extent upon the personality of the working proprietors who are selling the goodwill, it is necessary to consider with care the nature of what they have to sell. They are selling an annuity equal to the estimated future super-profit. But as the permanence of this super-profit depends upon the continued application of personal skill—something more than ordinary aptitude for business—and the personal skill of the vendors will be withdrawn, the super-profit arising out of the vendors' work should be treated as likely to diminish year by year over the particular number of years which may be selected as a suitable period, having regard to the nature of the connection. It is obvious that the super-profit must, under the most favourable circumstances, rapidly diminish, unless maintained by the capable work of others who in due course will expect and will be entitled themselves to enjoy the super-profit which may be attributable, in turn, to their recently done work.

Goodwill of professional practice; retirement of partner

Suppose the average profits of a professional practice amount to £6,000 per annum after providing interest on capital at 5 per cent., but before charging any sum for partners' services. In the case of a professional practice, the amount of capital employed being usually small and the risk less than the risk to capital engaged in trade, interest at the rate of 5 per cent. per annum on capital may be sufficient to answer normal requirements. Suppose there are in this case two equal partners, and that one is to retire selling his share of the goodwill to the remaining partner. First it is necessary to deduct from the annual profits of £6,000 a sum, to be agreed, for the personal remuneration of the partners, say £1,200 each per annum. This will leave £3,600 super-profit, of which the out-going partner has been receiving one half, or £1,800, during the period of his active participation.

Over how many years is it likely that the already done work and influence of the retiring partner will extend? Supposing ten years is agreed upon, and that it is assumed the first year's annuity will be £1,800, less one-tenth—equal to £1,620. It will be found on reference to the Tables in the Appendix that, allowing interest at 5 per cent. per annum, the present value of an annuity commencing with £100 and diminishing by equal sums over ten years is £455·65. On the assumptions made therefore, the value of the goodwill, subject to proper adjustment in respect of future income tax, is £455·65 × 16·2 = £7,382, which proves to amount to rather less than two and a half times the retiring partner's former total annual income of £3,000 from the practice.

Decease of partner

As another example, take a case in which one of two equal partners in an old-established professional practice dies, and it becomes necessary to value the goodwill. The first step should be to ascertain the average annual amount of super-profit which the practice has, in recent years, yielded to the partners. The period of years taken may be three years or longer, but unless there is some reason for taking more than three years it is probable that this short period will reflect most closely the existing state of the practice. Assume it is found that the deceased partner has been in receipt of super-profit to the amount of £1,800 per annum, and that it is agreed between his executors and the surviving partner that his estate is entitled to an amount equal to the present value of future super-profit commencing the first year at £1,600 and diminishing by £200 each year, so that for the first year the super-profit will be £1,600, for the second year the super-profit is computed at £1,400, and so on, until for the eighth and final year the amount will have fallen to £200. Allowing interest on the purchase price at the rate of 5 per cent. per annum, the result is as under—

End of year.	*Present value of £1, allowing 5% interest.*		*Share of super-profit.*	*Present value allowing 5% interest.*
1	·95238	×	1,600	1524·4
2	·90703	×	1,400	1269·8
3	·86384	×	1,200	1036·6
4	·82270	×	1,000	822·7
5	·78353	×	800	626·8
6	·74622	×	600	447·7
7	·71068	×	400	284·3
8	·67684	×	200	135·4
				£6147·7

and this sum of £6,148 is the value of the deceased partner's share of the goodwill on the agreed basis. The results are calculated on the ordinary mathematical 5 per cent. interest tables, showing the present value of £1 due at end of each of the eight years. This so computed value is, as in the previous example, subject to proper adjustment in respect of future income tax.

Private partnership converted into limited company with additional partners

The case may now be considered of a private undertaking hitherto carried on by two partners, A and B, which it is proposed to register as a private limited company and to admit two other partners, C and D. The business is an old-established connection of East India merchants and agents. It is agreed that the value of the goodwill is £18,000, of which seven-twelfths equal to £10,500 belongs to A, and five-twelfths, equal to £7,500 to B. The average profits of recent years amount to £6,000 per annum before charging interest on capital and remuneration for partners' services.

The proposal in connection with the private limited company is that the two present partners, A and B, shall each put in, or leave, £2,000 in the business, and that the two new partners, C and D, shall each bring in £2,000. This will represent a share capital of £8,000 in addition to the value of the goodwill. At the date of the proposed transfer, each of the partners, A and B, has in fact in the business a sum larger than £2,000, and it is proposed to link up the accounts of the old firm with those of the limited company in the following manner.

A balance sheet of the old firm will be prepared as at the date of the proposed transfer. Apart from goodwill this balance sheet will show a surplus of assets over liabilities. Of this surplus £4,000 will be treated as capital of the partners in the old firm, and the remainder of the surplus will be carried to the credit of the partners' current or drawing accounts in the books of the limited company. These latter amounts may be drawn out by the partners at will, being considered as deposits at call. Shares will be issued fully paid to A and B in respect of £4,000 standing to the credit of their capital accounts. The transaction may be recorded by means of the new company handing to A and B cheques amounting to £4,000 in payment for the surplus assets over liabilities of the old firm purchased by the new company, and A and B then handing to the new company their cheque for £4,000 in payment in full for their shares. As consideration for the £4,000 paid by the company, A and B, the vendors, will hand over the whole of the assets shown on the balance sheet at the values stated therein.

Part of the consideration given by the new company for the acquisition of the assets of the old firm is an undertaking by the new company to pay and discharge all liabilities of the old firm, including the deposits at call which will be standing to the credit of A and B. The amount of the liabilities, ascertained in the usual way, will be shown on the balance sheet, but the undertaking on the part of the new company extends, of course, to an indemnity in respect of all liabilities, whether more or less than the amounts shown on the balance sheet. It is not intended that the goodwill, the value of which has been agreed at £18,000, shall be paid for in cash, and it will be interesting to consider the details and the respective merits of several alternative schemes of financing this, either of which might possibly be adopted.

Scheme No. 1

The authorized capital may consist of 30,000 shares of £1 each amounting to £30,000, of which 26,000 shares will be issued leaving 4,000 available for future issue. The capital to be issued in the first place will then be as under—

	For Goodwill.	*For Cash or its Equivalent.*	*Total.*
	£	£	£
A . . .	10,500	2,000	12,500
B . . .	7,500	2,000	9,500
C . . .	—	2,000	2,000
D . . .	—	2,000	2,000
	£18,000	£8,000	£26,000

Assuming the average profits of future years to be

£6,000 per annum, the amount will be available for division as follows—

		£
A	Salary	800
B	,, ...	800
C	,, ...	500
D	,, ...	500
		2,600
Dividend 12½% on £26,000 . . .		3,250
Balance available for contingencies .		150
		£6,000

Scheme No. 2

An alternative method would be to issue 10 per cent. Cumulative Preference shares—preferential also as to capital repayment—for £18,000 in payment for the goodwill, and £8,000 in ordinary shares of £1 each. In this case the profits available for distribution as dividends, amounting to £3,400—on the assumption of an average profit of £6,000 per annum, will be divisible as follows—

Dividend 10% on Preference shares . .	£1,800
Dividend 18% on £8,000 Ordinary shares .	1,440
Balance available for contingencies . .	160
	£3,400

If either of the above schemes be adopted in this case then, supposing that a profit of £6,000 per annum is in fact earned in future years, and that it is dealt with in the manner suggested, there will permanently remain an amount of £26,000 capital outstanding, and on the assets side of the balance sheet there will remain the item of £18,000 for goodwill.

Scheme No. 3

A more scientific financial arrangement, which would result in the gradual and automatic reduction and ultimate disappearance at the end of the ten years of the £18,000 goodwill, may be adopted. The value of goodwill being nothing but the present value of super-profit expected to arise out of the business in future years, it is clear that as those profits arise the value of the now existing goodwill will have been worked off and will have disappeared by the end of the term of years. It is true that valuable goodwill may then exist, but this will have arisen out of the good work done in the meantime by the directors, and out of the connection they have maintained and secured. The value of the then existing goodwill may be equal to or greater than the £18,000 computed as the present value of the now existing goodwill. This will depend upon the degree of success of the company during the period. The future outlook of the business will always regulate the value of the goodwill, and of the issued shares of the company, quite irrespective of any amount which may appear in the books as an asset under the head of goodwill. As a matter of fact, no amount should ever appear in the books of a profit seeking undertaking as the value of commercial goodwill, except during the period over which the actual cost of purchased goodwill is being liquidated out of current profits.

It would be a serious disadvantage to the shareholders of this private undertaking to retain permanently on the books as an asset the cost of the goodwill, because it entails the shares or other security issued for the goodwill forming a permanent part of the capital of the company. In Schemes Nos. 1 and 2, the holders of the 18,000 shares will be entitled permanently to receive a large share of the profits equal to a regular annual dividend of either 12½ per cent. or 10 per cent. on the £18,000. Instead of this there should be applied, out of the annual profits available for distribution, an annual sum of £2,331, payable in the form of an annuity, to A, £1,360, and to B, £971. This will result in completely extinguishing the £18,000—belonging as to £10,500 to A, and as to £7,500 to B—by the end of ten years in addition to paying in the meantime to A and to B interest at 5 per cent. per annum on the unpaid balances remaining outstanding at the end of each year, as shown by the following table—

A—		*Interest at 5%.*	*Capital Repayment.*
1st year.	5% on £10,500	£525	£835
2nd ,,	,, ,, £9,665	483	877
3rd ,,	etc., etc.	439	921
4th ,,		393	967
5th ,,		346	1,014
6th ,,		294	1,066
7th ,,		241	1,119
8th ,,		185	1,175
9th ,,		126	1,234
10th ,,		65	1,295
		£3,097	£10,503

B—		*Interest at 5%.*	*Capital Repayment.*
1st year.	5% on £7,500	£375	£596
2nd ,,	,, ,, £6,904	345	626
3rd ,,	etc., etc.	314	657
4th ,,		281	690
5th ,,		246	725
6th ,,		210	761
7th ,,		172	799
8th ,,		132	839
9th ,,		90	881
10th ,,		46	925
		£2,211	£7,499

Total, £13,600 = Annuity of £1,360 × 10.
Total, £9,710 = Annuity of £971 × 10.

The balance of annual profits estimated to amount, after paying directors' salaries, to £3,400, will then be divisible as follows—

Annuities to A and to B	£2,331
12½% on £8,000	1,000
Balance available for contingencies . .	69
	£3,400

In order to give effect to Scheme No. 3 an agreement for sale of the business would be entered into between A and B of the one part, and the new company of the other part, providing that in consideration of A and B handing over their business connection having an agreed value of £18,000 to the new company, A and B shall have a first charge by way of annuity on the annual profits of the new company, such profits being computed after providing for salaries as may be agreed. This amount payable out of the annual profits is to be cumulative so that if the amount of profits in any one year is less than sufficient to meet the annual payment, the deficiency in the annual payment is to be carried forward to the next year, and so on. Inasmuch as the profits of the new company will be assessed to income tax without deduction being allowed for the annuities payable thereout to A and B, the new company will deduct income tax at the current rate from time to time from the amounts of these annuities. The agreement will make it clear that the liability of £18,000 is not a liability which will rank *pari passu* with the claims of trade and other creditors of the new company, but is in the nature of a shareholders' arrangement *inter se*, and a note to this effect might be made on each annual balance sheet of the company.

The great advantage of Scheme No. 3 is that it provides for the payment off over the term of ten years of the consideration paid for a form of value which must necessarily diminish and disappear, being nothing but the right to receive an annuity, the whole of which will, by the end of the term, have been received. After the end of ten years, if the average annual distributable profits should continue to amount to £3,400 per annum, the holders of the 8,000 shares may receive a dividend thereon at the rate of 42½ per cent. per annum on the £8,000 of issued capital, and in the meantime during the ten years the shares will rapidly increase in value, owing to the sound basis upon which the business is being financed.

Under Scheme No. 1, A and B would receive between them out of the profits of the company during the ten years 12½ per cent. per annum, namely, £2,250 × 10 = £22,500 on the £18,000 to be issued under that scheme for goodwill, and at the end of the ten years they would still be the holders of the 18,000 shares which would continue to rank for dividends in future years, thus, of course, permanently handicapping the remaining 8,000 shares. Under Scheme No. 3 the 8,000 shares would gradually improve in value over the period of ten years until at the end of that time the holders became entitled to divide amongst themselves the whole of the annual profits of the company.

The effect of Scheme No. 2 is much the same as of Scheme No. 1 except that the amount received by A and B as dividends on their 18,000 shares would be £1,800 per annum, amounting over the ten years to £18,000, the shares afterwards remaining in like manner as a permanent part of the capital of the company.

The operation of either of these two schemes, Nos. 1 and 2, constitutes a handicap upon the holders of the remaining 8,000 shares in their character as owners of the new undertaking. This remark applies as much to the original partners A and B, in their characters as part proprietors of the new undertaking, as it does to the new shareholders.

Scheme No. 3 has the following advantages for the original partners—

(*a*) In their character as out-going partners it assures to them to the fullest possible extent, short of the payment of the consideration in cash, the receipt over a period of ten years of £18,000 for their goodwill, together with interest at 5 per cent. per annum on the balances remaining from year to year outstanding.

(*b*) In their character as shareholders in the new company, they will receive the same dividends as under Scheme No. 1 on their holdings of 2,000 shares (which excludes the value of goodwill), while at the same time these 2,000 shares will constantly tend to improve in value, because they will participate in the value of any goodwill of the business which may arise to the new shareholders, out of the work of the directors and managers of the new company.

Scheme No. 3 has the following advantages for the new shareholders—

The capital of the new company will not be permanently loaded with the £18,000 representing the cost of the goodwill because this will be gradually paid off by applying, in the form of an annuity, a portion of the profits earned over the first ten years of the company's existence, instead of applying the whole of the divisible profits to pay a high rate of dividend on the capital, including that created to buy the goodwill. The effect is to add every year to the value of the shares held by the new shareholders, thus ensuring that any value which may arise out of the good work and connection of the present proprietors will accrue to their benefit. This is equitable and provides the proper stimulus to good work.

Private limited company. Death of one of two partners; valuation of shares

A business of importers and exporters of chemicals, drugs, etc., was carried on during many years by two partners, A and B, as a private partnership. It was afterwards registered as a private limited company, the issued capital being 70,000 shares of £1 each fully paid. Of these shares, 35,000 belonged to A, and 35,000 to B. At the date of registration of the private limited company, £42,700 was included among the assets as the value of the goodwill, patents, trade marks, and designs.

About three years after the registration of the private limited company one of the partners, A, died, and it was necessary for the Executors to ascertain the fair selling value of A's shares, which it was intended should be purchased by B who would continue the business. The last annual balance sheet showed the following position—

	£	£
Assets—		
Cash	1,400	
Furniture, etc.	1,000	
Temporary investments, consisting of Government securities at market price, 31st March, 1920	12,900	
Debtors :		
Sundry Persons	3,500	
A, Loan Account	5,000	
B, Loan Account	9,000	
Stock on hand	23,000	
Goodwill, patents, trade marks and designs	42,700	
		98,500
DEDUCT.		
Liabilities—		
Creditors	16,300	
Bank Loan	5,000	
Reserves for Income Tax and Excess Profits Duty	7,200	
		28,500
Representing Capital, 70,000 shares of £1 each		£70,000

The average capital employed, apart from goodwill, is estimated at £30,000.

What is the fair selling value of the shares at the date of the last balance sheet, assuming that the values of the assets other than goodwill, and the amounts of the liabilities, are correctly stated in the balance sheet? The value of the goodwill depends upon the future super-profit likely to be earned by the business after providing sums each year adequate for management and for interest, at a reasonable rate, on capital invested in the business other than goodwill. The business has hitherto been managed jointly by A and B as Governing Directors. During the last three years sums averaging together £6,000 per annum have been charged to Profit and Loss Accounts for salaries and income tax of the Governing Directors. Income tax under Schedule D and excess profits duty have also been charged to the Profit and Loss Accounts.

The profit on trading as shown by the Profit and Loss accounts, after charging the above mentioned amounts, but adjusted in certain other respects, is as follows—

	£	£
Year ended 31st March, 1918:		
Balance as per Profit and Loss Account .	4,600	
Preliminary Expenses charged to Profit and Loss and now written back . . .	1,200	
		5,800
Year ended 31st March, 1919:		
Balance as per Profit and Loss Account .		11,200
Year ended 31st March, 1920:		
Balance as per Profit and Loss Account .	2,500	
Depreciation of Investments, War Loans, etc., charged to Profit and Loss Account, and now written back . . .	1,000	
Special remuneration to Governing Directors charged to Profit and Loss Account, and now written back	7,000	
		10,500
		£27,500

This gives an average annual profit of about £9,000

after providing the average annual sum of £6,000 for salaries and income tax of the Governing Directors, and also providing income tax under Sch. D and excess profits duty. The very liberal provision for Governing Directors' services was in consideration of the strenuous years of work covered by the period. From the so computed average annual profit of £9,000 a sum of £3,000 should be deducted for interest at the rate of 10 per cent. per annum on a rough average sum of £30,000 capital invested in the business other than goodwill, leaving £6,000 per annum super-profit, on the experience of the last three years, after making ample provisions of every kind including income tax.

This is an old-established business having a wide and valuable connection. On the other hand the death of one of the two partners may cause the disposal of the goodwill to be to some extent in the nature of a forced sale. On the supposition that in the future the business may be expected to earn a super-profit of £6,000 per annum, what is the present value of the goodwill? The present value of an annuity of £6,000 per annum over a period of five years discounted at the rate of 10 per cent. is £22,740. As an alternative computation the present value of an annuity assumed to commence with £6,000 the first year, and to diminish by equal annual sums over a period of ten years—so that the annuity for the last year of the period is £600—discounted at the rate of 10 per cent. is £23,160. It is probable that the value of the goodwill of this business is not less than £23,000.

If, in order to test this against an old method of valuation, it is assumed that the profits of the business, while carried on as a private partnership for the seven years ended 31st March, 1917, prior to its registration as a private limited company, averaged about £8,000 per annum after adjusting certain fluctuations due to the late war, but before providing for partners' services, interest on capital or income tax, the value of the goodwill would, under the old method, be computed as equal to three years' average profits or £24,000, which tends to give support to the valuation at £23,000 on the reasoned basis set out above.

The value of the shares at the 31st March, 1920, is then ascertained by adding £23,000, the value of the goodwill, to £27,300, the balance sheet surplus of other assets over liabilities—after deducting £42,700 the book value of the goodwill—giving an amount of £50,300. If the shares are to be valued as at a date three months after the date of the last balance sheet, there must be added a further sum of £1,257, being 10 per cent. per annum interest on £50,300 for the three months ended 30th June, 1920, equals together £51,557. On this basis the 70,000 issued shares of £1 each are worth about 14s. 9d. per share, three months after the date of the last balance sheet, and the holding of A, the late partner, amounting to 35,000 shares is worth one moiety of £51,557 equal to £25,778.

Disadvantages of old method of valuing goodwill

In the above case the services of the two Governing Directors are considered to be fairly worth together £6,000 per annum, and an amount of £3,000 per annum is required to provide 10 per cent. interest on a capital of £30,000 exclusive of goodwill. Thus out of a total surplus revenue of £15,000 per annum, only £6,000 is super-profit. In the case of a business, otherwise identical, but requiring as fair remuneration for management, say, only £2,000 per annum, and for interest on capital other than goodwill only £1,000 per annum, the value of the goodwill would obviously be much greater than £23,000. If, for instance, in such case the value was computed on an expected future annual super-profit of £12,000 per annum instead of £6,000 per annum, the goodwill might be worth nearer £46,000 than £23,000. But under the old method of multiplying the average profits by three, five, or other number of years to measure the value of goodwill this difference in value is likely to be overlooked.

CHAPTER IV

PUBLIC COMPANIES AND GOODWILL

THE expression "public companies" is not intended to include all companies registered under the Limited Liability Acts, but to extend only to those undertakings in which the capital is, for the most part, owned by the public, that is, by persons who have little or nothing to do with the actual management of the business. It will be found that those descriptions of business which are commonly carried on by such public companies do not as a rule depend, to any great extent, upon the skilled work of particular individuals. The descriptions of business carried on by such undertakings usually fall under one of two well-defined classes— **Meaning of "public companies"**

(1) Established connections largely dependent on well-known trade names or trade marks;

(2) New undertakings formed to develop fresh enterprises, or to exploit patented inventions, etc.

An established connection may sometimes seem to be practically permanent. The value of the connection depends, of course, upon the amount of expected future super-profit. In the case of a business with a world-wide connection, carrying on a prosperous and increasing trade and earning a large amount of super-profit, it may seem that there is no reason to place any limit upon the period over which this may continue, and that, therefore, the value of goodwill may be permanent, but this is not so. Payments made for goodwill are represented by nothing more substantial than the hope of future abnormal success. There is **Value of established connection** no backing to show for such payments in the form of material security as in the case of capital invested in buildings, plant and machinery. And even if the expected super-profit is treated as receivable in perpetuity, the value is in all cases limited by the rate of discount which must be applied to the expected annuity (super-profit) in order to translate it into present value. Owing to the inevitable risk, the rate of discount needed in the case of capital embarked in the purchase of commercial goodwill is rarely less than 10 per cent. per annum. It will be found, on reference to the tables at the end of this work, that at this rate of discount the present value of an annuity of £100 for twenty years is £851, or eight and a half years' purchase; while the present value of an annuity of £100 for 100 years is only £1,000, or ten years' purchase. Thus the difference in value between a twenty years' annuity and a one hundred years' annuity is small.

It is clear, therefore, that in the case of capital risked in trade the necessary interest factor alone must severely limit the value of goodwill. But apart from the interest factor, super-profit will not continue to arise in perpetuity owing to ordinary trade competition and change of taste, fashion, and so on. Wherever super-profit exists, there exists also special inducement to others to set up rival and competing businesses. Again, in the case of large undertakings the directing ability may deteriorate as time goes on. This will cause the annual profits to fall. The larger the undertaking, the greater the ability required to direct it with success. Great amalgamations may become cumbersome and overgrown. There is in all profit-seeking undertakings what may be called an economic unit, the size of which depends upon the degree of directing and organizing ability available. It is always a vital question to ask—how long, in any particular case, will this exceptional advantage, the directing and organizing ability, so essential to the continued success of a great undertaking, be maintained?

Value of new undertaking

In the case of a new undertaking formed to develop a fresh enterprise or to exploit an unknown and speculative source of possible super-profit, such as a patented invention, a strong appeal is made to the gambling instinct of the inquiring investor, and wild estimates of future super-profit are too commonly found in prospectuses offering shares in such issues. The present value of such an undertaking must be measured by reference to the fact that the proposition is highly speculative, owing, amongst other things, to such unknown factors as—

(1) Cost of production or manufacture on a commercial basis.

(2) Cost of selling organization.

(3) Extent of public demand, and cost of advertising necessary to develop this demand.

(4) Probability of further new inventions which may at any time supersede the use of any patented invention.

A high rate of discount must, therefore, be applied to expected future super-profit to be derived from new undertakings of this character, including all fresh enterprises, patented inventions and the like. This rate cannot often be less than 20 per cent. On reference to the tables at the end of this work it will be seen that, discounted at 20 per cent., the present value of an annuity of £100 for twenty years is £487, or just under five years' purchase, and the present value of an annuity of £100 for 100 years is no more than £500, or five years' purchase.

Market quotation of shares at a premium, its causes and meaning discussed

The amount paid for purchased goodwill is in the nature of a premium given in the hope of an extra profitable investment. When the shares in a joint stock company are quoted at a premium this premium, unless distorted and rendered artificial by bull and bear operations in the shares, may represent the market's estimate of (1) the value per share of undistributed profits already earned, and (2) the value per share of expected future super-profit. In examining the published balance sheet of a joint stock company with the object of ascertaining how far the premium at which the shares are quoted is due to the amount of undistributed profits already earned, and how much is attributable to goodwill, a number of difficult questions will be found to arise.

Assume a case, for the sake of illustration, and suppose that the floating assets of the particular undertaking are all properly stated at their fair values in the balance sheet. The wasting assets are also properly stated at values arrived at after deducting from their cost all capital outlay expired to the date of the balance sheet according to the best available estimates. On the other side of the balance sheet the liabilities are fully and fairly stated. In such a case the amount (if any) by which the stated value of the assets exceeds the sum of the liabilities and paid up share capital will represent the amount of the undistributed profits in hand. It is then comparatively easy, after allowing for the undistributed profits, to compute the amount which is being paid for goodwill in the market price of the shares. This can be done by deducting from the premium (the amount by which the price exceeds the par value) an amount equal to the proportion of undisturbed profits apportionable to each share. The remainder of the premium is represented by nothing but the present value of expected future super-profit. It must be noted that in the case of a joint stock company with a capital divided into preference and ordinary shares, any attempt to allocate the premium on the preference shares between undistributed profits and goowill, will need considerable care and a knowledge of the rights of the several classes of shares.

Balance sheet values

There is another complication which must be considered. Unfortunately it cannot be assumed as a matter of course either that the assets or the liabilities are stated in the balance sheet of a joint stock company at their full and fair values. This fact adds greatly to the difficulty of estimating how much, if any, of the premium included in the price at which the shares of a joint stock company are quoted is attributable to goodwill. The price of the shares may be based on a more or less common knowledge that the value of the assets is either greater or less than is stated in the balance sheet, or this knowledge may be restricted to a favoured few whose market operations may raise or depress the price of the shares. The values at which assets and liabilities are stated in a balance sheet must, therefore, always be accepted with caution. The values of wasting assets are, of necessity, in the nature of long-distance estimates, but these should be based on the regular observation and record of the conditions affecting all such assets. The figures in the *pro forma* balance sheet set out below will provide an illustration of the method, in a simple case, of computing the amount representing goodwill in the market price of shares.

PRO FORMA BALANCE SHEET AT THE 31ST DEC., 19..

		£	s.	d.		£	s.	d.
Capital:					Freehold Land	5,000	–	–
50,000 shares of £1 each,					Buildings	7,750	–	–
fully paid		50,000	–	–	Leaseholds	750	–	–
Debentures		20,000	–	–	Plant and Machinery	16,500	–	–
Creditors		15,000	–	–	Stock of Raw and Partly			
Reserve		16,000	–	–	manufactured material	14,000	–	–
Profit and Loss—					Manufactured Stock	22,500	–	–
Balance as per last					Debtors	24,000	–	–
Balance Sheet . £6,500					Cash	16,500	–	–
DEDUCT.								
Dividend at 10 per cent. per annum in respect of previous year £5,000								
Transfer to Reserve 1,000								
	6,000							
	500							
Profit for the year	5,500							
		6,000	–	–				
		£107,000	–	–		£107,000	–	–

This balance sheet shows that the capital of the company concerned is £50,000, consisting of 50,000 shares of £1 each fully paid, and that the profit for the year ended at the date to which the balance sheet is prepared, amounted to £5,500. The dividend paid for the previous year was 10 per cent. on the share capital, and out of the balance of profits then remaining in hand the sum of £1,000 was transferred to reserve account, which was thereby raised to £16,000. It is clear from the balance sheet that, after paying a dividend of 10 per cent. for the year just ended, there will remain an undistributed balance of profit of £1,000, together with the reserve of £16,000. Assuming then that the assets and liabilities are stated in the balance sheet at their full and fair values, a sum of £17,000 will remain in hand after paying a dividend of 10 per cent. for the year, and this is undistributed profit, and is equal to about 6s. 9d. per £1 share.

If, therefore, the £1 fully paid shares are quoted on the Stock Exchange at £1 16s. 9d. each, the price includes a premium of 16s. 9d. per share, of which 10s. is represented by nothing but goodwill. The goodwill of the business is thus valued in the price at which the shares are quoted at £25,000, being 10s. × 50,000 = £25,000. Suppose the average profits of past years have been no more than, say, £6,000 per annum, this leaves a super-profit of only £1,000, after providing interest at 10 per cent. per annum on the £50,000 capital. The value of an annuity of £1,000 for twenty years allowing interest at 10 per cent. amounts to £8,510 or about 3s. 4d. per share. In order to justify a premium of 10s. per share for goodwill alone, a future average annual profit of about £8,000 is needed. This would include £3,000 super-profit, the value of which on the above basis is £25,530. But future prospects may, of course, fully warrant such a favourable anticipation as a future annual super-profit of £3,000.

In considering the *pro forma* balance sheet set out above it has been assumed that the assets and liabilities are stated at their full and fair values, but the determination of the values of assets at any given date is always a matter of estimate, with the exception of land, easily marketable securities, and cash at Bank and in hand, the values of which cannot be a matter of doubt. For accounting purposes land should be stated at cost, because the capital outlay thereon does not expire as it does in the case of wasting assets. The values of other assets may easily be either over-stated or under-stated. If they are understated the effect is to create what is called a hidden reserve, and this condition may be within the knowledge of some operators in the shares, as a consequence of which the demand for the shares may cause the price to rise to a premium which appears, to those unacquainted with the facts, to be excessive.

Suppose, on the other hand, that in the balance sheet set out above, the values of the wasting assets, such as buildings, leaseholds, and plant and machinery are overstated, owing to failure to deduct adequate provision for expired capital outlay (depreciation), to the extent of, say, £8,000. The effect of this is that one half the reserve of £16,000, appearing in the balance sheet, and purporting to be undistributed profits, is not represented by anything. The profit and loss accounts have, in that case, been prepared in previous years without making adequate charges for expired capital outlay to the extent of £8,000, and thus the profits of those years have been over-stated, and so transferred to the reserve, which is, therefore, overstated to a like amount. Again it is possible that the other assets appearing in the balance sheet, representing what is commonly called the floating capital, such as stock in trade and debtors, may be stated at sums which may ultimately prove to be excessive. If this further over estimate of value amounts to £8,000 or £9,000, it may be found that the whole of the supposed reserve is a myth. Sufficient has been said to show the difficulty of judging the value of shares by reference to the balance sheet of an undertaking. It will also be plain that the premium at which a share is quoted on the market may, or may not, represent estimated goodwill. The premium may be due to the accumulation of profits already earned but undistributed, and it may be due to nothing but market manipulation and baseless rumours.

Issue of shares at a premium

A successful public company with an established connection may need further capital to meet the requirements of a constantly increasing business. It may be decided to issue new shares at a premium to rank *pari passu* with shares already issued. It is important to examine the effect of such an issue on the already existing shares. Suppose a prosperous manufacturing company requires to extend its plant, and that its last published balance sheet shows the following position—

Liabilities.			*Assets.*	
		£		£
Capital—			Land, buildings, plant, stock, debtors, and cash . . .	152,000
50,000 6% Preference shares of £1 each	£50,000			
50,000 Ordinary shares of £1 each	50,000			
		100,000		
Creditors . . .		27,000		
Reserve . . .		25,000		
		£152,000		£152,000

The accounts of recent years show that the business and profits have steadily increased, and that the profits of the last year amounted to £10,500. After providing £3,000 for dividend on the preference shares there remained a balance of £7,500 which is equal to 15 per cent. on the ordinary shares, and which was distributed as dividend thereon. The ordinary shares are quoted on the market, and are in good demand. The market price is 40s. per share, being a premium of 20s. or 100 per cent. At this price the dividend of 15 per cent., equal to 3s. on each £1 share, gives a yield of 7½ per cent. on the price of 40s.

It is assumed that the assets and liabilities are all stated in the balance sheet at their full and fair values.

If this be so, and there has been no previous issue of shares at a premium, the £25,000 reserve must be undistributed profit. It is plain then that one moiety—or 10s. of the premium of 20s. on each £1 ordinary share—is represented by this £25,000 undistributed profit. The balance of the premium 10s. is represented by nothing but goodwill. This shows that the goodwill is valued in the market price at £25,000, being 10s. × by 50,000, the number of ordinary shares issued. The super-profit on the last year's trading is scarcely more than £2,500, being £7,500 less the amount of £5,000 required to provide a dividend at a normal rate of, say, 10 per cent. on the ordinary shares. The market valuation of the goodwill, £25,000, is roughly equal to the value of an annuity of £3,000 for a period of twenty years, allowing interest at 10 per cent. The market price, therefore, seems to be based on the expectation that the profits of the business will continue to increase.

In these circumstances suppose that an issue of 50,000 new ordinary shares of £1 each at the price of 40s. per share is offered for subscription and fully subscribed. The effect on the holders of the 6 per cent. preference shares will be to substantially increase the margin of their security, but not, in any event, to increase their dividends. The ordinary shares would still be quoted on the market at not less than 40s. per £1 share, being a premium of 20s. per share. This premium will now be represented, however, by 15s. per share reserve, and 5s. per share goodwill. The reason is that the reserve has been increased by £50,000, the premium on the 50,000 new ordinary shares, and it therefore stands at £75,000, equal to 15s. per share on the 100,000 ordinary shares now issued. The market valuation of the goodwill remains the same at £25,000. The subscribers to the 50,000 new ordinary shares have, in fact, brought in to the coffers of the company 10s. per new share to answer the 10s. undistributed profit per old share, and 10s. per new share to answer the 10s. per old share value of goodwill. The number of ordinary shares is, however, doubled, and therefore the same amount of future super-profit will suffice for only half the former distribution of super-profit per share, thus halving the value of the goodwill per share, but against this each of the 100,000 ordinary shares is now interested to the extent of 5s. in the £25,000 cash brought in to the coffers of the company for goodwill by the subscribers to the issue of new ordinary shares.

The future extension of the company's business consequent upon the introduction of fresh capital may soon result in the earning of more than £3,000 annual super-profit, but this cannot happen unless and until the additional earnings amount to upwards of 10 per cent. per annum on the fresh capital, this being the assumed normal rate of profit required to attract the capital. In the case here illustrated, the preference shareholders are not entitled to direct participation in the amount received as premium on the new ordinary shares, the ordinary shares being entitled to the whole of any surplus after payment of the fixed dividend of 6 per cent. on the preference shares. The ordinary shareholders are, in this respect, in the position of residuary legatees. It would be otherwise if the issue of preference shares had been in the form of 6 per cent. participating preference shares. In that case the preference shares would be entitled to some portion, according to their rights, of the premium and of any future increase in super-profit, and their future value would, therefore, have been more directly affected by the issue at a premium of new ordinary shares.

Undistributed profit and premiums on new shares distributed as dividend; deduction of income tax

If at any future time it happens that the £50,000 received as premium on the issue of the new ordinary shares is not required for use as capital by the business, it may be legally distributed in the form of dividends over the whole of the ordinary shares either in one payment, or in a number of payments spread over a series of years. It is obvious that this £50,000 premium may properly be looked upon as a sum deposited with the company by shareholders, which may, therefore, be withdrawn by them without encroaching on, or curtailing, the share capital. The £25,000 balance of the reserve £75,000 consists of profit previously earned by the company and retained in hand, and, therefore, this amount also may, at any time, be properly distributed *pari passu* to the holders of the 100,000 ordinary shares as dividend. When a compound reserve of this nature is distributed to shareholders, income tax should be deducted only on that part of the dividend which represents undistributed profit. Premiums received on a new issue of shares are not assessable to income tax.

Rule for ascertaining total value placed upon goodwill of undertaking issuing shares at a premium

Assuming, for the sake of simplicity, that there is no undistributed profit to complicate the question, the rule for ascertaining the total value placed upon the goodwill of an undertaking which issues, at a premium, new shares ranking *pari passu* with shares previously issued, is to multiply the number of the shares previously issued by the amount of the premium per share at which the new shares are issued. The premium on the new shares is paid in order to bring them up to the computed value of the old shares, and, therefore, the market value of the shares should not fall after the issue of the new shares and the receipt of the premium. Although one part of the value of the old shares is decreased in consequence of the sale of a proportion of the goodwill formerly attaching to them, the decrease is made up by the proportion of the premium received, which vests *pari passu* in each share. Thus, each share, of the greater number of shares issued, has then not less than the market value per share which formerly attached per share to the smaller number of old shares, part of this value being now represented by goodwill, and part by the common right to participate in the premium brought into the undertaking by the holders of the new shares.

The following table illustrates this rule. The issue, in each case, is assumed to be 50,000 new ordinary shares of £1 each at a premium of 10s. per share for goodwill, the premium amounting, therefore, to £25,000. What is the total value placed upon the goodwill, if the old ordinary shares in the undertaking are (*a*) 50,000, (*b*) 150,000, and (*c*) 450,000 respectively ?

Old ordinary shares of £1 each.	Amount of premium per share for goodwill.	Total computed value of goodwill.	Total ordinary shares of £1 each after the new issue.	How premium of 10s. per share is represented after the new issue.	
				Goodwill per share.	Cash £25,000 in reserve per share.
		£			
(*a*) 50,000	× 10/-	25,000	100,000	5/-	5/-
(*b*) 150,000	× 10/-	75,000	200,000	7/6	2/6
(*c*) 450,000	× 10/-	225,000	500,000	9/-	1/-

After the new issue the 10s. premium per share will be represented as shown above partly by goodwill—which remains the same in total, but is spread over a larger number of shares—and partly by cash which has been brought in to the coffers of the undertaking by the new shareholders. From the point of view of the old shareholders the issue of new shares at a premium is a convenient way of cashing, in advance, estimates of future super-profit, because, to the extent that the premium per old share is represented by nothing but goodwill, the transaction is an exchange of rights to expected future profit for cash down.

Industrial and commercial concerns

As already stated it will generally be found that industrial and commercial concerns of normal development carried on by public companies are less directly dependent upon the work and influence of any one particular individual than either small businesses on the one hand, or great amalgamations on the other hand. The term *normal development* must be construed according to the circumstances of each case. It may easily be applicable to any connection—irrespective of size—which does not need abnormal directing ability. A large and successful business generally has a well-organized executive and a widely-based connection. It may not need very exceptional ability to direct it. It may nevertheless have a world-wide reputation, and its goods may be recognized everywhere by a trade name, or trade mark. When this is so the value of the right to use this trade name, or trade mark, may be very great. This is well shown by the large sums paid for goodwill when privately owned undertakings, which have already attained to world-wide fame, are sold to the public. In other cases great success may have been attained by businesses created, developed, and carried on by public companies, the shares in which are quoted in the market at high premiums. These premiums will doubtless be represented partly by increased property other than goodwill, and partly by the market estimate of the value of the goodwill.

Test of Stock Exchange values; a great retail business

In considering the Stock Exchange values of the shares of profit-seeking undertakings a rough and ready test may be applied with the aid of the published balance sheets of the undertakings. Take the case of a supposed public company, registered thirty or forty years ago, with a fully paid capital of £20,000 divided into 20,000 shares of £1 each. It may be common knowledge that from small beginnings, in this case, a great and successful retail business has been developed, which has grown to enormous volume, and which supplies a very large number of customers. Suppose that the undertaking has been financed in such a sound and conservative manner that all its business assets are valued in the books at strictly fair going-concern values, and that, in the course of years, there has been gradually accumulated and invested out of past profits, retained in hand undistributed, sums amounting in all to, say, £480,000—equal to £24 per share on the 20,000 issued shares. This £480,000 stands in the last published balance sheet to the credit of a reserve account, and is represented on the other side of the balance sheet by gradually accumulated increase in assets. One half of this increase is in business assets, such as buildings, plant, and stock, and the other half is invested in trustee securities. Assume that for the first twenty-five or thirty years of its existence the annual profits of this undertaking increased steadily year by year, and enabled an increasing dividend to be paid to shareholders out of the profits available for distribution. Assume further that the annual dividend, which has been regularly paid on each £1 share for some years past, is £3 per share, equal to no less than 300 per cent. on the capital originally invested.

It must always happen in the case of an undertaking of this kind, which has expanded steadily and attained great prosperity, that a time comes when the annual increase in profits will show signs of flagging. It is probable that, as years go on, there may be even small decreases in the annual profits. But the financial position is now very sound. There is no further need to apply profits to extend the assets. All the profits can therefore be distributed, and the annual dividend of £3 per share may well be maintained.

What, then, is likely to be the market value of each of the £1 fully paid shares in this successful undertaking? The company pays 300 per cent., and has behind it a wonderful history of constant progress and expansion. Its name may have become almost a household word throughout the world. It is, perhaps, popularly spoken of as being as "safe as the Bank of England." It has never reduced its rate of dividend. In these circumstances it is possible that, at a time when the average normal rate of interest on trustee securities was 5 per cent., the market value of a £1 share in such an undertaking may have been as high as £60. At this price it would pay the purchaser only 5 per cent. on his money while the annual dividend remains at £3 per share. If the dividend rises again in future, as it has so often risen in the past, then if the dividend reaches £3 12s. 0d. per share it will pay 6 per cent. on the price of £60, and if it rises to £4 10s. 0d. per share it will pay 7½ per cent., and with each increase in dividend the price of the share is likely to continue to rise. The business has shown that it is second to none. That is the view of sanguine and conservative shareholders. The high price of the shares does not tempt them to sell, for surely, at the worst, say they, the dividend will be maintained.

But sooner or later the dividend paid out of current profits will surely decrease. It cannot always go on increasing, and the outside limit of success may already have been reached, or even passed. No dividend, depending principally upon super-profit, can be indefinitely maintained, owing to the laws of competition and of change, which must ultimately cause a decrease of profit. But when will the profit decrease? This can best be judged by reviewing the past history of the undertaking as revealed by the annual reports and balance sheets. If it is found that there has been a vigorous growth and development for many years, followed by a considerable period of fluctuating prosperity, it is likely that some of the first signs of decay may even now be observable. On the other hand, it may be, of course, that the marked halt in the progress of development is only temporary, and that the undertaking has not yet reached maturity. But in all probability the chances are the other way. A great business which has grown and developed ultimately reaches a fine maturity which, with continued good management, may endure for a long time, but decay is the next stage as surely in the case of a great business as it is in the case of a mature man. Neither can last for ever. There are not many men, or many businesses, in existence to-day which were in existence a hundred years ago, and a hundred years hence the same remark will surely be equally true.

Those who agree with this view will agree that whenever a great business is judged to have reached maturity the ordinary shares should only be held as an attractive investment, while the average dividend paid returns a high rate of interest on the market price. Now if £60 is paid for each share in this supposed undertaking the value will, on the assumptions made, be represented thus—

	£
Original share on which £1 has been paid . .	1
Undistributed profits represented by increased assets apart from goodwill, $\frac{1}{20000}$ of £480,000 !. . .	24
Balance represented by nothing but goodwill . .	35
	£60

Therefore £35 has been paid for goodwill by the purchaser of the share. It is obvious that this price can be justified only if there is likely to be further great growth and development, and this cannot be so when a business has already reached maturity. Yet in the past it has been a common thing to find the ordinary shares of great, and apparently fully developed, industrial and commercial undertakings changing hands on the market at a price which yields the purchaser only 5 or 6 per cent. on his money.

But to take a cheerful view of the future of this undertaking suppose it is assumed to have reached maturity, but to have before it a long and successful life during which the dividend of 300 per cent. (£3 on each £1 share) will be maintained, while all its assets including the investments of its great reserve fund will be kept intact. What would be a fair price for the shares, and one sufficiently tempting to attract a discriminating investor? Such an investor would probably refuse to attempt to look ahead more than twenty years at the outside, and if he thought it safe to count upon a long continuance of the high current rate of dividend, he would no doubt be willing to pay a price for the shares considerably greater than the full value of the existing tangible assets, including the outside investments.

The value per share might be computed by a discriminating investor as follows—

	£	s.	d.
Original share on which £1 has been paid .	1	–	–
Undistributed profits represented by increased assets, apart from goodwill, $\frac{1}{20000}$ of £480,000	24	–	–
Goodwill—based on super-profit of £1 2s. 6d. per share, for a period of twenty years, allowing 10% per annum interest on the cost	9	10	–
	£34	10	–

The super-profit of £1 2s. 6d. is computed by deducting from the dividend of £3 per share the sum of £1 17s. 6d. required to pay a dividend at a normal rate—say 7½ per cent. per annum—on £25, the capital per share invested in the business, apart from goodwill. The low rate of 7½ per cent. is accounted for by the large proportion of capital invested in trustee securities in this case. The fair value of the shares of this undertaking is certainly nearer to £34 10s. 0d. than to £60 per £1 share. At the price of £34 10s. 0d. a dividend of £3 per annum yields about 8¾ per cent., which is not an excessive rate in view of the risk, and of the doubt whether the average super-profit will be maintained over so long a period as twenty years.

Test of value of shares of an insurance company

The fair market value of the shares of a large undertaking, such as a great insurance company, may be roughly measured by a careful consideration of the financial position and results disclosed by the published balance sheets. Suppose that the last published balance sheet shows that 590,000 shares of £5 each have been issued. An amount of £2 10s. 0d. per share has been credited as paid up, including £1 per share applied to uncalled capital reduction out of the profits of the previous year as shown below.

The balance sheet shows that, after deducting an investment reserve of £1,000,000, the assets connected with the fire, marine, and accident insurance branches of the business amount in value to £21,000,000 net. Those assets consist almost wholly of sound investment securities. They do not include the investments connected with the life insurance branch, which are allocated to meet the liabilities under the life policies.

Then suppose that the liabilities, including the shareholders' capital credited as paid up, and the final dividend proposed to be paid in respect of the year, together with all the other liabilities, and the usual reserve of 40 per cent. on premiums received during the year to cover future claims, amount to £14,475,000. Deduct this amount from £21,000,000, the net assets, and there remains a surplus of £6,525,000, being undistributed profits in hand equal to about £11 per share on each of the 590,000 shares issued.

An examination of the published revenue accounts of the fire, marine, and accident departments, and of the profit and loss account to which the results of these are carried, discloses the fact that, before writing off the cost of certain businesses acquired, the total profits earned for the year amount to £2,163,333, which have been allocated as follows—

Dividends paid to shareholders and income tax thereon paid by the company on shareholders' behalf	£716,000
Uncalled capital reduction £1 per share, making the shares £2 10s. paid . .	590,000
Income tax balance paid by the company .	440,000
Written off cost of businesses acquired . .	215,000
Balance added to reserves	202,333
	£2,163,333

Nothing has been carried to credit of the profit and loss account from the life insurance branch. The annual accounts of previous years show clear evidence of very capable and enterprising management, and rapid increase in the volume and profits of the business. The recent accounts, however, seem to suggest a rather prodigal increase in administration expenses, which now exhibit an increasing instead of a decreasing ratio to the growing premium income.

The profits earned for the year just ended, amounting to £2,163,333, are equal to £3 13s. 4d. per share. Of this amount 13s. 4d. is required to provide 5 per cent. interest on £13 10s. 0d., representing paid up capital £2 10s. 0d. per share, and undistributed profits in hand £11 per share. It should be noted that this £13 10s. 0d. per share is represented by the sound securities in which the funds of the company are invested, and, therefore, interest at the rate of 5 per cent. per annum may, in this case, be considered a normal rate of interest. This leaves a super-profit of £3 per share, and the share value might be computed as follows—

	£	s.	d.
Amount credited as paid up on each £5 share, including £1 per share applied out of the profits of the year just ended . . .	2	10	0
Undistributed profits represented by surplus assets, $\frac{1}{590000}$ of £6,525,000 (say) . .	11	0	0
Goodwill, based on super profit of £3 per share for a period of twenty years, allowing 10% per annum interest on the cost . .	25	10	0
	£39	0	0

On this basis, therefore, each share is worth £39, being £13 10s. 0d. represented by the funds actually in hand, and £25 10s. 0d. for goodwill. The yield on the price of £39 is about 7½ per cent. If it is desired to value the shares upon a more conservative basis it will be found that the value of an annuity of £3 for a period of ten years, allowing interest on the cost at 10 per cent. per annum, is £18 10s. 0d., and so computed the value per share is £32, consisting of £13 10s. 0d. the funds in hand, and £18 10s. 0d. for goodwill. The yield on the price of £32 is about 9⅜ths per cent.

CHAPTER V

THE ACCOUNTING VALUE OF PURCHASED GOODWILL AND ITS RECORD AND TREATMENT IN ACCOUNTS

Fallacy of treating purchased goodwill as having permanent value

THE most difficult problem in connection with the subject of commercial goodwill has now been reached and must be carefully examined. There is at present no common agreement on the question of the accounting value of purchased goodwill. It is a usual practice to treat the amount paid for the purchase of goodwill as representing permanent value. It is sometimes loosely said that, if the profits of a business are well maintained, the value of the goodwill cannot diminish. This is not necessarily always the case, because the value of goodwill at any time depends on future prospects, and these may be deteriorating even while profits are maintained or are actually increasing. Supposing, however, that the value of the now existing goodwill is not less than the value of the goodwill which existed at the date of purchase, yet it is equally necessary gradually to write off the cost of the earlier existing goodwill because part of this cost has expired. There can be no question as to whether or not part of the cost has expired; the only question is as to the proportion which has expired. It may be safely stated that capital outlay on the purchase of goodwill inevitably expires year by year, whether the profits of an undertaking are increasing or decreasing.

Spasmodic writing-off is unsatisfactory

In the case of a limited liability company which purchases goodwill, some kind of permanent capital—usually in the form of ordinary shares—is issued in payment for the goodwill, and the cost of the goodwill thus continues to be included among the assets in the balance sheet year after year, just as if the value was as permanent as the value of the freehold land upon which the premises of the business are situated. It is true that although no definite policy may be laid down, yet in the case of prosperous undertakings spasmodic allocations of surplus profits may often be carried to a reserve account, or transferred direct to the goodwill account in reduction of the cost. But such writing off is generally considered to be unnecessary, and it is sometimes even resented by shareholders as a needless retention and allocation of profits which, they think, should be distributed to them in the form of dividends.

Why should cost of purchased goodwill be written off?

It is urged against the writing off of the cost of goodwill—and often it is a fact—that the goodwill of a prosperous undertaking earning large surplus profits is worth no less now than it was when it was purchased ten or twenty years ago. The question is asked: "Why, therefore, should the goodwill be written off?" The answer is that the present goodwill is, in the main, not the goodwill which was bought ten or twenty years ago. At that time—ten or twenty years ago—the now existing goodwill (which is the present value of super-profit expected to arise in still future years) would have been worth next to nothing.

Comparison between goodwill purchased and goodwill created

All presently existing value in the form of goodwill—whether the amount be great or small—has arisen mainly out of the good work of the past or present proprietors, or their agents—the directors and managers—done and exercised over a period falling within the last twenty years. This is as true in the case of undertaking A which, on its formation, may have purchased the rights to the connection of a business established ten or twenty years before, as it is in the case of undertaking B, which may have been formed and commenced business ten or twenty years earlier than A, and itself created and built up the businsss connection. If, at the present time, the future prospects of A and B are similar, and equally good, the present value of the goodwill of each will be equal in amount. In these circumstances, if A, having purchased the business connection, is entitled to retain the cost of this in the books of account as an asset of permanent value it follows that B, having an asset of equal value, is also entitled to bring a like amount into account under the head of "Goodwill." In each case the effect would be to improperly forestall the future by appropriating, in advance, the expected profits of later years.

Cost of purchased goodwill is a fixed and definite quantity

The price paid for anything is of necessity equal to some fixed and definite quantity. Therefore, the price of every right, or thing, having exchangeable value must—knowingly or unknowingly—be computable on some basis which is equivalent to, or measurable against, some other fixed and definite quantity. In fixing the price to be paid for goodwill it is necessary to have regard solely to future prospects, and no one can do more than estimate what will happen in the future. But a price must be settled, and therefore it is necessary for the vendor and purchaser to agree upon some reasonable compromise, which takes the form of some fixed and definite quantity.

Usual rough and ready method of computing value of goodwill

The rough and ready method hitherto commonly followed in arriving at a price is to compute the value of the goodwill of an established undertaking as being equal to some number of years' purchase of the average annual profits of past years. For this purpose the profits of past years are sometimes computed without allowing for the value of the owner's services, and also without allowing for interest at a normal rate on the capital invested. It is probable that this practice originally came to be adopted because it was found by common experience that a computation so made gave a rough and ready measure of the amount which purchasers, of more or less similar business connections, in the past, had been willing to pay.

The usual process connected with the fixing of the price of goodwill would thus appear to involve a rule of thumb method rather than a conscious exercise in detail of the reasoning faculties, but however that may be, it is quite clear that the value of goodwill, which has cost a sum equal in amount to the profits of the past three or five years, cannot properly be written off against the profits of the next following three or five years. The purchaser has, in fact, bought the right to an expected annuity for a longer term of future years, although he may have measured the value of this right as being equal to the amount of the profits for the last three or five years.

Rate of interest required, in view of risk, a determining factor of value

In considering the accounting value of purchased goodwill, and its record and treatment in accounts, it is important, therefore, to keep in mind the nature of an annuity. The price of an annuity varies with the term of years, and with the agreed rate of interest. In the case of all profit-seeking undertakings the term of years over which super-profit will continue to arise in the future is, of course, uncertain but limited, just as in the case of human life. It is, however, the particular rate of interest required which determines the value of goodwill, rather than the period of years over which the future super-profit is expected to arise, and it must be assumed that a suitable rate of interest, having regard to the nature of the risk, and to the circumstances of each particular case, has been adopted in fixing the value of any goodwill.

Interest required not often less than 10 per cent. per annum

This rate of interest must obviously depend particularly upon the degree of risk inherent to the trade or business concerned. The rate can, however, scarcely ever be less than 10 per cent. per annum, even when applied to an obviously strictly fair and reasonable estimate of the amount of future super-profit, and when the business concerned is considered to be safe and secure. When, on the other hand, the enterprise is of a speculative nature, or the estimate of future super-profit is apparently extravagant in amount, the appropriate rate of interest may be as much as 20 per cent. or even more.

Reason that accounting value of purchased goodwill must diminish

If it be granted that, in computing the fair present value of goodwill, interest at a minimum rate of 10 per cent. per annum on the cost must be allowed for, it is obvious that the accounting value of purchased goodwill must diminish, and, in fact, it diminishes rapidly year by year, and consequently it should be gradually written off. Those who still allege that the cost of purchased goodwill may properly be carried forward as a permanent asset in the balance sheet of an undertaking should consider the fact that, allowing interest at 10 per cent. per annum, no less than 95 per cent. of the present value of a perpetuity will have expired by the end of thirty-one years from the date of purchase. It is obvious, of course, that commercial super-profit cannot arise in perpetuity.

Permanent share capital should not be issued to pay for purchased goodwill

As there is no such thing, then, as perpetual goodwill, the present custom adopted by limited liability companies of issuing share capital in a permanent form, against the cost of purchased goodwill, is a very undesirable one. Share capital, in permanent form, should not be issued by limited liability companies, to provide for the payment for purchased goodwill. In the present state of the law, which does not allow facilities for repayment of share capital, the difficulty might be overcome by issuing that part of the capital of a company which is required to pay for purchased goodwill in some form of deferred debentures, repayable by annual drawings in future years. Applicants for the share capital of the company, represented by value other than goodwill, might, in that case—subject to some better arrangement being made—be allotted a *pro rata* proportion of such debentures. It has already been shown in an illustration given in Chapter III that the issue of share capital in a permanent form to pay for purchased goodwill results in unfairly encroaching upon the rights of future shareholders, by taking away from them a large proportion of the earnings which may arise at any subsequent time out of the good work done by themselves, or their agents—the directors and managers.

Purchased goodwill may be written off in thirty-one years by applying only 5 per cent. of amount equal to expected super-profit

The cost of purchased goodwill may be written off within a limited period of years by regularly providing an annual sum, even though this is not larger than 5 per cent. of the amount of the expected annual super-profits. For instance, the cost of goodwill purchased on the basis of a thirty-one years' period, allowing interest at 10 per cent. per annum, is £947·9 for each £100 of expected future super-profit. In order to write off the whole cost of this, by the end of thirty-one years, it is only necessary to apply a sum equal to 5·21 per cent. of the expected future super-profit. The following tables show the different periods of years needed to write off the whole cost of goodwill when the value has been based on rates of interest of either 5, 10 or 20 per cent. Table A shows the approximate number of years required if a sum equal to about 5 per cent. of the amount of the expected future super-profit is so applied, and Table B shows the approximate number of years required if about 10 per cent. thereof is so applied.

TABLES SHOWING APPROXIMATE NUMBER OF YEARS REQUIRED TO WRITE OFF THE COST OF GOODWILL

TABLE A

When it is proposed to apply about 5% of the expected future annual super-profit.

Rate of interest.	Cost of goodwill per £100 of super-profit.	Interest on cost available as dividend.	Amount to be written off being balance of £100 remaining after paying interest on cost.	Approximate number of years.
	£	£	£	
5%	1898·03	94·90	5·10	61
10%	947·90	94·79	5·21	31
20%	472·99	94·60	5·40	16

TABLE B

When it is proposed to apply about 10% of the expected future annual super-profit.

Rate of interest.	Cost of goodwill per £100 of super-profit.	Interest on cost available as dividend.	Amount to be written off being balance of £100 remaining after paying interest on cost.	Approximate number of years.
	£	£	£	
5%	1798·10	89·90	10·10	47
10%	898·47	89·85	10·15	24
20%	453·29	90·66	9·34	13

Illustration of plan for writing-off the cost of purchased goodwill

Suppose the case of a profit-seeking undertaking which has bought the manufacturing plant of a successful going-concern for £100,000, and the business connection for £85,000, this connection being, of course, estimated to yield a large annual super-profit. The actual amount of future super-profit is always unknown, but the profits of the past five years, though fluctuating, showed an increasing tendency and averaged £25,000 per annum, after providing full remuneration for management, but before allowing for interest on capital invested. It is assumed that the agreement to pay the vendor £85,000 for the goodwill was arrived at after a full investigation of the position.

It is also assumed that this is an undertaking of a nature which requires an ordinary trade-risk interest at the rate of 10 per cent. per annum in order to attract, and retain unimpaired in value, the necessary capital. If this be so, and supposing that, including working capital the amount of capital apart from goodwill is £150,000, then a future annual profit of £25,000 will be sufficient to yield £10,000 of super-profit. How much of this super-profit has been already allocated and paid in advance to the vendor in the price of £85,000 the cost of the goodwill? As the normal rate of interest on capital invested in the manufacturing plant and stock is 10 per cent. per annum, it may be assumed that no less rate of interest can have been allowed for in arriving at the value of the goodwill, £85,000, because capital invested in goodwill is invested in that which is considerably less substantial than capital invested in manufacturing plant and stock.

Assume, therefore, that the purchaser has taken good care, in computing the value of the goodwill, to provide for the retainer by him of a part of the expected annual super-profit sufficient to provide 10 per cent. per annum on the balance outstanding from year to year of the purchase price £85,000—or, to be exact, say £85,135. In that case he has paid in advance to the vendor sums equal approximately to the sums shown in the column headed " Vendor's share " in the Table below—

Year.	Estimated annual super-profit.	Balance of accounting value of purchased goodwill at beginning of year.	Purchaser's share equal to 10% per annum on the money remaining invested in purchased goodwill.	Vendor's share equal to £10,000, less 10% per annum on the balance of money advanced to him as price of goodwill.
	£	£	£	£
1	10,000	85,136	8,514	1,486
2	10,000	83,649	8,365	1,635
3	10,000	82,014	8,201	1,799
4	10,000	80,215	8,022	1,978
5	10,000	78,237	7,824	2,176
6	10,000	76,061	7,606	2,394
7	10,000	73,667	7,367	2,633
8	10,000	71,034	7,103	2,897
9	10,000	68,137	6,814	3,186
10	10,000	64,951	6,495	3,505
11	10,000	61,446	6,145	3,855
12	10,000	57,590	5,759	4,241
13	10,000	53,349	5,335	4,665
14	10,000	48,684	4,868	5,132
15	10,000	43,553	4,355	5,645
16	10,000	37,908	3,791	6,209
17	10,000	31,699	3,170	6,830
18	10,000	24,868	2,487	7,513
19	10,000	17,355	1,735	8,265
20	10,000	9,091	909	9,091
	£200,000		£114,865	£85,135

If, in this case, the future prospects of the business should improve at any time after the transfer the exchangeable value of the goodwill at that time would no doubt be greater than £85,000. On the other hand, if the future prospects should deteriorate, the value of the goodwill would be less, and the value might fall to little or nothing. But this profit-seeking undertaking, having made a bargain and paid to the vendor a share of the profits of future years, should set aside out of the profits of those years amounts equal to that share so paid in advance.

A reference to the column headed "Balance of accounting value of purchased goodwill" will show that by the beginning of the eleventh year the accounting value of the goodwill should appear in the books at the reduced amount of £61,446. Assuming that the £85,000 has been raised by the issue of some form of deferred security which can be gradually paid off, by annual drawings or otherwise, over the period of twenty years, the amount redeemed by the end of ten years will be £23,689, leaving still outstanding a balance of £61,446 of the security so issued to raise the capital for the purchase of the goodwill.

Other plans illustrated

If, in the case of this assumed undertaking, the profits earned, in the years following the purchase of the goodwill, do in fact amount to not less than £25,000 per annum, thus yielding not less than £10,000 per annum super-profit, the right method of gradually writing off the cost of the goodwill is plain enough, and no question of difficulty need arise. But supposing on the other hand that in the years following the purchase of the goodwill the profits turn out to be considerably less than expected, it will be found in that case that all kinds of difficulties are likely to be met with by those who desire to lay down and carry out a sound financial policy. There are various plans which might be adopted, some being sounder than others. It is only possible here to outline one or two of these.

Plans modified when annual profits prove to be less than expected

Suppose that the profits—which were estimated as likely to amount to £25,000 per annum in the future—amount for the first five years, after the purchase of the goodwill, to the following sums—

Year.	£
1	15,000
2	20,000
3	10,000
4	30,000
5	17,000

What policy, or modified policy, should be adopted in writing off the goodwill during these years? It will be remembered that the capital, apart from goodwill, is £150,000, and that the goodwill has cost £85,000.

In that case, if the undertaking is carried on in the form of a limited liability company, the policy adopted might be as follows—

Cost of goodwill	£85,000
First year, written off	Nil
because the profit of £15,000 is only sufficient to pay a dividend at the normal rate of 10% per annum on the £150,000 capital invested in the business apart from purchased goodwill.	
Second year, written off	750
because the super-profit being only £5,000 (instead of the expected £10,000), the shareholders' share can be no more than 5/10ths of 10% on £85,000 = £4,250, leaving a balance of £750 to be written off.	
	84,250
Third year, written off	Nil
because the profit of £10,000 is less than sufficient to pay a dividend at the normal rate of 10% on the £150,000 capital invested in the business apart from purchased goodwill.	
Fourth year, written off	6,575
because the super-profit being £15,000, the full shareholders' share of 10% on £84,250, the amount remaining invested in the goodwill, has been earned, and leaves a balance of £6,575 to be written off	
	77,675
Fifth year, written off	447
because the super-profit being only £2,000, the shareholders' share is only 2/10ths of 10% on £77,675 = £1,553, leaving a balance of £447 to be written off.	
	£77,228

If this method of writing off is adopted, the cost of the goodwill will have been reduced by the end of the fifth year from £85,000 to £77,228. On reference to the Table on page 85 it will be seen that—on the assumption that the £10,000 super-profit had been regularly earned in each of the five years and the proper proportion written off—the cost of the goodwill would then have been reduced by the beginning of the sixth year to £76,061. There has thus been written off a sum which is less than it should have been by £1,167; but the reason is that on the actual experience of the first five years the expectations which were formed at the time the goodwill was purchased have not been fully realized. The more this question is studied the clearer it will be that there are a variety of methods available for adoption in writing off the cost of goodwill. There ought to be general agreement that some method should, in each case, be laid down and systematically followed.

Plan involving a stricter policy

A stricter policy of writing off the cost of goodwill in the case of a limited liability company, when profits prove to be less than expected, might entail the adoption of a method which would result in allocating the profits of each year—first, in paying an agreed normal dividend on the capital invested in the business apart from purchased goodwill; second, in writing off the cost of goodwill to an amount necessary to reduce the balance of the accounting value of the purchased goodwill to the amount shown in the above Table in the column headed "Balance of accounting value"; third, in payment of a dividend at the agreed normal rate on the deferred security issued to provide the capital cost of the purchased goodwill; and fourth, in payment of a further dividend to the several classes of shareholders in accordance with their rights.

In that case, the fluctuating profits for the first five years after the purchase of the goodwill, as set out in the previous illustration, would be dealt with as follows—

Cost of Goodwill	£85,000
First year, written off . . . . because the profit of £15,000 is only sufficient to pay a dividend at the normal rate of 10% per annum on the £150,000 capital invested in the business apart from purchased goodwill	Nil
Second year, written off . . . . . . because out of the super-profit earned amounting to £5,000 there must be allocated under this scheme a sum of £3,000 to be written off the cost of goodwill in order to reduce the balance of accounting value of this at the beginning of the third year to £82,000 (see Table above)	3,000
	82,000
Third year, written off. . . . . . . because the profit of £10,000 is less than sufficient to pay a dividend at the normal rate of 10% on the £150,000 capital invested in the business apart from purchased goodwill.	Nil.
Fourth year, written off . . . . . . because out of the super-profit earned amounting to £15,000 it is only necessary to allocate £3,800 to be written off the cost of goodwill in order to reduce the balance of accounting value at the beginning of the fifth year to £78,200 (see Table above)	3,800
	78,200
Fifth year, written off . . . . because the super-profit being only £2,000, it is necessary to allocate the whole of this to be written off the cost of goodwill. This reduces the balance to £76,200, but on reference to the above Table it will be seen that the balance of accounting value at that date is only £76,061	2,000
	£76,200

Case of private partnership: more drastic plan

If the supposed profit-seeking undertaking mentioned above was carried on in the form of a private partnership it might be considered desirable to adopt a still more drastic method of writing off the cost of the purchased goodwill. The capital invested in the undertaking is supposed to be £150,000, apart from purchased goodwill, and £85,000 was paid for the goodwill, together £235,000. Assuming, then, that the profits for the first five years after the purchase of the goodwill proved to be as shown in the second column below, these might be allocated year by year, first to reduce the balance of accounting value of the purchased goodwill to the proper amount as shown in the above Table, and second for distribution among the partners as profits.

In that case the annual profits would be dealt with as follows—

Year.	*Annual Profits.*	*Written off Goodwill.*	*Distribution among the Partners as Profits.*
1	£15,000	£1,500	£13,500
2	20,000	1,600	18,400
3	10,000	1,800	8,200
4	30,000	2,000	28,000
5	17,000	2,100	14,900
		£9,000	£83,000

The total amount written off goodwill in the five years amounts to £9,000, thus reducing the balance of accounting value to £76,000 which, in round figures, is the amount shown in the above Table as the accounting value of the purchased goodwill at the beginning of the sixth year.

Need for adoption of sounder and more adequate rules of finance

The vast and constant extension of joint stock enterprise makes it increasingly desirable, for the protection of investors, that sounder and more adequate rules of finance should be, by common consent, adopted in connection with the value of goodwill, and its record and treatment in accounts. When the underlying principles relating to this matter are more widely understood and appreciated, a demand will inevitably arise that better, and more dependable, information shall be available for shareholders. As already explained in this work the exchangeable value of goodwill depends upon the future prospects of earning super-profit, and these may at any time be estimated, by having regard to all the known factors, and to past events, as guides to the future. The existing value of goodwill is not at all dependent upon whether or not there happens to appear, in the balance sheet of a profit-seeking undertaking, an asset under the head of goodwill. The value of commercial goodwill, at any particular time, depends solely upon the future prospects of the undertaking at that time.

Balance sheet note of present value of goodwill computed on reasoned basis

Information might well be available in the published balance sheets of profit-seeking undertakings showing—in the form of a note—the estimated value of the goodwill based on a continued earning of super-profit equal to, say, the average amount earned in recent years, discounted at a stated rate of interest. There is no reason why the annual balance sheet of every profit-seeking undertaking should not contain a note of this kind, stating that on an estimated ..... years annual super-profit of £...., discounted at ..... per cent. per annum, the present value of the goodwill is £..... being equal to £..... per share. Shareholders would then have some reasoned basis to assist them in forming an opinion as to the value of their shares. Shareholders might themselves adopt a higher, or a lower, estimate of future annual super-profit, or they might discount the amount at another rate of interest. At present the price at which a share is quoted on the market depends principally upon the amount of dividend paid, but this is often no true indication of the value of the share when regarded in the light of all the known factors affecting future probabilities.

Securities issued against cost of goodwill should be in a redeemable form

The question of the form of security which should be issued by joint stock companies against that part of the capital which is represented by nothing but goodwill is a difficult one. It is clear, however, that such security should always be in a form which can be redeemed by drawings, as and when the means are available for redemption. Some form of deferred debentures might be devised. The security should not carry a fixed rate of interest as it is obvious that, whatever financial policy is adopted for writing off the goodwill, the amount of interest payable in any year on the outstanding balance of the security must depend upon the profits of that year. If the profits are less than sufficient to pay a normal rate of interest on the capital invested apart from goodwill, there can be no dividend properly available for the deferred debentures, or other form of security which has been issued against the cost of the purchased goodwill.

CHAPTER VI

ANNUAL INCOME TAX AND PURCHASED GOODWILL

The two classes of wasting assets

In considering the method of computing annual profits assessable to annual income tax, it is important to keep clearly in mind the fact that deduction cannot be allowed for expired capital outlay (depreciation) on that class of wasting assets which is represented by purchased goodwill, consisting of rights to the enjoyment of the profits of future years. There are two distinct classes of wasting assets represented respectively by—

(*A*) Capital invested in the purchase of assets necessarily required to be wasted in seeking the profits of future years;

(*B*) Capital invested in the purchase of rights to the enjoyment of the profits of future years.

Wasting assets, falling within the first-mentioned class, are termed inherently wasting assets, and are always represented by some form of existing material or commodity necessarily required to be wasted when applied in seeking profits; assets falling within the last-mentioned class are represented by nothing but rights to profits, which may, or may not, arise in future years. If, and when, such profits do arise, in future years, they must at that time be assessed to income tax, because income tax is a tax on profits, increase of value, or other advantage, actually arising within each year, and it must be collected at the source. Thus the income tax on business profits must be collected on the profits as they arise year by year, from those in physical possession of a business, without any regard to the fact that those persons may themselves have paid away part of the profits in advance of their arising—as payment for goodwill to the founder of the business. And so also the income tax on the annual value of land, for instance, must be collected from a lessee in possession, although he, as the lease-holder, may have paid the rent under discount, years in advance of its arising, in the payment made to the lessor at the time the lease was granted.

Inherently wasting assets

In computing annual profits, for income tax purposes, deduction should be allowed from revenue in respect of the annual waste of all inherently wasting assets. Wasting assets of this character include—

(*a*) Industrial plant.

(*b*) Natural raw materials including coal, minerals, stone, gravel, earths, oil, nitrate, and, when intended for sale, land.

(*c*) Shaft sinking and development undertaken to obtain access to all such raw materials.

(*d*) Purchased life, and other terminable, annuities.

In all the above cases annual profit is dependent on—because it cannot arise without—the employment and gradual waste of the inherently wasting assets, and therefore the annual profit ceases when these have been exhausted.

As stated above all inherently wasting assets are represented by some form of existing material or commodity, necessarily required to be wasted when applied or dedicated to the purpose of seeking profits. This is as true in the case of a purchased annuity as it is in the case of industrial plant, but this important fact is not very plain at first sight. In order to make clear the distinction between the two classes of wasting assets it seems desirable to consider the matter in some detail. It may appear at first sight that a purchased annuity is a wasting asset which has more points of resemblance to a lease of land, for instance, than to anything in the nature of material or commodity, but this is not so. Both annuity and lease are concerned with the future receipt of money or money's worth, but otherwise they are very different in character.

Fundamental difference between annuity and lease

In order to illustrate the fundamental difference between the two classes of wasting assets, suppose that A and B are each possessed of the sum of £272·32 in money on a gold basis. Money on a gold basis is of course a commodity, and as such at any given time forms part of the world's stock of existing wealth. In order to emphasize the fact that true money has full commodity character, suppose that A and B have each a pile of gold sovereigns, each pile amounting to £272·32

Suppose, further, that A elects to exchange his money amounting to £272·32 for the purchase of an annuity, on a basis which will yield him 5 per cent. per annum thereon, and so entitle him to receive £100 at the end of each of the next three years. B, on the other hand, exchanges his £272·32 for the purchase of a lease of land for three years, the value of the land being £100 per annum. This will entitle B to the use of land, worth £100 per annum, for a period of three years. Thus B's investment will also yield him interest at the rate of 5 per cent. per annum.

The nature of the investment, for which £272·32 has been exchanged in each case, will be clearer by reference to the table on page 96.

PRESENT VALUE OF £100 PER ANNUM FOR THREE YEARS,

ALLOWING INTEREST AT 5% ON UNEXPIRED CAPITAL OUTLAY.

	Present value.	Allocation between capital and income. 1st £100.	2nd £100.	3rd £100.	Annual instalment.
	£	£	£	£	£
Instalment due at end of 1st year	95·24	4·76	—	—	100
Instalment due at end of 2nd year	90·70	4·54	4·76	—	100
Instalment due at end of 3rd year	86·38	4·32	4·54	4·76	100
	£272·32				£300
Interest (income) . .		13·62	9·30	4·76 =	27·68
Capital		86·38	90·70	95·24 =	272·32
		£100·	£100·	£100·	£300·

The capital, consisting originally of the two piles of gold sovereigns, must be kept intact during the three years, but assuming a yield of 5 per cent. per annum, the annual income arising on each £272·32 will, in the meantime, be £13·62, which sum may be spent and consumed each year by A and B respectively, without diminishing the capital. Let us see, then, how A and B must each manage his different investment in order to secure that he shall spend and consume the annual income of £13·62, and shall also have his pile of gold sovereigns remaining intact at the end of the three years.

A, who has exchanged his £272·32 for an annuity, must apply the proceeds of that annuity as follows—

	To replace capital.	To spend as income. From annuity.	From simple interest earned on replaced capital.	Total income.
1st year .	86·38	13·62	—	13·62
2nd year .	90·70	9·30	5% on £86·38 : 4·32	13·62
3rd year .	95·24	4·76	5% on £177·08 : 8·86	13·62
	£272·32			

At the end of the three years A will have replaced his capital of £272·32, which will thus still remain intact, and he will have spent and consumed the income of £13·62 per annum. The grantor of the annuity may, of course, during the three years himself have made a further profit, by earning interest greater than the 5 per cent. per annum allowed by him to A in fixing the purchase price of the annuity, but this is not material to the argument.

B, who has purchased a lease of land having an annual value of £100, covering a period of three years, may perhaps let the land at an annual rent greater than £100 per annum, but for present purposes it is assumed that B lets the land to another person at a rent of £100 per annum. B must then set aside to replace his capital, out of the annual amounts of £100 which he receives, the same amounts as shown above in the case of A. B will also, at the end of the three years, have recovered the whole of his capital, and in the meantime he will have spent and consumed the annual income of £13·62 which represents his profit, and is all that he is entitled to spend. If B himself occupies the land, he consumes the annual value, and must set aside similar sums each year to replace his capital, and the balance, together with the simple interest earned on replaced capital, as shown above, will represent his annual income.

And in the meantime what is the position of the lessor who received from B, at the time the lease was granted, a transfer of capital represented by a pile of gold amounting to £272·32? The lessor being the owner of the land out of which an annual value of £100 arises, is obviously entitled to spend and consume that amount each year, and supposing that in the meantime he invests, as shown above, at 5 per cent. interest, the capital in his hands not yet translated into income, he will obtain the full income of £100 a year from the following sources—

	Capital in lessor's hands which becomes gradually translated into income.		Interest at 5% on capital remaining in lessor's hands.	Total.
	£		£	£
1st year .	86·38	↗ 5% on £272·32	13·62	100
2nd year .	90·70	↗ 5% on £185·94	9·30	100
3rd year .	95·24	→ 5% on £95·24	4·76	100

Thus the capital originally transferred by B to the lessor has become gradually translated in the lessor's hands, into income, and thereupon has been properly spent and consumed by the lessor. A and B have also spent their incomes, and each has his capital, or pile of gold sovereigns, still remaining intact.

Wasting assets other than inherently wasting assets

The whole income arising out of the annuity in which A invested his money amounts to only £27·68 over the period of three years, whereas the income arising out of the land amounts to £300 over the period. It will be observed that B, in purchasing a lease of land, did not invest his money in a form entitling him to repayment of the capital by the lessor, but entitling him only to a future income of £100 per annum, out of which he must set aside, to replace his capital, sums equal to the proportion of that income from land belonging to the lessor, which B has already advanced to the lessor in the cost of the lease.

It is true, therefore, to state that all inherently wasting assets, including purchased annuities, are represented by some form of existing material or commodity. In the case of a purchased annuity, the commodity is in the form of money. A lease of land, on the other hand, is not an inherently wasting asset, and is not represented by any form of existing material or commodity. Thus the exchangeable value of an annuity, at any time, is represented wholly by capital, and the exchangeable value of a lease of land, at any time, is represented wholly by a right to the enjoyment of annual value to arise in the future. The same conditions which apply to a lease of land apply also to all other non-material wasting assets, including purchased terminable concessions, copyrights, patent-rights, goodwill, and trade marks.

An annual income tax should be assessed only on the balance of an annuity after deducting the capital element, because the annuitant must replace the capital cost out of the annuity, spending only the income, as otherwise more than the annual income will have been spent. British income tax is at present wrongly assessed upon the whole amount of an annuity. In the case of a lease of land, although the lessee must refund to himself sums equal to the capital cost out of the annual value of the land, yet the lessor may spend similar sums out of the consideration paid to him for the lease without causing more than the annual income to have been spent. Thus an annual income tax is properly assessable upon the whole net annual value arising out of land, whether the land is in the occupation of the actual owner or of a lessee or tenant.

Income tax must be levied on profits in the year they actually arise

Income tax must be levied periodically on profits at the source as they arise from property, professions, trades, and offices, notwithstanding the common practice for the owner of a particular source from which profits arise, such as either land, buildings, copyrights, patentrights, or other business undertaking, to sell or dispose of his personal interest in that source to another party either absolutely or for a term of years. The original owner receives in one sum the agreed present value of the future annual income. The amount is paid to him in advance of the years in which the future profits are expected to arise, and the payment is therefore made under discount. In fixing the purchase price allowance should always be made to the purchaser, not only for the annual discount, but also for the estimated future liability shifted on to him to pay income tax.

Transfer from owner to owner of rights to future profits

The new owner enters into possession of the particular source of profits arising, and while in possession he is liable to pay income tax annually thereon. He may, in his turn, at any time sell his interest either absolutely or for a term of years to a third party, and so on indefinitely. It is obvious that those responsible for assessing and collecting income tax could not undertake to follow the ever-changing interests and equities of individuals in sources of taxable annual profits back into the hands of the original owner. The Inland Revenue authorities must assess annually at the source the annual profits arising, and collect the tax annually from the individual in possession of that source. The individual in possession of a source of profits must be assumed to have made all necessary adjustments with other parties, in regard to future liability to income tax, at the time those other parties received the sums of money representing the then-value of the pure annual profits expected to arise in future years.

Depreciation, or expired capital outlay, which is not allowable as a deduction in assessing profits to an annual income tax is, therefore, that which takes place only in the hands of the individual owner arising out of the fact that he has purchased the future income from another man. Clearly such depreciation is something quite different from depreciation of inherently wasting assets arising out of, and necessarily incidental to, the earning of future annual profits. The claim to an allowance in respect of wasting assets which are not inherently wasting assets arises simply out of the fact that the ownership of the source of profit has been transferred, by purchase, from one individual to another. There is no equitable ground for claiming allowance on this account, because such transfer, from one to another, does not of itself impair the annual value, or profit-earning capacity, which must in all cases be taxed, in one sum, at the source, as it arises annually.

The purchase for a lump sum of the right to the profits which may arise in future years from the work of the author (represented by copyrights), or from the work of the inventor (represented by patentrights), or from the work of the industrial and business organizer (represented by legal goodwill) does not diminish these future profits. What has happened is that the original owner, or creator of the source, has himself anticipated the receipt and enjoyment of those taxable profits, by assigning to others, for valuable consideration, his right to receive them, if and when they arise.

In these cases the charging of income tax on the full income, or profit, arising each year may seem, at first sight, to bear unjustly upon those who have invested their capital in the purchase of temporary rights of this description unless, in fixing the purchase price, due allowance has been specifically made to the purchaser for the future liability shifted on to him to pay income tax. No doubt it may be argued that, although the tax must be paid, it falls on the wrong shoulders, but until some practical means can be found to charge with income tax those who have received expected future taxable profit, in advance of the year of its arising, there seems to be no remedy.

Different case where vendor is outside United Kingdom

But deduction of depreciation or expired capital outlay on wasting assets, other than inherently wasting assets, should be allowed, in computing annual profits for assessment to income tax, whenever, and to the extent that, the vendor would not have been subject to British income tax if the source of income had remained in his hands. An instance of such an exception is capital invested in the purchase of a terminable concession outside the United Kingdom. In such a case the original owner of the source of the future annual profit would not have been subject to British income tax, and therefore the expired capital outlay, necessary to be refunded out of the revenue receipts, before any annual profit can be earned by the purchaser domiciled in the United Kingdom, should be allowed as a deduction from revenue receipts in assessing British income tax. The assessment to British income tax of the whole of the annual profits arising from such a foreign concession tends to restrict, and sometimes even to prohibit, as between a foreigner and a British subject, all transfer business of this nature which is, of course, always open to the bids of other purchasers in all countries of the world.

The reason for distinguishing between a British vendor and a foreign vendor is, thus, that the present value of goodwill belonging to a British vendor is a right to future profits which will be assessable to British income tax, as and when those profits arise in future years, while the present value of goodwill belonging to a foreign vendor is a right to future profits which would not be assessable to British income tax, unless that right had been transferred to a purchaser domiciled in the United Kingdom. While profits arising outside the jurisdiction of the British income tax continue to be taxed, the effect is to tax persons domiciled here on amounts including profits which have come into the hands of foreigners. Such a practice prevents persons domiciled in the United Kingdom from having an equal chance with persons in other countries of the world to purchase the rights to those future profits arising outside the United Kingdom.

CHAPTER VII

PUBLIC COMPANY PROSPECTUS AND OTHER PITFALLS

Public company prospectuses

It is sometimes difficult, even for the practical man of business, to judge from the information contained in a public company prospectus of the merits of an offer to subscribe for shares in a profit-seeking undertaking. This difficulty arises from various causes. There is the difficulty of knowing the value basis which has been adopted in valuing the assets of the undertaking. Does the value placed upon these assets include any and what sum for goodwill? Another difficulty is to estimate correctly the real effect upon the particular class of shares offered for subscription of the rights which may attach to other classes of shares. It sometimes happens that innocent-looking issues of deferred shares "no par value" or of nominal value 1s. each, amounting perhaps in all to no more than £100 of nominal capital, carry in either case the right to a large part of the profits of the undertaking after a minimum dividend has been paid on the other class of shares. In either case a statement may be contained in the prospectus that nothing is being paid for goodwill, or that the amount paid for goodwill is the nominal amount of the deferred shares. Such statements may be made in all good faith, but nevertheless they are not in accordance with fact, because such deferred shares carry the right to future super-profit out of which alone the value of goodwill arises.

Mills, factories, etc., valued "as going-concern"

In considering the merits of a prospectus caution is always desirable, even in the absence of deferred shares "no par value" or of low nominal value, and even when there is a statement to the effect that no payment is to be made for goodwill. In estimating the value of industrial undertakings, such as mills and factories, for the purpose of sale and transfer to a company, it is a common practice to obtain a certificate from a firm of valuers drawn in a form which states that the value of the land, buildings, plant, and stock "as a going-concern" is £.... This certificate is usually printed in the body of the prospectus, and it may be specifically stated in the prospectus that "nothing is paid for goodwill." It is clear, however, that valuations drawn in this form must often include large sums over and above the "then-value"—a term explained below—of the plant, and such additional amounts are represented by nothing but goodwill. This form of certificate of value, therefore, should be accepted with caution by a discriminating purchaser or investor.

Object of a valuation

The object of a valuation, made at the time of a proposed sale of a commercial enterprise to a public company, is to give the purchasers—represented by applicants for shares—information sufficient in detail to enable them to judge, on good authority, of the nature and attractiveness of the offer. It is quite impossible to form a fair opinion as to the value of an undertaking unless adequate details of the assets are available. The valuation certificate of a profit-seeking enterprise should, therefore, always state separately the values of—

(*a*) Freehold Land;
(*b*) Buildings and Plant;
(*c*) Goodwill, Patents, Trade marks, etc.

Freehold land is not a wasting asset. Buildings and plant are wasting assets which are necessarily required to be used, and will be gradually wasted, in seeking the profits of future years. Goodwill, Patents, Trade marks, etc., are wasting assets represented by rights growing out of past endeavour in seeking profit, the present value of which—being based on expected future super-profit—must diminish as the future super-profit is received. A prospectus, therefore, which lumps these different classes of value together is unsatisfactory.

"Then-value" of plant

The common commercial view of the economic value, to a going-concern, of plant in use (including mills, factories, and all kinds of machinery) is that the value is based upon the unexpired capital outlay on that plant computed by deducting from the cost—less estimated residual value—an equal annual instalment of the cost in respect of each year of the estimated efficient life which has expired. This is called the "going-concern" value. In selling to a company, or individual, the proper basis of value of plant is the so ascertained "going-concern" value, adjusted in respect of subsequent fluctuations in the cost of material and labour, as bearing upon the possible price of new plant. This so adjusted value is called the "then-value," and will be found very fully discussed in the several arbitration proceedings in the well-known Tramways and National Telephone cases.

To what extent is the value of goodwill included in plant valuations?

To what extent is the value of goodwill sometimes inadvertently included in valuations made at the time of the proposed sale of a profit-seeking undertaking to a company? It is not possible to answer this question with any degree of precision, because of the absence of any generally accepted basis of valuing plant when selling an undertaking as a going-concern. The answer, in any particular case, would probably depend largely on the personal view taken by the valuer in each case. The words " value " and " valuation " are, of course, quite properly used to express the present exchangeable value of any particular kind of property. But while, for the purposes of a going-concern, the " going-concern " value of each class of plant is the right basis of value, for the purposes of a sale to a company the " then-value " of each class of plant should be adopted and strictly adhered to. Both the " going-concern " value and the " then-value " are based strictly on cost, the " then-value " being, as previously explained, the unexpired original cost adjusted to present cost. Both these methods involve the taking of actual inventories of existing plant, and the values, being thus based on cost, should not be in any way affected by the question of whether the undertaking is earning a small, or a large, profit. Thus the valuation of plant should be made without any regard to future profit prospects, or the estimated amount of future earnings.

Illustration of goodwill included in plant valuation

As an illustration of the inclusion, in the value of plant, of value in the nature of goodwill, take the case of an industrial undertaking which is to be sold to a company. Suppose that suitable records have been kept, in a register of wasting assets, and it is known that the going-concern value of the plant is £50,000, and suppose it is computed that there has been an average rise in the cost of materials and labour of 50 per cent. since the plant was installed. The then-value of the existing plant, in this case, would be £50,000 plus an addition of 50 per cent. thereon, amounting to £75,000. Now, if the annual profits of the undertaking averaged, say, £10,000, being 10 per cent. on the capital of, say, £100,000, is it not more likely that the value of the plant " as a going-concern " would be stated in the valuers' certificate at £75,000—and no more—than if the undertaking was earning an average annual profit of £20,000 ? In the latter case, the value of the plant "as a going-concern" might well be estimated at, say, £100,000, which it might, perhaps, actually cost to replace, and it might, at the same time, be stated in perfect good faith that nothing is paid for goodwill, although the valuation includes a sum of £25,000 over and above the "then-value" of the plant, which—fairly stated—is in fact represented by nothing but goodwill. And again, suppose the undertaking was earning £40,000 a year, might not the value of the plant "as a going-concern" be certified at even more than £100,000 ?

Three distinct bases of plant valuation

Thus it seems that there are three distinct methods or bases in common use for valuing industrial plant. The first method may be defined as the "going-concern cost-basis value." This is the value at which industrial plant should always be carried in the accounts of a going-concern. It is based upon the unexpired capital outlay on that plant (viz., cost) computed by deducting from cost less estimated scrap value, an equal annual instalment in respect of each year of the estimated efficient life which has expired. The second method of plant valuation is the "then-value" which is, as already explained, the "going-concern cost-basis value," adjusted in respect of subsequent fluctuations in the cost of material and labour, as bearing upon the possible price of new plant. This is the basis which gives the true value of industrial plant for the purpose of transfer as a going-concern from a seller to a purchaser. It is the basis recognized in the Tramways and National Telephone arbitration cases. The "then-value" method is based strictly upon cost, and has no regard whatever to the amount of profits which the undertaking may be earning, or likely to earn. The third method of valuation may be defined as the "going-concern profits-basis value." In valuing industrial plant on this basis it is natural and inevitable that some regard is had to the degree of success enjoyed, and likely to be enjoyed by the undertaking. The future prospects of the undertaking are taken into account, and thus the value of goodwill is, to some extent, reflected in a valuation made on this basis as suggested in the above illustration.

Need of a register of wasting assets

All profit-seeking undertakings, using any class of industrial plant, should keep suitable accounting records in the form of a register of wasting assets, to enable annual expired capital outlay to be calculated on a settled basis, and deducted each year from the cost of each class of plant. A convenient form of register of plant[1] is a loose-leaf book of suitable size, having a page, which can be followed by others when required, known as "Class Record," allotted to each class of industrial plant. Each page is ruled with twelve separate decimal cash columns, one column for each year. Each page should be headed with a description of a particular class of the industrial plant, its declared length of life in years, and its scrap value. Each year's capital outlay on each class of plant is recorded, at the end of the year, in total in the appropriate column. The register also contains ruled sheets known as "Class Summary" and "Annual General Summary." The Annual General Summary is also written up once a year, and shows in one sum the amount to be written off the balance of the Plant

[1] *Leake's Register of Industrial Plant for the Measurement of Depreciation* is published by Messrs. Henry Good & Son, 50 Moorgate Street, E.C.2.

Account in the financial books, and charged to the annual Profit and Loss Account as expired capital outlay.

If it became customary for a record of this nature to be kept by industrial undertakings, this would enable annual profits to be computed with much greater accuracy than is the case at present. Annual depreciation would be measured and recorded on a proper system, based on a settled and continuous financial policy. There would always be a permanent record available showing the classification of all capital outlay on industrial plant, and a direct connection would be maintained between the existing plant and the going-concern value of that plant, as shown in the financial books, and in the annual balance sheet of the undertaking. Many years' history of any number of different classes of industrial plant can be recorded in a register of this kind without any confusion. The whole subject is fully discussed and illustrated in the author's work on *Depreciation and Wasting Assets*, published by Sir Isaac Pitman & Sons, Ltd.

Periods of currency inflation

When considering any class of values expressed in terms of money there is another point which should not be overlooked. Money is, of course, a commodity, and, prior to the commencement of the great War in August, 1914, was freely interchangeable with gold coin and bullion, and possessed full commodity-character. Owing to the necessary temporary abandonment, at the outbreak of war, of the gold standard, the currency, which has to do duty for money in such circumstances, does not possess full commodity-character. Thus, for the time being, such currency is not comparable with real money—which is in fact a commodity. Exchangeable value expressed in terms of money possessing full commodity-character is a true measure of wealth or capital, but this is not so when exchangeable value is expressed in terms of currency which does not possess full commodity-character. These facts should not be overlooked by investors, because they have a direct bearing upon values. The existence of a condition of general inflation cannot be permanent. It is also a matter of great importance to consider in what manner, and to what extent, the gradual, but inevitable, return to the gold standard basis of value will affect the interests, *inter se*, of different classes of shares in public companies. But these subjects are outside the scope of this work.

Ordinary shares issued as fully paid

It often happens that the shares offered to the public, for subscription in cash, are in the form of fixed interest, or limited participation, preference shares, and that the consideration payable to the vendors is in the form of ordinary shares to be issued to the vendors as fully paid. These ordinary shares may be entitled to take the whole of that part of the profits available for dividend which remains, in any year, after providing the dividend on the preference shares. A more common plan is to offer shares for subscription in the form of participating preference shares. This means that after payment of, say, 7½ per cent. on these participating preference shares, a dividend at the same rate is payable to the holders of the ordinary shares, and any balance of the annual profits, available for dividend, is divisible, in some stated proportions, as further dividend, between the holders of the participating preference, and the holders of the ordinary, shares. The participating preference shares may be entitled to a further dividend limited to, say, an additional 7½ per cent., making a total dividend of 15 per cent.

In that case the whole of the remainder of the annual profits available for dividend is usually to be applied in payment of a further dividend to the holders of the ordinary shares.

Founders' shares

In some cases the financial scheme embodied in a prospectus provides for the issue to the vendors of what are often called "founders' shares," of the nominal value of, perhaps, 1s. each, but the holders of such shares may be entitled to take the whole balance of the annual profits available for dividend, remaining after the payment of the limited dividend due to the holders of the preference shares. Such shares are also called "deferred shares" and sometimes "ordinary shares"; and they may be shares of any denomination. But suppose the shares are of the nominal value of 1s. each, then 100,000 shares will amount to only £5,000—an apparently insignificant and unimportant sum. If, according to the prospectus, the vendor is selling the goodwill, contracts, patents, and manufacturing rights of a prosperous profit-seeking undertaking for shares of the nominal value of £5,000, the price may appear to be extremely small. But everything depends, not upon the nominal value of the shares, but upon the proportion of the future annual profits to which those shares are entitled.

Ordinary shares 1s. nominal value

Take the case of a prospectus offering an issue of preference shares—in a form which is somewhat common. The prospectus may include the following statements—

PROSPECTUS

This company has been formed to acquire the freehold lands and works, plant, machinery, patent rights, and other assets for the purpose of manufacturing the well-known Ajax car, and with the object of raising the necessary capital to enable the company to execute the orders now in hand.

Share Capital	£280,000
Divided into	
275,000 8% Cumulative Participating Preference Shares of £1 each . .	275,000
100,000 Ordinary Shares of 1s. . .	5,000
	£280,000

The preference shares carry a cumulative preferential dividend of 8 per cent. per annum, and the right to participate in any surplus profit, available for dividend in each year, to the extent of 20 per cent. of such surplus profits, the balance being payable to the holders of the ordinary shares.

The preference shares are also entitled, on a winding up, to payment off of capital paid up and arrears of cumulative dividend, whether declared or not, up to the commencement of the winding up in priority to the ordinary shares, and, after payment off of the capital paid up on the ordinary shares, to one-fifth of the remaining surplus assets.

Present issue—

250,000 8 per cent. Cumulative Participating Preference Shares of £1 each are offered for subscription at par.

PURCHASE

The purchase consideration is £30,000, consisting of £25,000 payable in fully paid preference shares in respect of the freehold lands, works, plant, and machinery and loose tools, and £5,000 in fully paid 1s. shares for the goodwill, contracts, patents, and manufacturing rights for Great Britain and the colonies. The freehold property with fixtures, plant and machinery, are valued by a firm of valuers at £25,000.

Estimated Profits

An estimate of expected future profits is usually included in such a prospectus, but this is sometimes framed in a loose and unconvincing way as follows—

> The annual profits, estimated on the basis of an output of 200 cars per week, should amount to £200,000.

To the uninitiated, however, this may appear to be a remarkably attractive offer. The vendor may seem at first sight to be selling the goodwill for £5,000. But what are the facts? The public are invited to subscribe capital to the extent of £250,000 in cash to enable the company to execute orders for cars now in hand, and expected to be received in the future to an extent sufficient to secure an output at the rate of 200 cars per week, on which an annual profit of £200,000 is expected to arise. There is obviously great risk as to whether this expected output and future annual profit can be secured. If the company is not a success, the preference shareholders may lose all, or part of, their capital. The preference shareholders take all the risk.

But supposing that the company is successful, and that annual profits of £200,000 are actually realized, how will they be divided? It is clear that, in this case, the greater part of the annual profits will go into the pockets of the vendors, the £200,000 being divisible as follows—

	£
Dividend of 8% on 275,000 Preference Shares	22,000
20% of £178,000, the surplus profit available for dividend (equal to 13·3%) . .	35,600
Balance of surplus profit payable to holders of Ordinary Shares	142,400
	£200,000

Thus the preference shares would receive a dividend at the rate of 21·3 per cent. per annum.

And while the vendors appear to be receiving only £5,000 for the goodwill, they are really getting that which entitles them to take the whole balance of surplus profit, estimated to amount to £142,400 per annum. The present value of £142,400 per annum, on the basis of an annuity over a period even as short as five years, and discounted at 20 per cent. per annum, amounts to £426,000. It is obvious then, in this case, either that the consideration payable to the vendors is very excessive, or that the future annual profits are grossly over-estimated, and, therefore, the offer to the public of participating preference shares on such terms will be disregarded by the discriminating investor.

Preferred shares ranking between debentures and deferred shares

Another case may be taken of a prospectus offering simultaneously issues of first mortgage debenture stock, and of participating preferred shares. This is a particularly unattractive position for investors. The prospectus may include the following statements—

PROSPECTUS

The company has been formed to acquire the freehold site of the St. Martin's Hotel, London, together with the buildings erected thereon. It is intended to re-construct the building so as to provide a high-class picture theatre, a restaurant, café, shops and offices.—

Share Capital, £380,000.

	£
Divided into 130,000 7% First Mortgage Debenture Stock	130,000
200,000 8% Participating Preferred Shares of £1 each	200,000
1,000,000 Deferred Shares of 1s. each . .	50,000
	£380,000

The debenture stock will be secured by a Trust Deed constituting a mortgage on the company's freehold property and fixed plant, and a first floating charge on all the assets, except uncalled capital.

The participating preferred shares shall confer on the holders the right to a fixed cumulative preferential dividend at the rate of 8 per cent. per annum, and the right to 25 per cent. of the surplus profits available for dividend in any year after the deferred shares shall have received a dividend of 8 per cent. per annum on the capital paid up thereon.

Applicants for the participating preferred shares are entitled to apply for and have allotted to them one deferred share for every two participating preferred shares.

Present Issue

130,000 7 per cent. first mortgage debenture stock at par.

200,000 8 per cent. participating preferred shares of £1 each at par.

100,000 deferred shares of 1s. each at par.

Purchase Price

The purchase consideration is £191,000 consisting of £146,000 in cash, and £45,000 in 900,000 deferred shares of 1s. each.

Estimated Profits

An estimate of the annual profits has been carefully prepared by two of the Directors and amounts to £114,875.

In this case the freehold property of the company is specifically mortgaged to secure the issue of the 7 per cent. Debenture Stock which is further protected by a first floating charge on all the assets of the company. It is plain, therefore, that those who are invited to subscribe £200,000 for the participating preferred shares have little or no security, unless the company should prove successful. According to the estimate of profits prepared by two of the directors, the company is likely to be phenomenally successful. The point to be considered by intending subscribers is whether the terms of the offer are such as to give them reasonable security, and a reasonable share of the future profits. It is a matter of common knowledge that undertakings of this nature are sometimes very successful for a few years and then, owing to competition or to change of taste on the part of the public, the profits may rapidly decrease and ultimately disappear altogether. In such circumstances, the mere right to a fixed preferential dividend of 8 per cent. would be very little advantage to the holders of the participating preferred shares. In view of the existence of the mortgage debenture stock, it is probable that, in the event of failure and a winding up, the holders of the participating preferred shares might lose their capital.

In order to discover whether the proposed division of the future profits is, in these circumstances, a fair one, let it be assumed that the company actually earns future annual profits equal to the amount of the estimate stated in the prospectus. In that case, the profits would be divisible between the parties as on page 118.

	£	£
Debenture Holders—		
Interest at 7% on 130,000 Debentures	9,100	
Sinking fund on same	2,500	
		11,600
Public Shareholders—		
8% dividend on 200,000 Participating Preferred Shares	16,000	
8% dividend on 100,000 Deferred Shares of 1s. each, subscribed for by holders of Participating Preferred Shares	400	
$\frac{1}{10}$th of 75% of £83,275 surplus profits after payment of 8% on each class of shares	6,245	
25% of £83,275 surplus profits after payment of 8% on each class of shares	20,820	
		43,465
Vendor Shareholders—		
8% dividend on 900,000 Deferred Shares of 1s. each	3,600	
$\frac{9}{10}$ths of 75% of £83,275 surplus profits after payment of 8% on each class of shares	56,210	
		59,810
		£114,875

The present value of £59,810 per annum, on the basis of an annuity of £59,810 over a period of ten years (and a shorter period can scarcely be taken having regard to the nature of the enterprise) discounted at 20 per cent. per annum, amounts to more than £250,000, equal to nearly six times £45,000 the nominal value of the 900,000 deferred shares of 1s. each. These 900,000 deferred shares form that portion of the purchase consideration paid to the vendors for goodwill, and appear to represent £45,000. But on the vendors' own estimate of future profits these shares have a present value of upwards of £250,000. Viewed in the light of the facts it is clear that such an offer should not be accepted by the investing public.

Shares "no par value"

The issue of part of the capital of a company in the form of shares "no par value" is perhaps more common in America than in this country. The plan is to issue the capital in the form of (*a*) cumulative preferred stock divided into shares, say, $100 par value, and (*b*) common stock divided into shares " no par value." In order to illustrate the effect of this, an example may be given, as, in such case, those invited to subscribe to the cumulative preferred stock may easily over-rate the advantages offered to them. Suppose a manufacturing company, originally started in a small way and registered a year or two before, desires to develop its manufacturing capacity in order to meet increased demands for its product, and with that object seeks to issue further capital. The proposed capital will consist of—

	$
7% Cumulative Preferred Stock divided into 2,500 shares of $100 par value . .	250,000
Common Stock divided into 5,000 shares " no par value "	—
	$250,000

It is important to understand the meaning and effect of this harmless-looking financial arrangement.

A prospectus referred to as " descriptive circular " is issued, with a printed form of application called " Preferred Stock Subscription Agreement." The prospectus contains the following, amongst other material statements—

1. 7 per cent. cumulative preferred stock is preferred as to assets and dividends.

2. Dividends payable semi-annually on 1st January and 1st July.

3. With every five shares of preferred stock purchased a bonus of two shares of common stock will be given.

4. The corporation contemplates the sale of approximately 1,500 shares of preferred stock at the present time.

5. Sales of the product in previous year amounted to $340,000.

6. Earnings in previous year amounted to seven times the dividend requirements on the preferred stock then outstanding.

7. Sales in current year (about six months still to run) estimated at $800,000.

8. Earnings in current year estimated $64,000, at the very least.

9. Sinking fund. There will be set aside annually, out of surplus or net profits, a sum equal to 5 per cent. of the greatest par amount of preferred stock at any time outstanding for the purchase and for redemption of preferred stock.

10. The corporation reserves the right to redeem the whole or any part of the 7 per cent. preferred stock, on any dividend date, at 110 and accrued dividends.

11. Upon any dissolution or distribution of capital the preferred stock will receive $110 per share, plus accrued dividends, before the remaining assets are distributed to the common stock.

12. Two-thirds of the outstanding preferred stock must consent to any increase in the authorized amount of preferred stock, or to the creation of any stock having preference over the existing preferred stock, or to the mortgage or pledge of the corporate property; except as to these matters, the common stock possesses the exclusive voting rights, with cumulative voting for directors, unless two semi-annual dividends on the preferred stock are in arrears, whereupon the preferred stock becomes entitled to vote until all arrears in cumulative dividends are paid.

The prospectus calls attention to the recent phenominal development of the particular kind of trade with which the product of the corporation is concerned. The story of the success and growth of the great companies in America doing similar business is amazing. Factories which ten years ago had a capital of $250,000 each, to-day have a capital of over $100,000,000 each. The phenomenal developments of the past decade should be repeated in the coming years. These and similar optimistic statements are contained in the prospectus.

If the prospectus estimate of earnings ($64,000 in the current year) is realized, what dividend will the preferred stock-holders receive? It may be assumed that 1,000 shares of preferred stock had been previously issued, and that all the 1,500 shares of the same stock offered for subscription by the prospectus have been allotted to subscribers. In that case 1,000 shares of common stock, given as bonus-out of a total issue of 5,000 shares, of common stock—will have passed to the preferred stockholders. On these assumptions the preferred stockholders' share of the estimated earnings in the current year will be equal to a dividend of just under 10 per cent. as shown below—

Allocation of earnings, $64,000.

	$	$
Sinking fund 5% on $250,000 .		12,500
Preferred Stockholders—		
7% on $250,000 Preferred Stock	$17,500	
$\frac{1000}{5000}$ of balance of earnings, $34,000	6,800	
		24,300
Vendors—		
$\frac{4000}{5000}$ of balance of earnings, $34,000		27,200
Estimate of current year's earnings .		$64,000

But in view of the great risk inseparable from a new enterprise of this kind, it is surely not unreasonable for the subscribers to expect an annual income which would be nearer to 20 per cent. than to 10 per cent.

on the capital invested. The term " capital risked " is a more accurate description than the term " capital invested" in cases of this kind. It will be found that, in order to yield a return equal to 20 per cent. to the holders of the preferred stock, an average annual profit of $192,500 is needed. This is more than 75 per cent. per annum profit on the subscribed capital, and would fall to be dealt with thus—

Allocation of earnings, $192,500.

Sinking fund 5% on $250,000 .	$	$12,500
Preferred Stockholders—		
7% on $250,000 Preferred Stock	17,500	
$\frac{10000}{50000}$ of balance of earnings, $162,500	32,500	
		50,000
Vendors—		
$\frac{40000}{50000}$ of balance of earnings, $162,500		130,000
Average annual earnings needed to yield 20% to Preferred Stockholders . .		$192,500

It will be noted that many statements, material as guides to enable an opinion to be formed as to the position and prospects of this enterprise, are omitted from the prospectus. It is stated in the prospectus that an independent inventory of machinery and equipment would show at least $15,000 in excess of the value carried on the books, but no particulars are given of the existing assets and liabilities of the corporation or, except by inference, of the capital issued. There is no definite statement of profits earned to date, and no information as to what provisions have been made, in computing profits, for remuneration of management, and for expired capital outlay on inherently wasting assets. The sinking fund provisions are not clear; the statement that—" the corporation will annually set aside . . . . . . a sum equal to 5 per cent. of the greatest par amount of preferred stock at any time outstanding "—being too indefinite.

This is an offer which should be ignored by the discriminating investor. It is too much in the nature of "heads I win, tails you lose." If phenomenal success is attained, as it may be, the vendors take the bulk of the annual profits. If moderate success comes to the enterprise the vendors still take the greater part of the profits. If, and when, bad times come it is probable the preferred stockholders may be induced to consent to the issue of some form of priority stock. In that case they may ultimately find that on a dissolution of the corporation the whole of their capital has been lost. This may possibly happen after some years of great success, and in the meantime the bulk of the profits of such years will have been paid out to the vendors holding 4,000 out of the 5,000 shares "no par value" common stock.

A more equitable offer in this case would seem to be for the subscribers of 7 per cent. preferred stock, and the vendors, to share the future super-profit equally between them. If, for every $100 share of preferred stock purchased, a bonus of one share of common stock was given, this would result in one moiety of the common stock being allotted to those who provide and risk the capital, and one moiety to the vendors. The above estimated future earnings would then be divisible as follows—

Allocation of earnings, $64,000 or $192,500.

	$	$	$	$
Sinking fund, 5% on $250,000		12,500		12,500
Preferred Stockholders—				
7% on $250,000 Preferred Stock	17,500		17,500	
$\frac{2500}{5000}$ of balance of earnings	17,000		81,250	
		34,500		98,750
Vendors—				
$\frac{2500}{5000}$ of balance of earnings		17,000		81,250
		$64,000		$192,500

An amount of $34,500 is equal to about 14 per cent. on the $250,000 preferred stock, and an amount of $98,750 is equal to 39½ per cent. thereon. Under such an arrangement the preferred stockholders, and the vendors, would share equally in future success; while in the event of failure the preferred stockholders might probably lose the greater part, or even the whole, of their capital.

CHAPTER VIII

COMMERCIAL GOODWILL AND NATIONAL CAPITAL

Is value of goodwill included in valuations of national capital?

BEFORE concluding the consideration of the subject of commercial goodwill, it may be useful to enquire whether, and if so to what extent, the value of commercial goodwill enters into and forms part of the estimates of the value of national capital as computed from time to time by economists.

Stamp's valuation of British national capital

It is necessary in the first place to inquire (*a*) what national capital really consists of, and (*b*) how its value is usually estimated. For this purpose it is proposed to refer to the valuation of British national capital prepared by Sir Josiah Stamp, C.B.E., D.Sc. (Lond.), and published in his recent work *British Incomes and Property*. This valuation will be discussed and the figures re-stated in such a way as to indicate, as nearly as possible, the various forms in which national capital actually exists. It will be found as a result of these enquiries, that the basis on which valuations of national capital are commonly made includes the full value of commercial goodwill.

Nothing exists except materials and commodities

There is nothing in existence to represent capital except exchangeable materials and commodities in their various forms. Such things include lands, buildings, railways, shipping, mines, factories, mills, and manufactured goods. In the case of Great Britain some of these are located in the United Kingdom, and some outside the United Kingdom. Some of them are utilized for the purposes of industry and production, and some for the purposes of leisure and consumption —the latter consisting principally of lands, buildings, furniture and other contents used for private dwellings. There must be added also Government and local property, such as lands, dockyards, public buildings, etc. And finally—the least important and merely fractional factor—money consisting of gold and silver coins and bullion. All these things are represented by some form of exchangeable materials and commodities. The only part of national capital which is not material is that represented by Foreign, Indian, and Colonial Government securities held by persons domiciled in the United Kingdom. The meaning and effect of the British national debt and local loans will be considered later. Trade and other debtors must be set off against creditors, and thus they cancel each other and do not affect the amount of national capital.

Meaning of present exchangeable value

Capital value, as distinct from capital itself, which is material, is rightly defined as "present exchangeable value," and it is necessary, therefore, to consider the meaning of the term "present exchangeable value." "Present exchangeable value" is expressed in terms of currency, and applied to all existing materials and commodities, and to rights growing out of all kinds of past effort in profit-seeking, and being stated in currency it includes, of course, currency inflation whenever this condition prevails. But capital itself actually in existence at any time can consist only of all kinds of exchangeable materials and commodities. Values are attached to these in figures—either high or low—according to the circumstances of the time. These figures, in which the usual estimates of value of national capital are stated, will be found to include (*a*) the gold value of existing commodities in their present condition of usefulness, (*b*) the gold value of goodwill based on the expectation that past profits will be maintained in the future, and (*c*) in each case the inflated value of the currency, whenever the currency is anything other than money possessing full gold or commodity-character.

All exchange is barter. Meaning of barter power

All free and natural exchange is barter. When money is—as is the case in normal times — on a commodity or gold basis, then, apart from the effect of temporary disturbances due to the constant variations in supply and demand, the principle of barter can be easily understood. The barter power of a stated quantity of any commodity is equal to that quantity of gold which calls for a unit of human effort, to produce and deliver, equal in quality and quantity to the unit of human effort required to produce and deliver the stated quantity of the commodity. Money is based on quantity of gold. One troy ounce of standard gold is coined into £3 17s. 10½d sterling, and, therefore, a British sovereign is roughly equal to one quarter of a troy ounce of standard gold. This calls for a certain average unit of human effort to produce and deliver, and the term "unit of human effort" is used to indicate some standard measure of effective ability exercised in producing and delivering respectively the commodity and the gold to be exchanged against it.

Usual method of valuing national capital

In valuing national capital there is no attempt at anything like the making of inventories of existing exchangeable materials and commodities. The common method of valuation adopted by economists is the capitalization of income tax statistics so far as these cover the ground, supplementing the results by estimates for the remaining items. For instance, separate estimates must be made of (*a*) income of the non-income tax paying classes derived from capital; (*b*) movable property, etc., not yielding income, such as furniture, clothing, jewellery, and works of art; (*c*) Government and local property. This accepted method is considered to be the only one available to present anything like a comprehensive attempt at the measurement of national capital.

British income tax statistics

British income tax is collected under five schedules, A, B, C, D and E. Schedules A and B, in combination, form the charge upon landed property, including buildings. Schedule C includes income from public revenue—either Imperial, colonial, or foreign—and Schedule D relates to income from trades, businesses and other occupations, as well as to any income not included in the other schedules. Incomes assessed under Schedule D are for the most part computed on the average statutory profits of the three previous years. The income tax statistics under these four schedules, A to D, only are utilized in valuing British national capital. Schedule E relates to persons in State employment (civil servants, etc.), and to persons in any other public employments of profit, including public corporations and limited companies. The returns under this schedule are, therefore, omitted from consideration in valuing British national capital as representing the reward of human effort only, quite apart from the employment of capital.

Multiplier applied to annual income of capital

The actual method of procedure in estimating British national capital is as follows. Having first ascertained the amount of the income tax income of the selected year under Schedules A to D—the Schedule D income being based on the average of the three preceding years—the next step is to endeavour to eliminate from the amount the proportion of that income estimated to represent the personal remuneration of those income tax paying classes who are assessed under Schedule D, because they are not public officials, etc., assessable under Schedule E. The second step is to apply, to the balance of income remaining, a multiplier—varying with the class of income. This is done in order to capitalize the remaining balance of income as representing the annual profits attributable to capital, as distinct from the annual profits attributable to human effort.

Method of estimating annual income of capital

The magnitude of the resulting capital depends, of course, upon the number of years purchase or rate of interest employed. The multiplier used varies according to the class of income, from under ten to over twenty-five years. The treatment of the important group in the Schedule D income tax statistics classed under the heading "Businesses not otherwise detailed," which represents nearly half of all the assessments made under Schedule D, presents great difficulties. It is assumed by Sir L. Chiozza Money that one-half of the net profits included in this group are from capital, and the number of years purchase taken by him for this half is ten, or 10 per cent. interest. Sir Josiah Stamp considers that this plan of taking the whole profits assessed under this particular group in Schedule D, dividing the amount into two equal parts, and allocating one part as attributable to capital earnings, and one part as attributable to the earnings of human effort, has much to recommend it.

Method is subject to serious limitations and difficulties

Unfortunately, income tax statistics are not statistics of actual profits earned. Income tax statistics are based on statutory profits, and these differ in many respects very materially from true profits. But even if the income tax statistics are accepted as giving some indication of the profits earned by capital there are serious limitations and difficulties inseparable from this method of estimating national capital. One of these is the transfer of income tax assessments which is constantly taking place from the included Schedule D to the excluded Schedule E, owing to firms and partnerships becoming incorporated under the Limited Liability Acts. In all these cases the assessment of the income of the managers and other employees concerned is at once automatically shifted from Schedule D to Schedule E. For instance, suppose a private firm having six employees liable to tax—with salaries aggregating £5,000—is converted into a private limited company, the profits will continue to be assessed under Schedule D, but the salaries are thereupon transferred to Schedule E. Before the conversion from firm to company the profits and salaries were both included under Schedule D, and as the returns under this schedule form an important part of the statistics used in valuing national capital, the continuity of the results obtained is seriously interrupted.

Another difficulty which arises in connection with the valuation of British national capital by the application of a multiplier to the statutory income of the income tax statistics is caused by the fact that losses are, to a great extent, unrepresented in these statistics. This is so whenever losses are continuous enough or sufficiently heavy to produce an average loss over any three years' period. But the fact that an average loss may have been incurred by a profit-seeking undertaking over a period of three years does not necessarily render the capital of the concern valueless. The plant and stock will still possess some value against the coming of more prosperous times. Another considerable difference between the income tax statistics and actual profits arises from the fact that interest paid on debentures, and on other permanent loans, is assessed to income tax and included in the income tax statistics as profit, although the undertaking may be incurring losses greater than the interest paid to the holders of the debentures and loans, and therefore there is no profit, the interest being paid out of capital.

Further, there is the fact that in computing profits, for income tax purposes, of undertakings and individuals with capital invested in wasting assets such as mines, annuities, etc., no deduction is allowed to be made from the receipts on account of depreciation or expired capital outlay. The result is that the profits assessed to income tax exceed the true profits earned. The same thing applies in regard to wasting assets consisting of plant and machinery, using the term "plant and machinery" in its widest sense. In the case of plant and machinery some deduction is allowed, but the amount is usually less than the actual depreciation incurred in earning the profits. It may no doubt be said that the discrepancies between true annual profits, and the income of the income tax statistics, have been in some way allowed for in fixing the various multipliers applied to the different classes of income in making valuations of national capital. However this may be, it is clear that valuations of national capital, based on income tax statistics, must be accepted with caution. It seems that there are, in fact, no statistics in existence suitable for the purpose.

New valuation of British national capital

Sir Josiah Stamp's new valuation of British national capital referred to above is based on 1913-1914 income tax statistics. The amount is £14,319,000,000, and it is arrived at as follows—

NEW VALUATION.

Source of Income.	Capital value (millions £)
1. Lands	1,155
2. Houses, etc.	3,330
3. Other profits (Sch. A)	22
4. Farmers' capital	340
5. Sch. C., National Debt, etc.	1,148
6. Railways in the United Kingdom . .	1,143
7. Railways out of the United Kingdom . .	655
8. Coal and other mines	179
9. Ironworks	37
10. Gasworks	182
11. Waterworks, canals, and other concerns (Sch. A)	278
12. Indian, colonial, and foreign securities. .	621
13. Coupons	383
14. Other profits and interest	276
15. Businesses not otherwise detailed . .	2,770
16. Income arising abroad and not remitted .	400
17. Income of non-income tax paying classes derived from capital	200
18. Movable property, etc., not yielding income (furniture, etc.)	800
19. Government and local property . . .	400
	£14,319

Existing things which represent British national capital

It will be observed that this valuation is arranged under the various heads and groups into which the statistics of income are gathered in the course of assessment, these being supplemented by such additional items as estimates of (17) income of non-income tax paying classes derived from capital, (18) movable property, etc., not yielding income, (19) Government and local property. It is now proposed to consider the character and location of the existing things which represent the valuation, and to endeavour to allocate these under their appropriate heads in such a way as to present a statement in the form of an analysis which will show in an easily comprehensible form the constituent parts of British national capital.

The total value of lands in the United Kingdom, estimated in the valuation at £1,155 millions, is allocated in the analysis as to three-fourths, amounting to £867 millions, as being used for purposes of industry or production, and as to one-fourth, or £288 millions, as being occupied by private dwelling-houses, or used as parks, gardens, etc. The estimated value of houses, etc., in the United Kingdom, amounting in the valuation to £3,330 millions, is allocated in the analysis as to one-third, or £1,110 millions, to industrial buildings such as factories, mills, etc., and as to two-thirds, or £2,220 millions, to buildings such as private dwelling-houses, including stables, etc. The headings in the valuation "Other profits (Sch. A)" and "Farmers' capital," amounting to £362 millions, are treated together in the analysis as representing farmers' capital, growing crops, implements, stock, etc. Lands, houses, and farmers' capital

The next items in the new valuation are as follows— Industrial capital

	Capital value (millions £)
5. Sch. C., National Debt, etc.	1,148
6. Railways in the United Kingdom	1,143
7. Railways out of the United Kingdom	655
8. Coal and other mines	179
9. Ironworks	37
10. Gasworks	182
11. Waterworks, canals, and other concerns (Sch. A)	278
12. Indian, colonial, and foreign securities	621
13. Coupons	383
14. Other profits and interest	276
15. Businesses not otherwise detailed	2,770
16. Income accruing abroad and not remitted	400
17. Income of non-income tax paying classes derived from capital	200
Millions	£8,272

It is difficult to allocate this amount, but it is clear the total includes the capitalized value of foreign and colonial Government securities, the national debt before the war, and local loans. The total also includes gold and silver coin in circulation, and coin and bullion at the banks before the war. These several items, which must be deducted and shown separately in the analysis, are estimated as follows—

	Millions £
Foreign Government securities	250
Indian and Colonial Government securities . .	500
National debt before the war and local loans (say)	1,200
Money, viz., gold and silver coin in circulation and coin and bullion at the banks before the war .	150
Millions . .	£2,100

Location of industrial capital

Deducting this amount, £2,100 millions, from the total £8,272 millions, there remains a balance of £6,172 millions, represented by lands and buildings outside the United Kingdom, growing crops, railways, shipping, mines, works, the contents of factories, mills, and other property (municipal undertakings appear separately below under the head of Government and local property), including plant, and stocks of raw materials, manufactured goods, etc. All these materials and commodities are used for purposes of industry or production. It is estimated for the purposes of the analysis that $\frac{9}{16}$ths of this balance of £6,172 millions, amounting to £3,472 millions, is located in the United Kingdom, and $\frac{7}{16}$ths, amounting to £2,700 millions, is located outside the United Kingdom, although belonging to individuals domiciled within the United Kingdom. The next item in the valuation, movable property, etc., not yielding income (furniture, etc.) estimated at £800 millions, does not call for further explanation.

Household furniture, works of art, wearing-apparel, etc.

Details of Government and local property

The value of Government and local property was estimated in 1905 by Sir L. Chiozza Money as follows, and—subject to deducting £50 millions from the value put upon roads—Sir Josiah Stamp regards this estimate as probably the most reasonable that has been made. The estimate, with Sir Josiah Stamp's adjustment, is as follows—

	Millions £	Millions £
Government property—		
The Navy (at a written-down value) . .	114	
Naval works	80	
Army works and military arsenals . .	120	
Telegraphs and telephones	60	
Suez Canal shares	28	
Other property	98	
	——	500
Local property—		
Two million acres of common land . .	50	
22,000 miles of main roads and 97,000 miles of minor roads (Money, £600 millions) . .	550	
Parks, bridges, sewers, lighting, etc., electric light works, water works, reservoirs, etc., and other municipal undertakings . .	500	
	——	1,100
		£1,600

Sir Josiah Stamp in his new valuation includes Government and local property at a net amount of £400 millions. This amount is arrived at by deducting £1,200 millions, the estimated amount of the national debt before the war and local loans, from £1,600 millions, the estimated value of then existing Government and local property. The plan adopted in the analysis—as being clearer and more convenient—is to include in the national capital the £1,600 millions for Government and local property, and from the total of the analysis to deduct £1,200 millions for the national debt and local loans. The principal and interest of the national debt and local loans constitute, in fact, a charge on future production rather than on any presently existing capital, whether Government or otherwise owned. National and local debts are not, therefore, part of the net national capital. If the amount of these debts outstanding is counted among the assets it must be deducted from the total as a

Treatment of Government and local property, and Government and local debts liability. Such debts are nothing but a record, in legal and binding form, of the indebtedness of the whole nation to individual units of the nation.

Analysis of new valuation

The following analysis of the new valuation, based on the allocations stated above, has been prepared after careful consideration of the available evidence—

Analysis of new valuation of British national capital before the war.	*Millions* £	*Per cent. of* £14,319.
Property in the United Kingdom used for purposes of industry or production—		
(*a*) Lands used for agriculture and other industries . . .	867	
(*b*) Buildings such as factories, mills, etc.	1,110	
(*c*) Farmer's capital, growing crops, implements, stock, etc. . .	362	
(*d*) Railways, shipping, mines, works, the contents of factories, mills, businesses, and other property, including plant and stocks of raw materials, manufactured goods, etc., but excluding municipal undertakings such as water, light, heat, and power, which are included below under Government and local property . . .	3,472	40·58
Property outside the United Kingdom used for purposes of industry or production belonging to individuals domiciled in the United Kingdom—		
(*e*) Lands, buildings, growing crops, railways, mines, works, the contents of factories, mills, and other property including plant and stocks of raw materials and manufactured goods.	2,700	18·86
Property in the United Kingdom used for purposes of leisure or consumption—		
(*f*) Lands used as sites for private dwelling-houses, gardens, parks, etc.	288	
(*g*) Buildings such as private dwelling-houses, including stables, etc. .	2,220	23·10
(*h*) Household funiture, works of art, wearing apparel, etc. . .	800	
(*i*) Government and local property such as lands, dockyards, arsenals, public buildings, main roads, bridges, sewers, etc. . .	1,600	11·17
Carried forward	13,419	93·71

Brought forward	13,419	93·71
(*j*) Money, viz. gold and silver coin in circulation, and bullion at the banks before the war . .	150	1·05
(*k*) Foreign Government securities .	250	5·24
(*l*) Indian and Colonial Government securities	500	
	14,319	100·00
(*m*) National debt before the war and local loans (say) . . .	1,200	
NOTE.—These debts are represented by Government and local securities owned by individuals forming part of the nation		
	15,519	
Deduct : National debt before the war, and local loans (say)	1,200	
Millions	£14,319	

The amounts of the national debt, and of local loans, are deducted because they constitute a charge on the future production of the whole nation which will result from the co-operation of capital and human effort. It may be noted that the regular provision of an amount of no more than one-half of 1 per cent. per annum, in addition to the annual interest, would operate to repay these debts and loans in rather less than fifty years, allowing interest at 5 per cent. per annum.

National capital consists of materials and commodities with one exception

This analysis shows that the value of British national capital before the war, based on the 1913–14 income tax statistics, was £14,329 millions. This national capital consisted wholly of some form of then existing exchangeable materials and commodities, except as to £750 millions representing debts due from foreign, Indian, and Colonial Governments. Debts due to individuals domiciled in the United Kingdom from foreign, Indian, and Colonial Governments constitute the only portion of British national capital which is not represented by some form of existing materials and commodities. Such debts are in the same position as the British national debt and local loans, except that as they are not a charge upon the future production of Great Britain, the amount does not fall to be deducted from the assets constituting the national capital of Great Britain.

Extent and location of capital used in industry or production

The analysis shows that nearly 60 per cent. of British national capital before the war was represented by materials and commodities used for purposes of industry or production including agricultural lands, farmers' capital, growing crops, railways, shipping, mines, factories, and mills, together with plant and stock, and that rather more than two-thirds of all this property was located in the United Kingdom, the remaining one-third being located outside the United Kingdom. The greater part of this capital was held by joint stock companies, and was represented by debentures, share certificates, etc.

Extent of capital used for purposes of leisure or consumption

About 23 per cent. of British national capital was used for purposes of leisure or consumption, and existed in the form of private dwelling-houses with the lands on which they stand, including gardens, parks, etc., and household furniture, works of art, wearing apparel, etc. The great bulk of all this property was in the form of small dwelling-houses.

Government and local property. Foreign, Indian and colonial securities. Cash

The balance of the national capital consisted of Government and local property to the extent of about 11 per cent.; foreign, Indian, and Colonial securities 5 per cent.; and money in circulation and at the banks 1 per cent.

It will be seen, on reference to the above analysis, that the amount of the national debt before the war and local loans has been added to the valuation as representing securities owned by individuals forming part of the nation, but that on the other hand it has been deducted as representing a charge on the future production of the whole nation, which production results only from the future co-operation of capital and human effort.

Pre-war absence of the factor of inflation

The various items enumerated above amount to £14,319 millions, being Sir Josiah Stamp's valuation of British national capital before the war. At that time there existed an effective gold standard so that, then, the now dominating factor of inflation was absent. It has been shown that, with the exception of foreign, Indian, and Colonial Government securities, British national capital consists wholly of exchangeable materials and commodities in their various forms. In estimating national capital, existing at any given time, the important consideration is the quality and quantity of exchangeable materials and commodities actually in being, rather than their value in money. It is clear that their present value, even stated in gold standard money, and so excluding inflation, is swayed and influenced to a very great extent by estimates, optimistic or otherwise, of future prospects. The basis of value of materials and commodities which should be aimed at is the gold or commodity value—*i.e.*, the true barter value—and when there is an effective gold standard in operation, this is generally near to the cost.

Valuations of national capital include the value of commercial goodwill

The effect of valuing existing materials and commodities by applying a multiplier to the income tax statistics must be to place a high valuation upon them when the valuation is based on the statistics of a period of high profits, and a comparatively low valuation upon them when it is based on the statistics of a period of low profits. But the actual extent of national capital, which is represented only by existing exchangeable materials and commodities, is not directly affected by whether the profits of a particular period are high or low. The valuation, being based upon the results of a period of trade, whether prosperous or otherwise, must obviously include the full present value of all existing goodwill, by capitalizing past profits; and this is quite irrespective of whether the goodwill has been purchased or not. The reason is that a multiplier has been applied to all profits earned, which include, of course, all super-profit, and when an undertaking is earning super-profit as defined in this work, it is earning an amount which yields more than a normal interest on the capital invested. Normal true profit, equal to a normal interest on the capital invested in an undertaking, if increased by a normal multiplier, should theoretically amount to round about the gold value of the existing materials and commodities representing industrial capital. It is probable, because otherwise industry would soon cease, that profit in the aggregate is never less than the normal rate of interest on the gold value of materials and commodities representing industrial capital. This being so, the application of a normal multiplier to an amount which is greater than mere normal profit must result in a valuation which includes both the gold value of existing materials and commodities, and also a further amount which is represented by nothing but the gold value of goodwill.

Valuations of national capital are dependent upon the future maintenance of industry

Valuations of national capital, as usually made, thus clearly depend upon certain assumptions such as (*a*) that there will be a continuance of public security and confidence, (*b*) that the volume of trade and industry will be maintained undiminished, and (*c*) that capital will in future still attract as its reward profits equal to those earned in the past. It is interesting here to note that valuations of national capital which have been prepared on the basis of the estate duty statistics—a basis more nearly approximating in character to an inventory of materials and commodities—have been found to result in a smaller valuation of national capital than estimates based on the income tax statistics.

Difficulties of making future valuations of national capital

In view of the course of events since the outbreak of the European war, future valuations of national capital, based on the method, indicated in this chapter, of capitalizing the income tax statistics, will apparently be impracticable. As a consequence of the war it was necessary to abandon the gold (or commodity) standard of value, and prices have risen far above gold or commodity values; and now, as a further consequence of the war, all future production has become charged with the provision of interest and gradual repayment of a huge national debt—due almost wholly to ourselves—increased tenfold as compared with the debt before the war. The effect of these two factors has been to drive up and inflate nominal values, and nominal incomes, enormously. What multiplier, then, is to be applied in future to the swelling income tax statistics? The national debt being, for the most part, held by persons domiciled in the United Kingdom, does not represent a real diminution of British national capital; it represents rather a redistribution, amongst individuals, of existing capital or wealth. But will not the annual interest on the national debt swell the income tax statistics, and will not these statistics be further inflated by the great increase in nominal income and profits referred to above, though existing exchangeable materials and commodities—which alone represent British national capital—may remain in quality and quantity much the same as before the war?

Any valuations of national capital in the near future must be useless

The answers to these questions must be in the affirmative, and therefore any valuations of national capital, which may be made in the near future, based on the capitalization of recent income tax statistics, are likely to include, not only the full present value of all commercial goodwill, but also the dominating factor of inflation. It seems clear that the factor of inflation will operate to an extent which must for the time being render useless any attempts at the making of valuations of national capital by means of income tax statistics.

APPENDICES

I. Tables for Computing Value of Goodwill.

II. Trade Marks Act, 1905.

III. Patents and Designs Acts, 1907 and 1919,

IV. Copyright Act, 1911.

APPENDIX I

The tables contained in this appendix will be found useful in computing the value of commercial goodwill. The tables include—

A. Summary of tables showing present value at rates of interest from 4 per cent. to 20 per cent. of constant and diminishing annuity of £100.

B. Tables showing present value at rates of interest from 12½ per cent. to 20 per cent. of constant annuity of £100.

Note.—The lower rates of interest are omitted from this table because they are contained in the ordinary mathematical tables.

C. Tables showing present value at rates of interest from 4 per cent. to 20 per cent. of an annuity diminishing by equal sums.

A

SUMMARY OF TABLES SHOWING PRESENT VALUE, AT RATES OF INTEREST FROM 4% TO 20%, OF CONSTANT AND DIMINISHING ANNUITY OF £100.

Yrs.		4%	5%	6%	7%	8%	9%	10%	12½%	15%	17½%	20%
3	Constant	278	272	267	262	258	253	249	238	228	219	211
	Diminishing	187	185	182	179	176	174	171	165	159	154	149
5	Constant	445	433	421	410	399	389	379	356	335	316	299
	Diminishing	274	268	263	257	252	247	242	230	220	210	201
10	Constant	811	772	736	702	671	642	614	554	502	458	419
	Diminishing	472	456	440	425	411	398	386	357	332	310	291
15	Constant	1112	1038	971	911	856	806	761	663	585	521	468
	Diminishing	647	616	588	561	535	514	493	446	407	373	344
20	Constant	1359	1246	1147	1059	982	913	851	724	626	549	487
	Diminishing	801	754	711	672	636	604	574	510	458	417	378
30	Constant	1729	1537	1376	1241	1126	1027	943	777	657	567	498
	Diminishing	1059	975	902	838	781	731	685	593	521	464	417
50	Constant	2148	1826	1576	1380	1223	1096	991	798	666	572	500
	Diminishing	1426	1270	1141	1034	944	868	802	673	578	506	450
100	Constant	2450	1985	1662	1427	1249	1111	1000	800	667	572	500
	Diminishing	1887	1603	1390	1225	1094	988	900	736	622	539	475

B

TABLES SHOWING PRESENT VALUE, AT RATES OF INTEREST FROM 12½% TO 20%, OF CONSTANT ANNUITY OF £100.

Year.		12½%	15%	17½%	20%
1		88·89	86·96	85·11	83·34
2		79·01	75·62	72·44	69·45
3		70·23	65·76	61·65	57·87
	Present value three years' annuity.	238·13	228·34	219·20	210·66
4		62·45	57·18	52·47	48·23
5		55·51	49·72	44·66	40·19
	Present value five years' annuity.	356·09	335·24	316·33	299·08
6		49·34	43·24	38·01	33·49
7		43·86	37·60	32·35	27·91
8		38·99	32·70	27·53	23·26
9		34·66	28·44	23·45	19·38
10		30·81	24·73	19·96	16·15
	Present value ten years' annuity.	553·75	501·95	457·63	419·27
11		27·39	21·51	16·99	13·46
12		24·35	18·70	14·46	11·22
13		21·64	16·26	12·31	9·35
14		19·24	14·14	10·48	7·79
15		17·10	12·30	8·92	6·49
	Present value fifteen years' annuity.	663·47	584·86	520·79	467·58
16		15·20	10·70	7·59	5·41
17		13·51	9·30	6·43	4·51
18		12·01	8·09	5·47	3·76
19		10·68	7·04	4·66	3·13
20		9·49	6·12	3·97	2·61
	Present value twenty years' annuity.	724·36	626·11	548·91	487·00
21		8·44	5·32	3·38	2·18
22		7·50	4·63	2·88	1·82
23		6·67	4·03	2·45	1·52
24		5·93	3·51	2·09	1·27
25		5·27	3·05	1·78	1·06
26		4·68	2·65	1·51	·89
27		4·16	2·31	1·29	·74
28		3·70	2·01	1·10	·62
29		3·29	1·75	·94	·52
30		2·92	1·52	·80	·43
	Present value thirty years' annuity.	776·92	656·89	567·13	498·05

Year.		12½%	15%	17½%	20%
31		2·60	1·32	·68	·36
32		2·31	1·15	·58	·30
33		2·05	1·00	·49	·25
34		1·82	·87	·42	·21
35		1·62	·76	·36	·18
36		1·44	·66	·31	·15
37		1·28	·57	·26	·13
38		1·14	·50	·22	·11
39		1·01	·43	·19	·09
40		·90	·37	·16	·07
	Present value forty years' annuity.	793·09	664·52	570·80	499·90
41		·80	·32	·14	·06
42		·71	·29	·12	·05
43		·63	·25	·10	·04
44		·56	·22	·09	·03
45		·50	·19	·08	·02
46		·44	·17	·07	·01
47		·39	·15	·06	
48		·35	·13	·05	
49		·31	·11	·04	
50		·28	·10	·03	
	Present value fifty years' annuity.	798·06	666·45	571·58	
51		·25	·09		
52		·22	·08		
53		·20	·07		
54		·18	·06		
55		·16	·05		
56		·14	·04		
57		·12	·03		
58		·11	·03		
59		·10			
60		·09			
	Present value sixty years' annuity.	799·63			
61		·08			
62		·07			
63		·06			
64		·05			
65		·04			

C

PRESENT VALUE, AT VARIOUS RATES OF INTEREST, OF AN ANNUITY DIMINISHING BY EQUAL SUMS OVER SERIES OF YEARS COMMENCING WITH £100 DUE AT END OF THE FIRST YEAR.

Year.	Amount.	4%	5%	6%	7%	8%	9%	10%	12½%	15%	17½%	20%
1	100·00	96·15	95·24	94·34	93·46	92·59	91·74	90·91	88·89	86·96	85·11	83·34
2	66·67	61·64	60·47	59·34	58·23	57·16	56·11	55·10	52·67	50·42	48·29	46·30
3	33·33	29·63	28·80	27·98	27·21	26·46	25·77	25·04	23·41	21·92	20·55	19·29
	200·00	187·42	184·51	181·66	178·90	176·21	173·62	171·05	164·97	159·30	153·95	148·93
1	100	96·15	95·24	94·34	93·46	92·59	91·74	90·91	88·89	86·96	85·11	83·34
2	80	73·96	72·56	71·20	69·88	68·59	67·33	66·12	63·21	60·50	57·95	55·56
3	60	53·34	51·83	50·38	48·98	47·63	46·33	45·08	42·14	39·46	36·99	34·72
4	40	34·19	32·91	31·68	30·52	29·40	28·34	27·32	24·98	22·87	20·99	19·29
5	20	16·44	15·67	14·95	14·26	13·61	13·00	12·42	11·10	9·94	8·93	8·04
	300	274·08	268·21	262·55	257·10	251·82	246·74	241·85	230·32	219·73	209·97	200·95
1	100	96·15	95·24	94·34	93·46	92·59	91·74	90·91	88·89	86·96	85·11	83·34
2	90	83·21	81·63	80·10	78·61	77·16	75·75	74·38	71·11	68·06	65·20	62·50
3	80	71·12	69·11	67·17	65·30	63·51	61·77	60·10	56·18	52·61	49·32	46·30
4	70	59·84	57·59	55·45	53·40	51·45	49·59	47·81	43·72	40·03	36·73	33·76
5	60	49·32	47·01	44·84	42·78	40·83	39·00	37·26	33·31	29·83	26·80	24·11
6	50	39·52	37·31	35·25	33·32	31·51	29·81	28·22	24·67	21·62	19·00	16·75
7	40	30·40	28·43	26·60	24·91	23·34	21·88	20·53	17·54	15·04	12·94	11·96
8	30	21·92	20·30	18 82	17·46	16·21	15·06	14 00	11·70	9·81	8·26	6·98
9	20	14·05	12·89	11·84	10·88	10·00	9·21	8·48	6·93	5·69	4·69	3·88
10	10	6·76	6·14	5·58	5·08	4·63	4·22	3·86	3·08	2.47	2.00	1·62
	550	472·29	455·65	439·99	425·20	411·23	398·03	385·55	357·13	332·12	310·05	291·20

PRESENT VALUE, AT VARIOUS RATES OF INTEREST, OF AN ANNUITY DIMINISHING BY EQUAL SUMS OVER FIFTEEN YEARS, COMMENCING WITH £100 DUE AT END OF THE FIRST YEAR.

Year.	Amount.	4%	5%	6%	7%	8%	9%	10%	12½%	15%	17½%	20%
1	100·00	96·15	95·24	94·34	93·46	92·59	91·74	90·91	88·89	86·96	85·11	83·34
2	93·33	86·29	84·65	83·06	81·52	80·02	78·55	77·13	73·74	70·58	67·61	64·82
3	86·67	77·05	74·87	72·77	70·75	68·80	66·92	65·12	60·87	56·99	53·43	50·18
4	80·00	68·38	65·82	63·37	61·03	58·80	56·67	54·64	49·96	45·74	41·98	38·58
5	73·33	60·27	57·46	54·80	52·28	49·91	47·66	45·53	40·71	36·46	32·75	29·47
6	66·67	52·69	49·75	47·00	44·42	40·01	39·75	37·63	32·89	28·83	25·34	22·33
7	60·00	45·60	42·64	39·90	37·36	35·01	32·82	30·79	26·32	22·56	19·41	16·75
8	53·33	38·97	36·09	33·46	31·04	28·81	26·76	24·88	20·79	17·44	14·68	12·40
9	46·67	32·79	30·08	27·62	25·39	23·35	21·49	19·79	16·17	13·27	10·49	9·04
10	40·00	27·02	24·56	22·34	20·33	18·53	16·90	15·42	12·32	9·89	7·98	6·46
11	33·33	21·65	19·49	17·56	15·83	14·29	12·92	11·68	9·13	7·17	5·66	4·49
12	26·67	16·66	14·85	13·25	11·84	10·59	9·48	8·50	6·49	4·99	3·86	2·98
13	20·00	12·01	10·61	9·38	8·30	7·35	6·52	5·79	4·33	3·25	2·46	1·87
14	13·33	7·70	6·73	5·90	5·17	4·54	3·99	3·51	2·57	1·88	1·40	1·04
15	6·67	3·70	3·21	2·78	2·42	2·10	1·83	1·60	1·14	·82	·60	·43
	800·00	646·93	616·05	587·53	561·14	534·70	514·00	492·92	446·32	406·83	372·76	344·18

PRESENT VALUE, AT VARIOUS RATES OF INTEREST, OF AN ANNUITY DIMINISHING BY EQUAL SUMS OVER TWENTY YEARS, COMMENCING WITH £100 DUE AT END OF THE FIRST YEAR.

Year.	Amount.	4%	5%	6%	7%	8%	9%	10%	12½%	15%	17½%	20%
1	100	96·15	95·24	94·34	93·46	92·59	91·74	90·91	88·89	86·96	85·11	83·34
2	95	87·83	86·16	84·55	82·98	81·45	79·96	78·51	75·06	71·84	68·82	65·97
3	90	80·01	77·75	75·57	73·47	71·44	69·50	67·62	63·21	59·18	55·49	52·08
4	85	72·66	69·93	67·33	64·85	62·48	60·22	58·06	53·08	48·60	45·12	41·00
5	80	65·75	62·68	59·78	57·04	54·45	51·99	49·67	44·41	39·78	35·73	32·15
6	75	59·27	55·96	52·87	49·98	47·26	44·72	42·34	37·01	32·43	28·51	25·12
7	70	53·19	49·75	46·55	43·59	40·84	38·29	35·92	30·70	26·32	22·65	19·54
8	65	47·49	43·99	40·78	37·83	35·12	32·62	30·32	25·34	21·26	17·89	15·12
9	60	42·16	38·68	35·51	32·64	30·01	27·63	25·45	20·80	17·06	15·63	11·63
10	55	37·16	33·76	30·71	27·96	25·45	23·23	21·20	16·95	13·60	10·98	8·88
11	50	32·48	29·24	26·34	23·75	21·44	19·38	17·52	13·70	10·75	8·50	6·73
12	45	28·11	25·06	22·36	19·98	17·87	16·00	14·34	10·96	8·42	6·51	5·05
13	40	24·02	21·21	18·75	16·60	14·71	13·05	11·59	8·66	6·50	4·92	3·74
14	35	20·21	17·68	15·48	13·57	11·92	10·47	9·22	6·73	4·95	3·67	2·73
15	30	16·66	14·43	12·52	10·87	9·46	8·24	7·18	5·13	3·69	2·68	1·95
16	25	13·35	11·45	9·84	8·47	7·30	6·30	5·44	3·80	2·67	1·90	1·35
17	20	10·27	8·73	7·43	6·33	5·41	4·62	3·96	2·70	1·86	1·29	·90
18	15	7·40	6·23	5·25	4·44	3·75	3·18	2·70	1·80	1·21	·82	·56
19	10	4·75	3·96	3·30	2·76	2·32	1·94	1·64	1·07	·70	·47	·31
20	5	2·28	1·88	1·56	1·29	1·07	·89	·74	·47	·31	·20	·13
	1050	801·20	753·77	710·82	671·86	636·34	603·97	574·33	510·47	458·09	416·89	378·28

PRESENT VALUE, AT VARIOUS RATES OF INTEREST, OF AN ANNUITY DIMINISHING BY EQUAL SUMS OVER THIRTY YEARS, COMMENCING WITH £100 DUE AT END OF THE FIRST YEAR.

Year.	Amount.	4%	5%	6%	7%	8%	9%	10%	12½%	15%	17½%	20%
1	100·00	96·15	95·24	94·34	93·46	92·59	91·74	90·91	88·89	86·96	85·11	83·34
2	96·67	89·38	87·68	86·04	84·44	82·88	81·37	79·89	76·38	73·10	70·03	67·14
3	93·33	82·97	80·62	78·36	76·19	74·09	72·07	70·12	65·55	61·37	57·54	54·01
4	90·00	76·93	74·04	71·29	68·66	66·15	63·76	61·47	56·21	51·46	47·22	43·41
5	86·67	71·24	67·91	64·76	61·79	58·99	56·33	52·82	48·11	43·09	38·71	34·83
6	83·33	65·86	62·18	58·74	55·53	52·51	49·69	47·04	41·12	36·03	31·68	27·91
7	80.00	60·79	56·86	53·20	49·82	46·68	43·76	41·05	35·09	30·08	25·88	22·33
8	76·67	56·02	51·89	48·10	44·62	41·42	38·48	35·77	29·89	25·07	21·11	17·83
9	73·33	51·52	47·27	43·40	39·89	36·68	33·76	31·10	25·42	20·86	17·20	14·21
10	70·00	47·29	42·97	39·09	35·58	32·42	29·57	26·99	21·57	17·31	13·97	11·31
11	66·67	43·31	38·98	35·12	31·67	28·59	25·84	23·37	18·26	14·34	11·33	8·97
12	63·33	39·56	35·26	31·47	28·12	25·15	22·52	20·18	15·42	11·84	9·16	7·11
13	60,00	36·03	31·82	28·13	24·90	22·06	19·57	17·38	12·98	9·76	7·39	5·61
14	56·67	32·73	28·62	25·07	21·98	19·29	16·96	14·92	10·90	8·01	5·94	4·41
15	53·33	29·61	25·65	22·25	19·33	16·81	14·64	12·77	9·12	6·56	4·76	3·46
16	50·00	26·70	22·91	19·68	16·94	14·59	12·59	10·88	7·60	5·35	3·80	2·71
17	46·67	23·96	20·36	17·33	14·77	12·61	10·78	9·23	6·30	4·34	3·00	2·10
18	43·33	21·39	18·00	15·18	12·82	10·84	9·19	7·79	5.20	3·51	2·37	1·63
19	40·00	18·99	15·83	13·22	11·06	9·27	7·78	6·54	4·26	2·82	1·86	1·25
20	36·67	16·74	13·82	11·43	9·48	7·87	6·54	5·45	3·48	2·24	1·46	·96
21	33·33	14·63	11·96	9·80	8·05	6·62	5·46	4·50	2·81	1·77	1·13	·73
22	30·00	12·66	10·26	8·33	6·77	5·52	4·51	3·67	2·25	1·39	·86	·55
23	26·67	10·82	8·68	6·98	5·63	4·54	3·67	2·98	1·78	1·07	·65	·41
24	23·33	9·10	7·23	5·76	4·60	3·68	2·95	2·37	1·38	·82	·49	·30
25	20·00	7·50	5·91	4·66	3·68	2·92	2·32	1·85	1·05	·61	·36	·21
26	16·67	6·01	4·69	3·66	2·87	2·25	1·77	1·40	·78	·44	·25	·15
27	13·33	4·62	3·57	2·76	2·15	1·67	1·30	1·02	·55	·31	·17	·10
28	10·00	3·33	2·55	1·96	1·50	1·16	·90	·69	·37	·20	·11	·06
29	6·67	2·14	1·62	1·23	·94	·72	·55	·42	·22	·12	·06	·03
30	3·33	1·03	·77	·58	·44	·33	·25	·19	·10	·05	·03	·01
	1550·00	1059·01	975·15	901·92	837·68	780·90	730·62	684·76	593·04	520·88	463·63	417·08

PRESENT VALUE, AT VARIOUS RATES OF INTEREST, OF AN ANNUITY DIMINISHING BY EQUAL SUMS OVER FIFTY YEARS, COMMENCING WITH £100 DUE AT END OF THE FIRST YEAR.

Year.	Amount.	4%	5%	6%	7%	8%	9%	10%	12½%	15%	17½%	20%
1	100	96·15	95·24	94·34	93·46	92·59	91·74	90·91	88·89	86·96	85·11	83·34
2	98	90·61	88·89	87·22	85·60	84·02	82·48	80·99	77·43	74·11	70·99	68·06
3	96	85·34	82·93	80·60	78·36	76·21	74·13	72·12	67·42	63·13	59·18	55·56
4	94	80·35	77·33	74·46	71·71	69·09	66·59	64·20	58·70	53·75	49·31	45·34
5	92	75·62	72·08	68·75	65·59	62·61	59·79	57·12	51·07	45·74	41·09	36·97
6	90	71·13	67·16	63·45	59·97	56·72	53·66	50·80	44·41	38·92	34·21	30·14
7	88	66·87	62·54	58-53	54·80	51·35	48·14	45·16	38·60	33·09	28·47	24·56
8	86	62·84	58·21	53·96	50·05	46·46	43·16	40·12	33·53	28·12	23·68	20·00
9	84	59·02	54·15	49·72	45·69	42·02	38·68	35·62	29·11	23·89	19·70	16·28
10	82	55·40	50·34	45·79	41·68	37·98	34·64	31·61	25·26	20·28	16·37	13·24
11	80	51·97	46·77	42·14	38·00	34·31	31·00	28·04	21·91	17·21	13·59	10·77
12	78	48·72	43·43	38·76	34·63	30·97	27·73	24·85	18·99	14·59	11·28	8·75
13	76	45·64	40·30	35·63	31·54	27·95	24·79	22·01	16·45	12·36	9·36	7·11
14	74	42·73	37·38	32·73	28·70	25·19	22·14	19·49	14·24	10·46	7·76	5·76
15	72	39·98	34·63	30·04	26·10	22·70	19·77	17·24	12·31	8·86	6·42	4·67
16	70	37·37	32·07	27·56	23·71	20·43	17·63	15·23	10·64	7·49	5·31	3·79
17	68	34·91	29·67	25·25	21·53	18·38	15·71	13·45	9·19	6·32	4·37	3·07
18	66	32·58	27·42	23·12	19·53	16·52	13·99	11·87	7·93	5·34	3·61	2·48
19	64	30·38	25·33	21·15	17·70	14·83	12·45	10·46	6·84	4·51	2·98	2·00
20	62	28·30	23·37	19·33	16·02	13·30	11·06	9·22	5·88	3·79	2·46	1·62
21	60	26·33	21·54	17·65	14·49	11·92	9·82	8·11	5·06	3·19	2·03	1·31
22	58	24·47	19·83	16·10	13·08	10·67	8·71	7·13	4·35	2·69	1·67	1·06
23	56	22·72	18·23	14·66	11·81	9·54	7·72	6·25	3·74	2·26	1·37	·85
24	54	21·07	16·74	13·34	10·65	8·52	6·83	5·48	3·20	1·90	1·13	·69

25	52	19·51	15·36	12·12	9·58	7·59	6·03	4·80	2·74	1·59	·93	·55
26	50	18·03	14·06	10·99	8·61	6·76	5·32	4·20	2·34	1·33	·76	·45
27	48	16·65	12·84	9·95	7·72	6·00	4·69	3·66	2·00	1·11	·62	·36
28	46	15·34	11·73	9 00	6·92	5·33	4·12	3·19	1·70	·92	·51	·29
29	44	14·11	10·69	8·12	6·18	4·72	3·61	2·77	1·45	·77	·41	·23
30	42	12·95	9·72	7·31	5·52	4·17	3·17	2·41	1·23	·64	·34	·18
31	40	11·86	8·81	6·57	4·91	3·68	2·77	2·08	1·04	·53	·27	·14
32	38	10·83	7·98	5·89	4·36	3·24	2·41	1·80	·88	·44	·22	·11
33	36	9·87	7·20	5·26	3·86	2·84	2·10	1·55	·74	·36	·18	·09
34	34	8·96	6·47	4·69	3·41	2·48	1·82	1·33	·62	·30	·14	·07
35	32	8·11	5·80	4·16	3·00	2·16	1·57	1·14	·52	·24	·11	·06
36	30	7·31	5·18	3·68	2·63	1·88	1·35	·97	·43	·20	·09	·05
37	28	6·56	4·60	3·24	2·29	1·62	1·15	·82	·36	·16	·07	·04
38	26	5·86	4·07	2·84	1·99	1·40	·98	·69	·30	·13	·06	·03
39	24	5·20	3·56	2·47	1·71	1·19	·83	·58	·24	·10	·05	·02
40	22	4·58	3·13	2·14	1·47	1·01	·70	·49	·20	·08	·04	·02
41	20	4·01	2·71	1·83	1·25	·85	·58	·40	·16	·06	·03	·01
42	18	3·47	2·32	1·56	1·05	·71	·48	·33	·13	·05	·02	·01
43	16	2·96	1·96	1·31	·87	·58	·39	·27	·10	·04	·02	·01
44	14	2·49	1·64	1·08	·71	·47	·32	·21	·08	·03	·01	
45	12	2·05	1·34	·87	·57	·38	·25	·16	·06	·02	·01	
46	10	1·65	1·06	·69	·44	·29	·19	·12	·04	·02	·01	
47	8	1·27	·81	·52	·33	·21	·14	·09	·03	·01		
48	6	·91	·58	·37	·23	·15	·10	·06	·02	·01		
49	4	·59	·37	·23	·15	·09	·06	·04	·01			
50	2	·28	·17	·11	·06	·04	·03	·02	·01			
	2550	1425·91	1269·74	1141·28	1034·22	944·12	867·52	801·66	672·58	578·10	506·35	450·14

PRESENT VALUE, AT VARIOUS RATES OF INTEREST, OF AN ANNUITY DIMINISHING BY EQUAL SUMS OVER ONE HUNDRED YEARS, COMMENCING WITH £100 DUE AT END OF THE FIRST YEAR

Year	Amount	4%	5%	6%	7%	8%	9%	10%	12½%	15%	17½%	20%
1	100	96·15	95·24	94·34	93·46	92·59	91·74	90·91	88·89	86·96	85·11	83·34
2	99	91·53	89·80	88·11	86·47	84·88	83·33	81·82	78·22	74·86	71·72	68·76
3	98	87·12	84·66	82·28	80·00	77·80	75·67	73·63	68·83	64·44	60·42	56·71
4	97	82·92	79·80	76·73	74 00	71·30	68·72	66·25	60·58	55·46	50·90	46·78
5	96	78·91	75 22	71·74	68·45	65·34	62·39	59·61	53·29	47·73	42·87	38·58
6	95	75·08	70·89	66·97	63·30	59·87	56·65	53·62	46·87	41·08	36·11	31·82
7	94	71·43	66·80	62·52	58·54	54·85	51·42	48·24	41·23	35·34	30·41	26·24
8	93	67·95	62·95	58·35	54·13	50·25	46·67	43·39	36·26	30·41	25·60	21·63
9	92	64·64	59·30	54·45	50·04	46·02	42·36	39·02	31·89	26·16	21·57	17·83
10	91	61·48	55·87	50·81	46·26	42·15	38·44	35·08	28·04	22·50	18·16	14·70
11	90	58·46	52·62	47·41	42·76	38·60	34·88	31·54	24·65	19·36	15·29	12·11
12	89	55·59	49·56	44·23	39·52	35·34	31·64	28·36	21·67	16·64	12·87	9·99
13	88	52·85	46·67	41·26	36·52	32·36	28·70	25·49	19·04	14·31	10·83	8·23
14	87	50·24	43·94	38·48	33·74	29·62	26·03	22·91	16·74	12·30	9·12	6·78
15	86	47·75	41·37	35·89	31·17	27·11	23·61	20·59	14·71	10·58	7·67	5·58
16	85	45·38	38·94	33·46	28·79	24·81	21·41	18·50	12·92	9·10	6·45	4·60
17	84	43·12	36·65	31·19	26·59	22·70	19·41	16·62	11·35	7·81	5·40	3·79
18	83	40·97	34·49	29·08	24·56	20·77	17·60	14·93	9·97	6·71	4·54	3·12
19	82	38·92	32·45	27·10	22·67	19 00	15·95	13·41	8·76	5·77	3·82	2·57
20	81	36·97	30·53	25·26	20·93	17·38	14·45	12·04	7·68	4·96	3·22	2·11
21	80	35·11	28·72	23·53	19·32	15·89	13·10	10·81	6·75	4·26	2·70	1·74
22	79	33·33	27·01	21·92	17·83	14·53	11·86	9·70	5·93	3·66	2·28	1·44
23	78	31·65	25·39	20·42	16·45	13·28	10·75	8·71	5·20	3·14	1·91	1·19
24	77	30·04	23·88	19·02	15·18	12·14	9·73	7·82	4·57	2.70	1·61	·98
25	76	28·51	22·44	17·71	14 00	11·10	8·81	7·01	4·01	2·32	1·35	·81
26	75	27·05	21·09	16·49	12·91	10·14	7·98	6·29	3·51	1·99	1·13	·67
27	74	25·66	19·82	15·35	11·91	9·26	7·22	5·64	3·08	1·71	·95	·55
28	73	24·34	18·62	14·28	10·98	8·46	6·54	5·06	2·70	1·47	·80	·45
29	72	23·09	17·49	13·29	10·12	7·73	5·91	4·54	2·37	1·26	·68	·37
30	71	21·89	16·43	12·36	9·33	7·06	5·35	4·07	2·07	1·08	·57	·31
31	70	20·75	15·43	11·50	8·59	6·44	4·84	3·65	1·82	·92	·48	·25
32	69	19·67	14·48	10·69	7·92	5·88	4·38	3·27	1·59	·79	·40	·21
33	68	18·64	13·59	9·94	7·29	5·36	3·96	2·93	1·39	·68	·33	·17

34	67	17·66	12·75	9·24	6·71	4·89	3·58	2·62	1·22	·58	·28	·14
35	66	16·73	11·97	8·59	6·18	4·46	3·23	2·35	1·07	·50	·24	·12
36	65	15·84	11·22	7·98	5·69	4·07	2·92	2·10	·94	·43	·20	·10
37	64	15 00	10·52	7·41	5·24	3·71	2·64	1·88	·82	·36	·17	·08
38	63	14·19	9·87	6·88	4·82	3·38	2·38	1·68	·72	·32	·14	·07
39	62	13·43	9·25	6·39	4·43	3·08	2·15	1·51	·63	·27	·12	·06
40	61	12·71	8·67	5·93	4·01	2·81	1·94	1·35	·55	·23	·10	·04
41	60	12·02	8·12	5·50	3·74	2·56	1·75	1·21	·48	·19	·08	·04
42	59	11·36	7·60	5·11	3·44	2·33	1·58	1·08	·42	·17	·07	·03
43	58	10·74	7·12	4·73	3·16	2·12	1·43	·96	·37	·15	·06	·02
44	57	10·15	6·66	4·39	2·90	1·93	1·29	·86	·32	·13	·05	·02
45	56	9·59	6·23	4·07	2·67	1·75	1·16	·77	·28	·11	·04	·01
46	55	9·05	5·83	3·77	2·45	1·60	1·04	·69	·24	·09	·04	·01
47	54	8·55	5·45	3·49	2·25	1·45	·94	·61	·21	·08	·03	
48	53	8·07	5·09	3·23	2·06	1·32	·85	·55	·19	·07	·03	
49	52	7·61	4·76	2·99	1·89	1·20	·76	·49	·16	·06	·02	
50	51	7·18	4·45	2·77	1·73	1·09	·69	·43	·14	·05	·02	
51	50	6·77	4·15	2·56	1·59	·99	·62	·39	·13	·05		
52	49	6·37	3·88	2·37	1·45	·90	·55	·34	·11	·04		
53	48	6·00	3·62	2·19	1·33	·81	·50	·31	·10	·03		
54	47	5·65	3·37	2·02	1·22	·74	·45	·27	·08	·03		
55	46	5·32	3·14	1·87	1·11	·67	·40	·24	·07	·02		
56	45	5·00	2·93	1·72	1·02	·60	·36	·22	·06	·02		
57	44	4·70	2·73	1·59	·93	·55	·32	·19	·05	·01		
58	43	4·42	2·54	1·46	·85	·50	·29	·17	·05	·01		
59	42	4·15	2·36	1·35	·78	·45	·26	·15	·04	·01		
60	41	3·90	2·20	1·24	·71	·40	·23	·13	·04	·01		
61	40	3·66	2·04	1·14	·65	·37	·21	·12	·03	·01		
62	39	3·43	1·89	1·05	·59	·33	·19	·11	·03			
63	38	3·21	1·76	·97	·54	·30	·17	·09	·02			
64	37	3·01	1·63	·89	·49	·27	·15	·08	·02			
65	36	2·81	1·51	·82	·44	·24	·13	·07	·01			
66	35	2·63	1·40	·75	·40	·22	·12	·06				
67	34	2·46	1·29	·69	·36	·20	·11	·06				
68	33	2·29	1·20	·63	·33	·18	·09	·05				
69	32	2·14	1·10	·57	·30	·16	·08	·04				
70	31	1·99	1·02	·52	·27	·14	·07	·04				
71	30	1·85	·94	·48	·25	·13	·07	·03				

PRESENT VALUE, AT VARIOUS RATES OF INTEREST, OF AN ANNUITY DIMINISHING BY EQUAL SUMS OVER ONE HUNDRED YEARS, COMMENCING WITH £100 DUE AT END OF THE FIRST YEAR (*continued*)

Year.	Amount	4%	5%	6%	7%	8%	9%	10%	12½%	15%	17½%	20%
72	29	1·72	·86	·44	·22	·11	·06	·03				
73	28	1·60	·79	·40	·20	·10	·05	·03				
74	27	1·48	·73	·36	·18	·09	·05	·02				
75	26	1·37	·67	·33	·16	·08	·04	·02				
76	25	1·27	·61	·30	·15	·07	·04	·02				
77	24	1·17	·56	·27	·13	·06	·03	·02				
78	23	1·08	·51	·24	·12	·06	·03	·01				
79	22	·99	·47	·22	·10	·05	·02	·01				
80	21	·91	·42	·20	·09	·04	·02	·01				
81	20	·83	·38	·18	·08	·04	·02	·01				
82	19	·76	·35	·16	·07	·03	·02	·01				
83	18	·69	·31	·14	·07	·03	·01	·01				
84	17	·63	·28	·13	·06	·03	·01	·01				
85	16	·57	·25	·11	·05	·02	·01					
86	15	·51	·23	·10	·04	·02	·01					
87	14	·46	·20	·09	·04	·02	·01					
88	13	·41	·18	·08	·03	·01	·01					
89	12	·37	·16	·07	·03	·01	·01					
90	11	·32	·14	·06	·02	·01						
91	10	·28	·12	·05	·02	·01						
92	9	·24	·10	·04	·02	·01						
93	8	·21	·08	·04	·01	·01						
94	7	·18	·07	·03	·01	·01						
95	6	·14	·06	·02	·01							
96	5	·12	·05	·02	·01							
97	4	·09	·04	·01	·01							
98	3	·06	·03	·01								
99	2	·04	·02	·01								
100	1	·02	·01									
	5050	1887·35	1603·08	1389·62	1224·64	1093·83	987·65	899·97	736·18	622·49	538·96	475·15

APPENDIX II

TRADE MARKS ACT, 1905

[5 Edw. VII, Ch. 15]

Chapter 15

An Act to consolidate and amend the Law relating to Trade Marks. [11th August, 1905.] A.D. 1905

Be it enacted by the King's most Excellent Majesty, by and with the advice and consent of the Lords Spiritual and Temporal, and Commons, in this present Parliament assembled, and by the authority of the same, as follows—

1. This Act may be cited as the Trade Marks Act, 1905. Short title.

2. This Act shall, save as otherwise expressly provided, come into operation on the first day of April, one thousand nine hundred and six. Commencement of Act

Part I.

Definitions.

3. In and for the purposes of this Act (unless the context otherwise requires) :— Definitions

A " mark " shall include a device, brand, heading, label, ticket, name, signature, word, letter, numeral, or any combination thereof :

A " trade mark " shall mean a mark used or proposed to be used upon or in connexion with goods for the purpose of indicating that they are the goods of the proprietor of such trade mark by virtue of manufacture, selection, certification, dealing with, or offering for sale :

A " registrable trade mark " shall mean a trade mark which is capable of registration under the provisions of this Act :

" The register " shall mean the register of trade marks kept under the provisions of this Act :

A " registered trade mark " shall mean a trade mark which is actually upon the register :

" Prescribed " shall mean, in relation to proceedings before the Court, prescribed by rules of court, and in other cases, prescribed by this Act or the Rules thereunder :

" The Court " shall mean (subject to the provisions for Scotland, Ireland, and the Isle of Man) His Majesty's High Court of Justice in England.

Register of Trade Marks.

4. There shall be kept at the Patent Office for the purposes of this Act a book called the Register of Trade Marks, wherein shall be entered all registered trade marks with the names and addresses of their proprietors, notifications of assignments and transmissions, disclaimers, conditions, limitations, and such other matters relating to such trade marks as may from time to time be prescribed. The register shall be kept under the control and Register of trade marks

A.D. 1905

management of the Comptroller-General of Patents, Designs, and Trade Marks, who is in this Act referred to as the Registrar.

Trust not to be entered on register

5. There shall not be entered in the register any notice of any trust expressed, implied, or constructive, nor shall any such notice be receivable by the Registrar.

Incorporation of existing register

6. The register of trade marks existing at the date of the commencement of this Act, and all registers of trade marks kept under previous Acts, which are deemed part of the same book as such register, shall be incorporated with and form part of the register. Subject to the provisions of sections thirty-six and forty-one of this Act the validity of the original entry of any trade mark upon the registers so incorporated shall be determined in accordance with the statutes in force at the date of such entry, and such trade mark shall retain its original date, but for all other purposes it shall be deemed to be a trade mark registered under this Act.

Inspection of and extract from register

7. The register kept under this Act shall at all convenient times be open to the inspection of the public, subject to such regulations as may be prescribed; and certified copies, sealed with the seal of the Patent Office, of any entry in any such register shall be given to any person requiring the same on payment of the prescribed fee.

Registrable Trade Marks.

Trade mark must be for particular goods

8. A trade mark must be registered in respect of particular goods or classes of goods.

Registrable trade marks

9. A registrable trade mark must contain or consist of at least one of the following essential particulars:—

(1) The name of a company, individual, or firm represented in a special or particular manner;

(2) The signature of the applicant for registration or some predecessor in his business;

(3) An invented word or invented words;

(4) A word or words having no direct reference to the character or quality of the goods, and not being according to its ordinary signification a geographical name or a surname;

(5) Any other distinctive mark, but a name, signature, or word or words, other than such as fall within the descriptions in the above paragraphs (1), (2), (3), and (4), shall not, except by order of the Board of Trade or the Court, be deemed a distinctive mark:

Provided always that any special or distinctive word or words, letter, numeral, of combination of letters or numerals used as a trade mark by the applicant or his predecessors in business before the thirteenth day of August one thousand eight hundred and seventy-five, which has continued to be used (either in its original form or with additions or alterations not substantially affecting the identity of the same) down to the date of the application for registration shall be registrable as a trade mark under this Act.

For the purposes of this section "distinctive" shall mean adapted to distinguish the goods of the proprietor of the trade mark from those of other persons.

In determining whether a trade mark is so adapted, the tribunal may, in the case of a trade mark in actual use, take into consideration the extent to which such user has rendered such trade mark in fact distinctive for the goods with respect to which it is registered or proposed to be registered. A.D. 1905

10. A trade mark may be limited in whole or in part to one or more specified colours, and in such case the fact that it is so limited shall be taken into consideration by any tribunal having to decide on the distinctive character of such trade mark. If and so far as a trade mark is registered without limitation of colour it shall be deemed to be registered for all colours. Coloured trade marks

11. It shall not be lawful to register as a trade mark or part of a trade mark any matter, the use of which would by reason of its being calculated to deceive or otherwise be disentitled to protection in a court of justice, or would be contrary to law or morality, or any scandalous design. Restriction on registration

Registration of Trade Marks.

12.—(1) Any person claiming to be the proprietor of a trade mark who is desirous of registering the same must apply in writing to the Registrar in the prescribed manner. Application for registration

(2) Subject to the provisions of this Act the Registrar may refuse such application, or may accept it absolutely or subject to conditions, amendments, or modifications.

(3) In case of any such refusal or conditional acceptance the Registrar shall, if required by the applicant, state in writing the grounds of his decision and the materials used by him in arriving at the same, and such decision shall be subject to appeal to the Board of Trade or to the Court at the option of the applicant.

(4) An appeal under this section shall be made in the prescribed manner, and on such appeal the Board of Trade or the Court, as the case may be, shall, if required, hear the applicant and the Registrar, and shall make an order determining whether, and subject to what conditions, amendments, or modifications, if any, the application is to be accepted.

(5) Appeals under this section shall be heard on the materials so stated by the Registrar to have been used by him in arriving at his decision, and no further grounds of objection to the acceptance of the application shall be allowed to be taken by the Registrar, other than those stated by him, except by leave of the tribunal hearing the appeal. Where any further grounds of objection are taken the applicant shall be entitled to withdraw his application without payment of costs on giving notice as prescribed.

(6) The Registrar or the Board of Trade or the Court, as the case may be, may at any time, whether before or after acceptance, correct any error in or in connexion with the application, or may permit the applicant to amend his application upon such terms as they may think fit.

13. When an application for registration of a trade mark has been accepted, whether absolutely or subject to conditions, the Registrar shall, as soon as may be after such acceptance, cause the application as accepted to be advertised in the prescribed manner. Such advertisement shall set forth all conditions subject to which the application has been accepted. Advertisement of application

14.—(1) Any person may, within the prescribed time from the date of the advertisement of an application for the registration Opposition to registration

A.D. 1905

of a trade mark, give notice to the Registrar of opposition to such registration.

(2) Such notice shall be given in writing in the prescribed manner, and shall include a statement of the grounds of opposition.

(3) The Registrar shall send a copy of such notice to the applicant, and within the prescribed time after the receipt of such notice, the applicant shall send to the Registrar, in the prescribed manner, a counter-statement of the grounds on which he relies for his application, and, if he does not do so, he shall be deemed to have abandoned his application.

(4) If the applicant sends such counter-statement, the Registrar shall furnish a copy thereof to the persons giving notice of opposition, and shall, after hearing the parties, if so required, and considering the evidence, decide whether, and subject to what conditions, registration is to be permitted.

(5) The decision of the Registrar shall be subject to appeal to the Court or, with the consent of the parties, to the Board of Trade.

(6) An appeal under this section shall be made in the prescribed manner, and on such appeal the Board of Trade or the Court, as the case may be, shall, if required, hear the parties and the Registrar, and shall make an order determining whether, and subject to what conditions, if any, registration is to be permitted.

(7) On the hearing of any such appeal any party may either in the manner prescribed or by special leave of the tribunal bring forward further material for the consideration of the tribunal.

(8) In proceedings under this section no further grounds of objection to the registration of a trade mark shall be allowed to be taken by the opponent or the Registrar other than those stated by the opponent as herein-above provided except by leave of the tribunal hearing the appeal. Where any further grounds of objection are taken the applicant shall be entitled to withdraw his application without payment of the costs of the opponent on giving notice as prescribed.

(9) In any appeal under this section, the tribunal may, after hearing the Registrar, permit the trade mark proposed to be registered to be modified in any manner not substantially affecting the identity of such trade mark, but in such case the trade mark as so modified shall be advertised in the prescribed manner before being registered.

(10) The Registrar, or in the case of an appeal to the Board of Trade the Board of Trade, shall have power in proceedings under this section to award to any party such costs as they may consider reasonable, and to direct how and by what parties they are to be paid.

(11) If a party giving notice of opposition or of appeal neither resides nor carries on business in the United Kingdom, the tribunal may require such party to give security for costs of the proceedings before it relative to such opposition or appeal, and in default of such security being duly given may treat the opposition or appeal as abandoned.

Disclaimers

15. If a trade mark contains parts not separately registered by the proprietor as trade marks, or if it contains matter common

to the trade or otherwise of a non-distinctive character, the Registrar or the Board of Trade or the Court, in deciding whether such trade mark shall be entered or shall remain upon the register, may require, as a condition of its being upon the register, that the proprietor shall disclaim any right to the exclusive use of any part or parts of such trade mark, or of all or any portion of such matter, to the exclusive use of which they hold him not to be entitled, or that he shall make such other disclaimer as they may consider needful for the purpose of defining his rights under such registration: Provided always that no disclaimer upon the register shall affect any rights of the proprietor of a trade mark except such as arise out of the registration of the trade mark in respect of which the disclaimer is made. A.D. 1905

16. When an application for registration of a trade mark has been accepted and has not been opposed, and the time for notice of opposition has expired, or having been opposed the opposition has been decided in favour of the applicant, the Registrar shall, unless the Board of Trade otherwise direct, register the said trade mark, and the trade mark, when registered, shall be registered as of the date of the application for registration, and such date shall be deemed for the purposes of this Act to be the date of registration. Date of registration

17. On the registration of a trade mark the Registrar shall issue to the applicant a certificate in the prescribed form of the registration of such trade mark under the hand of the Registrar, and sealed with the seal of the Patent Office. Certificate of registration

18. Where registration of a trade mark is not completed within twelve months from the date of the application by reason of default on the part of the applicant, the Registrar may, after giving notice of the non-completion to the applicant in writing in the prescribed manner, treat the application as abandoned unless it is completed within the time specified in that behalf in such notice. Non-completion of registration

Identical Trade Marks.

19. Except by order of the Court or in the case of trade marks in use before the thirteenth day of August one thousand eight hundred and seventy-five, no trade mark shall be registered in respect of any goods or description of goods which is identical with one belonging to a different proprietor which is already on the register with respect to such goods or description of goods, or so nearly resembling such a trade mark as to be calculated to deceive. Identical marks

20. Where each of several persons claims to be proprietor of the same trade mark, or of nearly identical trade marks in respect of the same goods or description of goods, and to be registered as such proprietor, the Registrar may refuse to register any of them until their rights have been determined by the Court, or have been settled by agreement in a manner approved by him or (on appeal) by the Board of Trade. Rival claims to identical marks

21. In case of honest concurrent user or of other special circumstances which, in the opinion of the Court, make it proper so to do, the Court may permit the registration of the same trade mark, or of nearly identical trade marks, for the same goods or description of goods by more than one proprietor subject to such Concurrent user

A.D. 1905

conditions and limitations, if any, as to mode or place of user or otherwise, as it may think it right to impose.

Assignment.

Assignment and trans mission of trade marks

22. A trade mark when registered shall be assigned and transmitted only in connexion with the goodwill of the business concerned in the goods for which it has been registered and shall be determinable with that goodwill. But nothing in this section contained shall be deemed to affect the right of the proprietor of a registered trade mark to assign the right to use the same in any British possession or protectorate or foreign country in connexion with any goods for which it is registered together with the goodwill of the business therein in such goods.

Apportionment of marks on dissolution of partnership

23. In any case where from any cause, whether by reason of dissolution of partnership or otherwise, a person ceases to carry on business, and the goodwill of such person does not pass to one successor but is divided, the Registrar may (subject to the provisions of this Act as to associated trade marks), on the application of the parties interested, permit an apportionment of the registered trade marks of the person among the persons in fact continuing the business, subject to such conditions and modifications, if any, as he may think necessary in the public interest. Any decision of the Registrar under this section shall be subject to appeal to the Board of Trade.

Associated Trade Marks.

Associated trade marks

24. If application be made for the registration of a trade mark so closely resembling a trade mark of the applicant already on the register for the same goods or description of goods as to be calculated to deceive or cause confusion if used by a person other than the applicant, the tribunal hearing the application may require as a condition of registration that such trade marks shall be entered on the register as associated trade marks.

Combined trade marks

25. If the proprietor of a trade mark claims to be entitled to the exclusive use of any portion of such trade mark separately he may apply to register the same as separate trade marks. Each such separate trade mark must satisfy all the conditions and shall have all the incidents of an independent trade mark, except that when registered it and the trade mark of which it forms a part shall be deemed to be associated trade marks and shall be entered on the register as such, but the user of the whole trade mark shall for the purposes of this Act be deemed to be also a user of such registered trade marks belonging to the same proprietor as it contains.

Series of trade marks

26. When a person claiming to be the proprietor of several trade marks for the same description of goods which, while resembling each other in the material particulars thereof, yet differ in respect of—

(*a*) statements of the goods for which they are respectively used or proposed to be used ; or
(*b*) statements of number, price, quality, or names of places ; or
(*c*) other matter of a non-distinctive character which does not substantially affect the identity of the trade mark ; or
(*d*) colour ;

seeks to register such trade marks, they may be registered as a series in one registration. All the trade marks in a series of trade marks so registered shall be deemed to be, and shall be registered as, associated trade marks.

A.D. 1905

Assignment and user of associated trade marks

27. Associated trade marks shall be assignable or transmissible only as a whole and not separately, but they shall for all other purposes be deemed to have been registered as separate trade marks. Provided that where under the provisions of this Act user of a registered trade mark is required to be proved for any purpose, the tribunal may if and so far as it shall think right accept user of an associated registered trade mark, or of the trade mark with additions or alterations not substantially affecting its identity, as an equivalent for such user.

Renewal of Registration.

Duration of registration

28. The registration of a trade mark shall be for a period of fourteen years, but may be renewed from time to time in accordance with the provisions of this Act.

Renewal of registration

29. The Registrar shall, on application made by the registered proprietor of a trade mark in the prescribed manner and within the prescribed period, renew the registration of such trade mark for a period of fourteen years from the expiration of the original registration or of the last renewal of registration, as the case may be, which date is herein termed "the expiration of the last registration."

Procedure on expiry of period of registration

30. At the prescribed time before the expiration of the last registration of a trade mark, the Registrar shall send notice in the prescribed manner to the registered proprietor at his registered address of the date at which the existing registration will expire and the conditions as to payment of fees and otherwise upon which a renewal of such registration may be obtained, and if at the expiration of the time prescribed in that behalf such conditions have not been duly complied with, the Registrar may remove such trade mark from the register, subject to such conditions (if any) as to its restoration to the register as may be prescribed.

Status of unrenewed trade mark

31. Where a trade mark has been removed from the register for non-payment of the fee for renewal, such trade mark shall, nevertheless, for the purpose of any application for registration during one year next after the date of such removal, be deemed to be a trade mark which is already registered, unless it is shown to the satisfaction of the Registrar that there had been no *bona fide* trade user of such trade mark during the two years immediately preceding such removal.

Correction and Rectification of the Register.

Correction of register

32. The Registrar may, on request made in the prescribed manner by the registered proprietor or by some person entitled by law to act in his name,—

(1) Correct any error in the name or address of the registered proprietor of a trade mark; or

(2) Enter any change in the name or address of the person who is registered as proprietor of a trade mark; or

(3) Cancel the entry of a trade mark on the register; or

(4) Strike out any goods or classes of goods from those for which a trade mark is registered; or

A.D. 1905

(5) Enter a disclaimer or memorandum relating to a trade mark which does not in any way extend the rights given by the existing registration of such trade mark.

Any decision of the Registrar under this section shall be subject to appeal to the Board of Trade.

Registration of assignments, etc.

33. Subject to the provisions of this Act where a person becomes entitled to a registered trade mark by assignment, transmission, or other operation of law, the Registrar shall, on request made in the prescribed manner, and on proof of title to his satisfaction, cause the name and address of such person to be entered on the register as proprietor of the trade mark. Any decision of the Registrar under this section shall be subject to appeal to the Court or, with the consent of the parties, to the Board of Trade.

Alteration of registered trade mark

34. The registered proprietor of any trade mark may apply in the prescribed manner to the Registrar for leave to add to or alter such trade mark in any manner not substantially affecting the identity of the same, and the Registrar may refuse such leave or may grant the same on such terms as he may think fit, but any such refusal or conditional permission shall be subject to appeal to the Board of Trade. If leave be granted, the trade mark as altered shall be advertised in the prescribed manner.

Rectification of register

35. Subject to the provisions of this Act—

(1) The Court may on the application in the prescribed manner of any person aggrieved by the non-insertion in or omission from the register of any entry, or by any entry made in the register without sufficient cause, or by any entry wrongly remaining on the register, or by any error or defect in any entry in the register, make such order for making, expunging, or varying such entry as it may think fit:

(2) The Court may in any proceeding under this section decide any question that it may be necessary or expedient to decide in connexion with the rectification of the register:

(3) In case of fraud in the registration or transmission of a registered trade mark, the Registrar may himself apply to the Court under the provisions of this section:

(4) Any order of the Court rectifying the register shall direct that notice of the rectification shall be served upon the Registrar in the prescribed manner who shall upon receipt of such notice rectify the register accordingly.

Trade marks registered under previous Acts.

36. No trade mark which is upon the register at the commencement of this Act and which under this Act is a registrable trade mark shall be removed from the register on the ground that it was not registrable under the Acts in force at the date of its registration. But nothing in this section contained shall subject any person to any liability in respect of any act or thing done before the commencement of this Act, to which he would not have been subject under the Acts then in force.

Non-user of trade-mark

37. A registered trade mark may, on the application to the Court of any person aggrieved, be taken off the register in respect

of any of the goods for which it is registered, on the ground that it was registered by the proprietor or a predecessor in title without any *bona fide* intention to use the same in connexion with such goods, and there has in fact been no *bona fide* user of the same in connexion therewith, or on the ground that there has been no *bona fide* user of such trade mark in connexion with such goods during the five years immediately preceding the application, unless in either case such non-user is shown to be due to special circumstances in the trade, and not to any intention not to use or to abandon such trade mark in respect of such goods. A.D. 1905

Effect of Registration.

Powers of registered proprietor

38. Subject to the provisions of this Act—

(1) The person for the time being entered in the register as proprietor of a trade mark shall, subject to any rights appearing from such register to be vested in any other person, have power to assign the same, and to give effectual receipts for any consideration for such assignment:

(2) Any equities in respect of a trade mark may be enforced in like manner as in respect of any other personal property.

Rights of proprietor of trade mark

39. Subject to the provisions of section forty-one of this Act and to any limitations and conditions entered upon the register, the registration of a person as proprietor of a trade mark shall, if valid, give to such person the exclusive right to the use of such trade mark upon or in connexion with the goods in respect of which it is registered: Provided always that where two or more persons are registered proprietors of the same (or substantially the same) trade mark in respect of the same goods no rights of exclusive user of such trade mark shall (except so far as their respective rights shall have been defined by the Court) be acquired by any one of such persons as against any other by the registration thereof, but each of such persons shall otherwise have the same rights as if he were the sole registered proprietor thereof.

Registration to be *prima facie* evidence of validity

40. In all legal proceedings relating to a registered trade mark (including applications under section thirty-five of this Act) the fact that a person is registered as proprietor of such trade mark shall be *prima facie* evidence of the validity of the original registration of such trade mark and of all subsequent assignments and transmissions of the same.

Registration to be conclusive after seven years

41. In all legal proceedings relating to a registered trade mark (including applications under section thirty-five of this Act) the original registration of such trade mark shall after the expiration of seven years from the date of such original registration (or seven years from the passing of this Act, whichever shall last happen) be taken to be valid in all respects unless such original registration was obtained by fraud, or unless the trade mark offends against the provisions of section eleven of this Act:

Provided that nothing in this Act shall entitle the proprietor of a registered trade mark to interfere with or restrain the user by any person of a similar trade mark upon or in connexion with goods upon or in connexion with which such person has, by himself or his predecessors in business, continuously used such trade

A.D. 1905

mark from a date anterior to the user of the first-mentioned trade mark by the proprietor thereof or his predecessors in business, or to object (on such user being proved) to such person being put upon the register for such similar trade mark in respect of such goods under the provisions of section twenty-one of this Act.

Unregistered trade mark

42. No persons shall be entitled to institute any proceeding to prevent or to recover damages for the infringement of an unregistered trade mark unless such trade mark was in use before the thirteenth of August one thousand eight hundred and seventy-five, and has been refused registration under this Act. The Registrar may, on request, grant a certificate that such registration has been refused.

Infringement

43. In an action for the infringement of a trade mark the Court trying the question of infringement shall admit evidence of the usages of the trade in respect to the get-up of the goods for which the trade mark is registered, and of any trade marks or get-up legitimately used in connexion with such goods by other persons.

User of name, address, or description of goods

44. No registration under this Act shall interfere with any *bona fide* use by a person of his own name or place of business or that of any of his predecessors in business, or the use by any person of any *bona fide* description of the character or quality of his goods.

"Passing-off," action

45. Nothing in this Act contained shall be deemed to affect rights of action against any person for passing off goods as those of another person or the remedies in respect thereof.

Legal Proceedings.

Certificate of validity

46. In any legal proceeding in which the validity of the registration of a registered trade mark comes into question and is decided in favour of the proprietor of such trade mark, the Court may certify the same, and if it so certifies then in any subsequent legal proceeding in which such validity comes into question the proprietor of the said trade mark on obtaining a final order or judgment in his favour shall have his full costs, charges, and expenses as between solicitor and client, unless in such subsequent proceeding the Court certifies that he ought not to have the same.

Registrar to have notice of proceeding for rectification

47. In any legal proceeding in which the relief sought includes alteration or rectification of the register, the Registrar shall have the right to appear and be heard, and shall appear if so directed by the Court. Unless otherwise directed by the Court, the Registrar in lieu of appearing and being heard may submit to the Court a statement in writing signed by him, giving particulars of the proceedings before him in relation to the matter in issue or of the grounds of any decision given by him affecting the same or of the practice of the office in like cases, or of such other matters relevant to the issues, and within his knowledge as such Registrar, as he shall think fit, and such statements shall be deemed to form part of the evidence in the proceeding.

Costs.

Costs of proceedings before the Court

48. In all proceedings before the Court under this Act the costs of the Registrar shall be in the discretion of the Court, but the Registrar shall not be ordered to pay the cost of any other of the parties.

A.D. 1905

Evidence.

Mode of giving evidence

49. In any proceeding under this Act before the Board of Trade or the Registrar, the evidence shall be given by statutory declaration in the absence of directions to the contrary, but, in any case in which it shall think it right so to do, the tribunal may (with the consent of the parties) take evidence *vivâ voce* in lieu of or in addition to evidence by declaration. Any such statutory declaration may in the case of appeal be used before the Court in lieu of evidence by affidavit, but if so used shall have all the incidents and consequences of evidence by affidavit.

In case any part of the evidence is taken *vivâ voce* the Board of Trade or the Registrar shall in respect of requiring the attendance of witnesses and taking evidence on oath be in the same position in all respects as an Official Referee of the Supreme Court.

Sealed copies to be evidence

50. Printed or written copies or extracts of or from the register, purporting to be certified by the Registrar and sealed with the seal of the Patent Office, shall be admitted in evidence in all courts in His Majesty's dominions, and in all proceedings, without further proof or production of the originals.

Certificate of registrar to be evidence

51. A certificate purporting to be under the hand of the Registrar as to any entry, matter, or thing which he is authorised by this Act, or rules made thereunder, to make or do, shall be *primâ facie* evidence of the entry having been made, and of the contents thereof, and of the matter or thing having been done or not done.

Certificate of Board of Trade to be evidence

52.—(1) All documents purporting to be orders made by the Board of Trade and to be sealed with the seal of the Board, or to be signed by a secretary or assistant secretary of the Board, or by any person authorized in that behalf by the President of the Board, shall be received in evidence, and shall be deemed to be such orders without further proof, unless the contrary is shown.

(2) A certificate, signed by the President of the Board of Trade, that any order made or act done is the order or act of the Board, shall be conclusive evidence of the fact so certified.

PART II.

Powers and Duties of Registrar of Trade Marks.

Exercise of discretionary power by Registrar

53. Where any discretionary or other power is given to the Registrar by this Act or rules made thereunder he shall not exercise that power adversely to the applicant for registration or the registered proprietor of the trade mark in question without (if duly required so to do within the prescribed time) giving such applicant or registered proprietor an opportunity of being heard.

Appeal from Registrar

54. Except where expressly given by the provisions of this Act or rules made thereunder there shall be no appeal from a decision of the Registrar otherwise than to the Board of Trade, but the Court, in dealing with any question of the rectification of the register (including all applications under the provisions of section thirty-five of this Act), shall have power to review any decision of the Registrar relating to the entry in question or the correction sought to be made.

Recognition of agents

55. Where by this Act any act has to be done by or to any person in connexion with a trade mark or proposed trade mark or any procedure relating thereto, such act may under and in

A.D. 1905

accordance with rules made under this Act or in particular cases by special leave of the Board of Trade be done by or to an agent of such party duly authorized in the prescribed manner.

Registrar may take directions of law officers

56. The Registrar may, in any case of doubt or difficulty arising in the administration of any of the provisions of this Act, apply to His Majesty's Attorney-General or Solicitor-General for England for directions in the matter.

Annual reports of Comptroller. 46 & 47 Vict. c. 57

57. The Comptroller General of Patents, Designs, and Trade Marks shall in his yearly report on the execution by or under him of the Patents, Designs, and Trade Marks Act, 1883, and Acts amending the same, include a report respecting the execution by or under him of this Act as though it formed a part of or was included in such Acts.

Powers and Duties of the Board of Trade.

Proceedings before Board of Trade

58. All things required or authorized under this Act to be done by to or before the Board of Trade may be done by to or before the President or a secretary or an assistant secretary of the Board or any person authorized in that behalf by the President of the Board.

Appeals to Board of Trade

59. Where under this Act an appeal is made to the Board of Trade, the Board of Trade may, if they think fit, refer any such appeal to the Court in lieu of hearing and deciding it themselves, but, unless the Board so refer the appeal, it shall be heard and decided by the Board, and the decision of the Board shall be final.

Power of Board of Trade to make rules

60.—(1) Subject to the provisions of this Act the Board of Trade may from time to time make such rules, prescribe such forms, and generally do such things as they think expedient—

(*a*) For regulating the practice under this Act:

(*b*) For classifying goods for the purposes of registration of trade marks:

(*c*) For making or requiring duplicates of trade marks and other documents:

(*d*) For securing and regulating the publishing and selling or distributing in such manner as the Board of Trade think fit, of copies of trade marks and other documents:

(*e*) Generally, for regulating the business of the office in relation to trade marks and all things by this Act placed under the direction or control of the Registrar, or of the Board of Trade.

(2) Rules made under this section shall, whilst in force, be of the same effect as if they were contained in this Act.

(3) Before making any rules under this section the Board of Trade shall publish notice of their intention to make the rules and of the place where copies of the draft rules may be obtained in such manner as the Board consider most expedient, so as to enable persons affected to make representations to the Board before the rules are finally settled.

(4) Any rules made in pursuance of this section shall be forthwith advertised twice in the Trade Marks Journal, and shall be laid before both Houses of Parliament, if Parliament be in session at the time of making thereof, or, if not, then as soon as practicable after the beginning of the then next session of Parliament.

(5) If either House of Parliament within the next forty days after any rules have been so laid before such House, resolve that such rules or any of them ought to be annulled, the same shall after the date of such resolution be of no effect, without prejudice to the validity of anything done in the meantime under such rules or rule or to the making of any new rules or rule. A.D. 1905

Fees.

61. There shall be paid in respect of applications and registration and other matters under this Act, such fees as may be, with the sanction of the Treasury, prescribed by the Board of Trade. **Fees**

Special Trade Marks.

62. Where any association or person undertakes the examination of any goods in respect of origin, material, mode of manufacture, quality, accuracy, or other characteristic, and certifies the result of such examination by mark used upon or in connection with such goods, the Board of Trade may, if they shall judge it to be to the public advantage, permit such association or person to register such mark as a trade mark in respect of such goods, whether or not such association or person be a trading association or trader or possessed of a goodwill in connection with such examination and certifying. When so registered such trade mark shall be deemed in all respects to be a registered trade mark, and such association or person to be the proprietor thereof, save that such trade mark shall be transmissible or assignable only by permission of the Board of Trade. **Standardization, etc., trade marks**

Sheffield Marks.

63. With respect to the master, wardens, searchers, assistants, and commonalty of the Company of Cutlers in Hallamshire, in the county of York (in this Act called the Cutlers' Company), and the marks or devices (in this Act called Sheffield marks) assigned or registered by the master, wardens, searchers, and assistants of that company, the following provisions shall have effect— **Sheffield marks**

(1) The Cutlers' Company shall continue to keep at Sheffield the register of trade marks (in this Act called the Sheffield register) kept by them at the date of the commencement of this Act, and, save as otherwise provided by this Act, such register shall for all purposes form part of the register:

(2) The Cutlers' Company shall, on request made in the prescribed manner, enter in the Sheffield register, in respect of metal goods as defined in this section, all the trade marks which shall have been assigned by the Cutlers' Company and actually used before the first day of January one thousand eight hundred and eighty-four, but which have not been entered in such register before the passing of this Act:

(3) An application for registration of a trade mark used on metal goods shall, if made after the commencement of this Act by a person carrying on business in Hallamshire, or within six miles thereof, be made to the Cutlers' Company:

A.D. 1905

(4) Every application so made to the Cutlers' Company shall be notified to the Registrar in the prescribed manner, and, unless the Registrar within the prescribed time gives notice to the Cutlers' Company of any objection to the acceptance of the application, it shall be proceeded with by the Cutlers' Company in the prescribed manner:

(5) If the Registrar gives notice of an objection as aforesaid, the application shall not be proceeded with by the Cutlers' Company, but any person aggrieved may in the prescribed manner appeal to the Court:

(6) Upon the registration of a trade mark in the Sheffield register the Cutlers' Company shall give notice thereof to the Registrar, who shall thereupon enter the mark in the register of trade marks; and such registration shall bear date as of the day of application to the Cutlers' Company, and have the same effect as if the application had been made to the Registrar on that day:

(7) The provisions of this Act, and of any rules made under this Act with respect to the registration of trade marks, and all matters relating thereto, shall, subject to the provisions of this section (and notwithstanding anything in any Act relating to the Cutlers' Company), apply to the registration of trade marks on metal goods by the Cutlers' Company, and to all matters relating thereto; and this Act and any such rules shall, so far as applicable, be construed accordingly with the substitution of the Cutlers' Company, the office of the Cutlers' Company, and the Sheffield register, for the Registrar, the Patent Office, and the Register of Trade Marks respectively; and notice of every entry, cancellation, or correction made in the Sheffield register shall be given to the Registrar by the Cutlers' Company:

(8) When the Registrar receives from any person not carrying on business in Hallamshire or within six miles thereof an application for registration of a trade mark used on metal goods, he shall in the prescribed manner notify the application and proceedings thereon to the Cutlers' Company:

(9) Any person aggrieved by a decision of the Cutlers' Company in respect of anything done or omitted under this Act may, in the prescribed manner, appeal to the Court:

(10) For the purposes of this section the expression "metal goods" means all metals, whether wrought, unwrought, or partly wrought, and all goods composed wholly or partly of any metal:

(11) For the purpose of legal proceedings in relation to trade marks entered in the Sheffield register a certificate under the hand of the Master of the Cutlers' Company shall have the same effect as the certificate of the Registrar.

Cotton Marks.

64.—(1) The Manchester Branch of the Trade Marks Registry of the Patent Office (herein-after called "the Manchester Branch") shall be continued according to its present constitution. A chief officer of the Manchester Branch shall be appointed who shall be styled "the Keeper of Cotton Marks," and shall act under the direction of the Registrar. The present keeper of the Manchester Branch shall be the first Keeper of Cotton Marks. A.D. 1905

Cotton marks

(2) As regards cotton goods which have hitherto constituted classes 23, 24, and 25, under the classification of goods under the Patents, Designs, and Trade Marks Acts, 1883 to 1902, the Register of Trade Marks for all such goods, except such as may be prescribed, shall be called "the Manchester Register," and a duplicate thereof shall be kept at the Manchester Branch.

(3) All applications for registration of trade marks for such cotton goods in the said classes (herein-after referred to as "cotton marks") shall be made to the Manchester Branch.

(4) Every application so made to the Manchester Branch shall be notified to the Registrar in the prescribed manner together with the report of the Keeper of Cotton Marks thereon, and unless the Registrar, after considering the report and hearing, if so required, the applicant, within the prescribed time gives notice to the Keeper of Cotton Marks of objection to the acceptance of the application, it shall be advertised by the Manchester Branch and shall be proceeded with in the prescribed manner.

(5) If the Registrar gives notice of objection as aforesaid the application shall not be proceeded with, but any person aggrieved may in the prescribed manner appeal to the Court or the Board of Trade, at the option of the applicant.

(6) Upon the registration of a trade mark in the Manchester Register the Keeper of Cotton Marks shall upon notice thereof from the Registrar thereupon enter the mark in the duplicate of the Manchester Register, and such registration shall bear date as of the day of application to the Manchester Branch, and shall have the same effect as if the application had been made to the Registrar on that day.

(7) When any mark is removed from or any cancellation or correction made in the Manchester Register notice thereof shall be given by the Registrar to the Keeper of Cotton Marks, who shall alter the duplicate register accordingly.

(8) For the purpose of all proceedings in relation to trade marks entered in the Manchester Register a certificate under the hand of the Keeper of Cotton Marks shall have the same effect as a certificate of the Registrar.

(9) In every application for registration of a cotton mark, if such mark has been used by the applicant or his predecessors in business prior to the date of application, the length of time of such user shall be stated on the application.

(10) As from the passing of this Act—

(*a*) In respect of cotton piece goods and cotton yarn no mark consisting of a word or words alone (whether invented or otherwise) shall be registered, and no word or words shall be deemed to be distinctive in respect of such goods:

A.D. 1905

(b) In respect of cotton piece goods no mark consisting of a line heading alone shall be registered and no line heading shall be deemed to be distinctive in respect of such goods:

(c) No registration of a cotton mark shall give any exclusive right to the use of any word, letter, numeral, line heading, or any combination thereof.

(11) The right of inspection of the Manchester Register shall extend to and include the right to inspect all applications whatsoever that have been since the passing of the Trade Marks Registration Act, 1875, and hereafter shall have been made to the Manchester Branch in respect of cotton goods in classes 23, 24, and 25, whether registered, refused, lapsed, expired, withdrawn, abandoned, cancelled, or pending.

39 & 40 Vict. c. 33

(12) The Keeper of Cotton Marks shall, on request, and on production of a facsimile of the mark, and on payment of the prescribed fee, issue a certified copy of the application for registration of any cotton mark, setting forth in such certificate the length of time of user (if any) of such mark as stated on the application, and any other particulars he may deem necessary.

(13) As regards any rules or forms affecting cotton marks which are proposed by the Board of Trade to be made, the draft of the same shall be sent to the Keeper of Cotton Marks and also to the Manchester Chamber of Commerce. And the said Keeper, and also the said Chamber, shall, if they or either of them so request, be entitled to be heard by the Board of Trade upon such proposed rules before the same are carried into effect.

(14) The existing practice whereby the keeper of the Manchester Branch consults the Trade and Merchandise Marks Committee appointed by the Manchester Chamber of Commerce upon questions of novelty or difficulty arising on applications to register cotton marks shall be continued by the Keeper of Cotton Marks.

International and Colonial Arrangements.

International and colonial arrangements. 48 & 49 Vict. c. 63

65. The provisions of sections one hundred and three and one hundred and four of the Patents, Designs, and Trade Marks Act, 1883 (as amended by the Patents, Designs, and Trade Marks (Amendment) Act, 1885), relating to the registration of trade marks both as enacted in such Acts and as applied by any Order in Council made thereunder, shall be construed as applying to trade marks registrable under this Act.

Offences.

Falsification of entries in register

66. If any person makes or causes to be made a false entry in the register kept under this Act, or a writing falsely purporting to be a copy of an entry in any such register, or produces or tenders or causes to be produced or tendered in evidence any such writing, knowing the entry or writing to be false, he shall be guilty of a misdemeanor.

Penalty on falsely representing a trade mark as registered

67.—(1) Any person who represents a trade mark as registered which is not so, shall be liable for every offence on summary conviction to a fine not exceeding five pounds.

(2) A person shall be deemed, for the purposes of this enactment, to represent that a trade mark is registered, if he uses in connection with the trade mark the word "registered," or any

words expressing or implying that registration has been obtained for the trade mark. A.D. 1905

Royal Arms.

Unauthorized assumption of Royal Arms

68. If any person, without the authority of His Majesty, uses in connexion with any trade, business, calling, or profession, the Royal Arms (or arms so closely resembling the same as to be calculated to deceive) in such manner as to be calculated to lead to the belief that he is duly authorized so to use the Royal Arms, or if any person without the authority of His Majesty or of a member of the Royal Family, uses in connexion with any trade, business, calling, or profession any device, emblem, or title in such manner as to be calculated to lead to the belief that he is employed by or supplies goods to His Majesty or such member of the Royal Family, he may, at the suit of any person who is authorized to use such arms or such device, emblem, or title, or is authorized by the Lord Chamberlain to take proceedings in that behalf, be restrained by injunction or interdict from continuing so to use the same: Provided that nothing in this section shall be construed as affecting the right, if any, of the proprietor of a trade mark containing any such arms, device, emblem, or title to continue to use such trade mark.

Courts.

General saving for jurisdiction of Courts

69. The provisions of this Act conferring a special jurisdiction on the Court as defined by this Act shall not, except so far as the jurisdiction extends, affect the jurisdiction of any court in Scotland or Ireland in any proceedings relating to trade marks; and with reference to any such proceedings in Scotland the term "the Court" shall mean the Court of Session; and with reference to any such proceedings in Ireland the term "the Court" shall mean the High Court of Justice in Ireland.

Isle of Man

70. This Act shall extend to the Isle of Man, and—

(1) Nothing in this Act shall affect the jurisdiction of the Courts in the Isle of Man in proceedings for infringement or in any action or proceeding respecting a trade mark competent to those courts:

(2) The punishment for a misdemeanor under this Act in the Isle of Man shall be imprisonment for any term not exceeding two years, with or without hard labour and with or without a fine not exceeding one hundred pounds, at the discretion of the Court:

(3) Any offence under this Act committed in the Isle of Man which would in England be punishable on summary conviction may be prosecuted, and any fine in respect thereof recovered at the instance of any person aggrieved, in the manner in which offences punishable on summary conviction may from the time being be prosecuted.

Jurisdiction of Lancashire Palatine Court

71. The Court of Chancery of the County Palatine of Lancaster shall, with respect to any action or other proceeding in relation to trade marks, the registration whereof is applied for in the Manchester Branch, have the like jurisdiction under this Act as His Majesty's High Court of Justice in England, and the

A.D. 1905

expression "the Court" in this Act shall be construed and have effect accordingly:

Provided that every decision of the Court of Chancery of the County Palatine of Lancaster in pursuance of this section shall be subject to the like appeal as decisions of that Court in other cases.

Offences in Scotland

72. In Scotland any offence under this Act declared to be punishable on summary conviction may be prosecuted in the Sheriff Court.

Repeal; Savings.

Repeal and saving for rules etc.

73. The enactments described in the schedule to this Act are repealed to the extent mentioned in the third column, but this repeal shall not affect any rule, table of fees, or classification of goods made under any enactment so repealed, but every such rule table of fees, or classification of goods shall continue in force as if made under this Act until superseded by rules, tables of fees, or classification under this Act.

Application of 46 & 47 Vict. c. 57. ss. 82-84

74. The provisions of sections eighty-two to eighty-four of the Patents, Designs, and Trade Marks Act, 1883, as amended by any subsequent enactment, shall continue to apply with respect to the administration at the Patent Office of the Law relating to the registration of trade marks, and shall accordingly be construed as if this Act formed part of that Act.

SCHEDULE.

Section 73

ENACTMENTS REPEALED.

Session and Chapter.	Short Title.	Extent of Repeal.
46 & 47 Vict. c. 57.	The Patents, Designs, and Trade Marks Act, 1883.	Sections sixty-two to eighty-one, and, so far as they respectively relate to trade marks, sections eighty-five to ninety-nine, one hundred and one, one hundred and two, one hundred and five, one hundred and eight, and one hundred and eleven to one hundred and seventeen.
51 & 52 Vict. c. 50.	The Patents, Designs, and Trade Marks Act, 1888.	Sections eight to twenty, and, so far as they respectively relate to trade marks, sections twenty-one to twenty-six.

APPENDIX III

PATENTS AND DESIGNS ACT, 1907

[7 Edw. VII, Ch. 29]

Chapter 29

An Act to consolidate the enactments relating to Patents for Inventions and the Registration of Designs and certain enactments relating to Trade Marks. A.D. 1907

[28th August 1907.]

Be it enacted by the King's most Excellent Majesty, by and with the advice and consent of the Lords Spiritual and Temporal, and Commons, in this present Parliament assembled, and by the authority of the same, as follows—

Part I.

Patents.

Part I Patents

Application for and Grant of Patent.

1.—(1) An application for a patent may be made by any person who claims to be the true and first inventor of an invention, whether he is a British subject or not, and whether alone or jointly with any other person. Application

(2) The application must be made in the prescribed form, and must be left at, or sent by post to, the Patent Office in the prescribed manner.

(3) The application must contain a declaration to the effect that the applicant is in possession of an invention, whereof he, or in the case of a joint application one at least of the applicants, claims to be the true and first inventor, and for which he desires to obtain a patent, and must be accompanied by either a provisional or complete specification.

(4) The declaration required by this section may be either a statutory declaration or not, as may be prescribed.

2.—(1) A provisional specification must describe the nature of the invention.

(2) A complete specification must particularly describe and ascertain the nature of the invention and the manner in which the same is to be performed.

(3) In the case of any provisional or complete specification where the comptroller deems it desirable he may require that suitable drawings shall be supplied with the specification, or at any time before the acceptance of the same, and such drawings shall be deemed to form part of the said specification. Specifications

(4) A specification, whether provisional or complete, must commence with the title, and in the case of a complete specification must end with a distinct statement of the invention claimed.

(5) Where the invention in respect of which an application

A.D. 1907

PART I
PATENTS

is made is a chemical invention, such typical samples and specimens as may be prescribed shall, if in any particular case the comptroller considers it desirable so to require, be furnished before the acceptance of the complete specification.

Proceeding upon application

3.—(1) The Comptroller General of Patents, Designs, and Trade Marks (herein-after referred to as the comptroller) shall refer every application to an examiner.

(2) If the examiner reports that the nature of the invention is not fairly described, or that the application, specification, or drawings have not been prepared in the prescribed manner, or that the title does not sufficiently indicate the subject-matter of the invention, the comptroller may refuse to accept the application or require that the application, specification, or drawings be amended before he proceeds with the application; and in the latter case the application shall, if the comptroller so directs, bear date as from the time when the requirement is complied with.

(3) Where the comptroller refuses to accept an application or requires an amendment, the applicant may appeal from his decision to the law officer, who shall, if required, hear the applicant and the comptroller, and may make an order determining whether and subject to what conditions (if any) the application shall be accepted.

(4) The comptroller shall, when an application has been accepted, give notice thereof to the applicant.

Provisional protection

4. Where an application for a patent in respect of an invention has been accepted, the invention may during the period between the date of the application and the date of sealing such patent be used and published without prejudice to the patent to be granted for the invention; and such protection from the consequences of use and publication is in this Act referred to as provisional protection.

Time for leaving complete specification

5.—(1) If the applicant does not leave a complete specification with his application, he may leave it at any subsequent time within six months from the date of the application:

Provided that where an application is made for an extension of the time for leaving a complete specification, the comptroller shall, on payment of the prescribed fee, grant an extension of time to the extent applied for but not exceeding one month.

(2) Unless a complete specification is so left the application shall be deemed to be abandoned.

Comparison of provisional and complete specification

6.—(1) Where a complete specification is left after a provisional specification, the comptroller shall refer both specifications to an examiner.

(2) If the examiner reports that the complete specification has not been prepared in the prescribed manner, the comptroller may refuse to accept the complete specification until it has been amended to his satisfaction.

(3) If the examiner reports that the invention particularly described in the complete specification is not substantially the same as that which is described in the provisional specification the comptroller may—

(*a*) refuse to accept the complete specification until it has been amended to his satisfaction; or

(b) (with the consent of the applicant) cancel the provisional specification and treat the application as having been made on the date at which the complete specification was left, and the application shall have effect as if made on that date:

Provided that where the complete specification includes an invention not included in the provisional specification, the comptroller may allow the original application to proceed so far as the invention included both in the provisional and in the complete specification is concerned, and treat the claim for the additional invention included in the complete specification as an application for that invention made on the date at which the complete specification was left.

(4) A refusal of the comptroller to accept a complete specification shall be subject to appeal to the law officer, who shall, if required, hear the applicant and the comptroller and may make an order determining whether and subject to what conditions (if any) the complete specification shall be accepted.

(5) Unless a complete specification is accepted within twelve months from the date of the application, the application shall (except where an appeal has been lodged) become void:

Provided that where an application is made for an extension of time for the acceptance of a complete specification, the comptroller shall, on payment of the prescribed fee, grant an extension of time to the extent applied for but not exceeding three months.

Investigation of previous specifications in United Kingdom on applications for patents

7.—(1) Where an application for a patent has been made and a complete specification has been left, the examiner shall, in addition to the other inquiries which he is directed to make by this Act, make a further investigation for the purpose of ascertaining whether the invention claimed has been wholly or in part claimed or described in any specification (other than a provisional specification not followed by a complete specification) published before the date of the application, and left pursuant to any application for a patent made in the United Kingdom within fifty years next before the date of the application.

(2) If on investigation it appears that the invention has been wholly or in part claimed or described in any such specification, the applicant shall be informed thereof, and the applicant may, within such time as may be prescribed, amend his specification, and the amended specification shall be investigated in like manner as the original specification.

(3) If the comptroller is satisfied that no objection exists to the specification on the ground that the invention claimed thereby has been wholly or in part claimed or described in a previous specification as before mentioned, he shall, in the absence of any other lawful ground of objection, accept the specification.

(4) If the comptroller is not so satisfied, he shall, after hearing the applicant, and unless the objection is removed by amending the specification to the satisfaction of the comptroller, determine whether a reference to any, and, if so, what prior specifications ought to be made in the specification by way of notice to the public:

Provided that the comptroller, if satisfied that the invention claimed has been wholly and specifically claimed in any

A.D. 1907

Part I
Patents

specification to which the investigation has extended, may, in lieu of requiring references to be made in the applicant's specification as aforesaid, refuse to grant a patent.

(5) An appeal shall lie from the decision of the comptroller under this section to the law officer.

(6) The investigations and reports required by this section shall not be held in any way to guarantee the validity of any patent, and no liability shall be incurred by the Board of Trade or any officer thereof by reason of, or in connexion with, any such investigation or report, or any proceeding consequent thereon.

Investigation of specifications published subsequently to application

8.—(1) An investigation under the last preceding section shall extend to specifications published after the date of the application in respect of which the investigation is made, and being specifications which have been deposited pursuant to prior application; and that section shall, subject to rules under this Act, have effect accordingly.

(2) Where, on such an extended investigation, it appears that the invention claimed in the specification deposited pursuant to an application is wholly or in part claimed in any published specification deposited pursuant to a prior application, the applicant shall, whether or not his specification has been accepted or a patent granted to him, be afforded such facilities as may be prescribed for amending his specification, and in the event of his failing to do so the comptroller shall, in accordance with such procedure as may be prescribed, determine what reference, if any, to other specifications ought to be made in his specification by way of notice to the public.

(3) For the purposes of this section an application shall be deemed to be prior to another application if the patent applied for when granted would be of prior date to the patent granted pursuant to that other application.

(4) This section shall come into operation at such date as the Board of Trade may by order direct, and shall apply only to applications made after that date, and the order shall be laid before both Houses of Parliament.

Advertisement on acceptance of complete specification

9. On the acceptance of the complete specification the comptroller shall advertise the acceptance; and the application and specifications with the drawings (if any) shall be open to public inspection.

Effect of acceptance of complete specification

10. After the acceptance of a complete specification and until the date of sealing a patent in respect thereof, or the expiration of the time for sealing, the applicant shall have the like privileges and rights as if a patent for the invention had been sealed on the date of the acceptance of the complete specification: Provided that an applicant shall not be entitled to institute any proceeding for infringement until a patent for the invention has been granted to him.

Opposition to grant of patent

11.—(1) Any person may at any time within two months from the date of the advertisement of the acceptance of a complete specification give notice at the Patent Office of opposition to the grant of the patent on any of the following grounds:—

(*a*) that the applicant obtained the invention from him, or from a person of whom he is the legal representative; or

(b) that the invention has been claimed in any complete specification for a British patent which is or will be of prior date to the patent the grant of which is opposed, other than a specification deposited pursuant to an application made more than fifty years before the date of the application for such last-mentioned patent; or

(c) that the nature of the invention or the manner in which it is to be performed is not sufficiently or fairly described and ascertained in the complete specification; or

(d) that the complete specification describes or claims an invention other than that described in the provisional specification, and that such other invention forms the subject of an application made by the opponent in the interval between the leaving of the provisional specification and the leaving of the complete specification,

but on no other ground.

(2) Where such notice is given the comptroller shall give notice of the opposition to the applicant, and shall, on the expiration of those two months, after hearing the applicant and the opponent, if desirous of being heard, decide on the case.

(3) The decision of the comptroller shall be subject to appeal to the law officer, who shall, if required, hear the applicant and the opponent, if the opponent is, in his opinion, a person entitled to be heard in opposition to the grant of the patent, and shall decide the case; and the law officer may, if he thinks fit, obtain the assistance of an expert, who shall be paid such remuneration as the law officer with the consent of the Treasury may determine.

Grant and sealing of patent

12.—(1) If there is no opposition, or, in case of opposition, if the determination is in favour of the grant of a patent, a patent shall, on payment of the prescribed fee, be granted to the applicant, or in the case of a joint application to the applicants jointly, and the comptroller shall cause the patent to be sealed with the seal of the Patent Office.

(2) A patent shall be sealed as soon as may be, and not after the expiration of fifteen months from the date of application, provided that—

(a) Where the comptroller has allowed an extension of the time within which a complete specification may be left or accepted, a further extension of four months after the said fifteen months shall be allowed for the sealing of the patent:

(b) Where the sealing is delayed by an appeal to the law officer, or by opposition to the grant of the patent, the patent may be sealed at such time as the law officer may direct:

(c) Where the patent is granted to the legal representative of an applicant who has died before the expiration of the time which would otherwise be allowed for sealing the patent, the patent may be sealed at any time within twelve months after the date of his death:

(d) Where in consequence of the neglect or failure of the applicant to pay any fee a patent cannot be sealed within the period allowed by this section, that period

A.D. 1907

PART I
PATENTS

may, on payment of the prescribed fee and on compliance with the prescribed conditions, be extended to such an extent as may be prescribed, and this provision shall, in such cases as may be prescribed and subject to the prescribed conditions, apply where the period allowed for the sealing of the patent has expired before the commencement of this Act.

Date of patent

13. Except as otherwise expressly provided by this Act, a patent shall be dated and sealed as of the date of the application: Provided that no proceedings shall be taken in respect of an infringement committed before the publication of the complete specification.

Effect, extent, and form of patent

14.—(1) A patent sealed with the seal of the Patent Office shall have the same effect as if it were sealed with the Great Seal of the United Kingdom, and shall have effect throughout the United Kingdom and the Isle of Man:

Provided that a patentee may assign his patent for any place in or part of the United Kingdom, or Isle of Man, as effectually as if the patent were originally granted to extend to that place or part only.

(2) Every patent may be in the prescribed form and shall be granted for one invention only, but the specification may contain more than one claim; and it shall not be competent for any person in an action or other proceeding to take any objection to a patent on the ground that it has been granted for more than one invention.

Fraudulent applications for patents

15.—(1) A patent granted to the true and first inventor shall not be invalidated by an application in fraud of him, or by provisional protection obtained thereon, or by any use or publication of the invention subsequent to that fraudulent application during the period of provisional protection.

(2) Where a patent has been revoked on the ground of fraud, the comptroller may, on the application of the true inventor made in accordance with the provisions of this Act, grant to him a patent in lieu of and bearing the same date as the patent so revoked:

Provided that no action shall be brought for any infringement of the patent so granted committed before the actual date when such patent was granted.

Single patent for cognate inventions

16.—(1) Where the same applicant has put in two or more provisional specifications for inventions which are cognate or modifications one of the other, and has obtained thereby concurrent provisional protection for the same, and the comptroller is of opinion that the whole of such inventions are such as to constitute a single invention and may properly be included in one patent, he may accept one complete specification in respect of the whole of such applications and grant a single patent thereon.

(2) Such patent shall bear the date of the earliest of such applications, but in considering the validity of the same and for the purpose of the provisions of this Act with respect to oppositions to the grant of patents, the court or the comptroller, as the case may be, shall have regard to the respective dates of the provisional specifications relating to the several matters claimed therein.

Term of Patent.

A.D. 1907

PART I PATENTS

Term of patent

17.—(1) The term limited in every patent for the duration thereof shall, save as otherwise expressly provided by this Act, be fourteen years from its date.

(2) A patent shall, notwithstanding anything therein or in this Act, cease if the patentee fails to pay the prescribed fees within the prescribed times; provided that the comptroller, upon the application of the patentee, shall, on receipt of such additional fee, not exceeding ten pounds, as may be prescribed, enlarge the time to such an extent as may be applied for but not exceeding three months.

(3) If any proceeding is taken in respect of an infringement of the patent committed after a failure to pay any fee within the prescribed time, and before any enlargement thereof, the court before which the proceeding is proposed to be taken may, if it thinks fit, refuse to award any damages in respect of such infringement.

Extension of term of patent

18.—(1) A patentee may, after advertising in manner provided by rules of the Supreme Court his intention to do so, present a petition to the court praying that his patent may be extended for a further term, but such petition must be presented at least six months before the time limited for the expiration of the patent.

(2) Any person may give notice to the court of objection to the extension.

(3) On the hearing of any petition under this section the patentee and any person who has given such notice of objection shall be made parties to the proceeding, and the comptroller shall be entitled to appear and be heard, and shall appear if so directed by the court.

(4) The court, in considering its decision, shall have regard to the nature and merits of the invention in relation to the public, to the profits made by the patentee as such, and to all the circumstances of the case.

(5) If it appears to the court that the patentee has been inadequately remunerated by his patent, the court may by order extend the term of the patent for a further term not exceeding seven, or, in exceptional cases, fourteen years, or may order the grant of a new patent for such term as may be specified in the order and containing any restriction, conditions, and provisions the court may think fit.

Patents of addition

19.—(1) Where a patent for an invention has been applied for or granted, and the applicant or the patentee, as the case may be, applies for a further patent in respect of any improvement in or modification of the invention, he may, if he thinks fit, in his application for the further patent, request that the term limited in that patent for the duration thereof be the same as that of the original patent or so much of that term as is unexpired.

(2) Where an application containing such a request is made, a patent (herein-after referred to as a patent of addition) may be granted for such term as aforesaid.

(3) A patent of addition shall remain in force so long as the patent for the original invention remains in force, but no longer, and in respect of a patent of addition no fees shall be payable for renewal.

A.D. 1907

PART I
PATENTS

(4) The grant of a patent of addition shall be conclusive evidence that the invention is a proper subject for a patent of addition, and the validity of the patent shall not be questioned on the ground that the invention ought to have been the subject of an independent patent.

Restoration of lapsed Patents.

Restoration of lapsed patents

20.—(1) Where any patent has become void owing to the failure of the patentee to pay any prescribed fee within the prescribed time, the patentee may apply to the comptroller in the prescribed manner for an order for the restoration of the patent.

(2) Every such application shall contain a statement of the circumstances which have led to the omission of the payment of the prescribed fee.

(3) If it appears from such statement that the omission was unintentional and that no undue delay has occurred in the making of the application, the comptroller shall advertise the application in the prescribed manner, and within such time as may be prescribed any person may give notice of opposition at the Patent Office.

(4) Where such notice is given the comptroller shall notify the applicant thereof.

(5) After the expiration of the prescribed period the comptroller shall hear the case and, subject to an appeal to the court, issue an order either restoring the patent or dismissing the application: Provided that in every order under this section restoring a patent such provisions as may be prescribed shall be inserted for the protection of persons who may have availed themselves of the subject-matter of the patent after the patent had been announced as void in the illustrated official journal.

Amendment of Specification.

Amendment of specification by comptroller

21.—(1) An applicant or a patentee may at any time, by request in writing left at the Patent Office, seek leave to amend his specification, including drawings forming part thereof, by way of disclaimer, correction, or explanation, stating the nature of, and the reason for, the proposed amendment.

(2) The request and the nature of the proposed amendment shall be advertised in the prescribed manner, and at any time within one month from its first advertisement any person may give notice at the Patent Office of opposition to the amendment.

(3) Where such a notice is given the comptroller shall give notice of the opposition to the person making the request, and shall hear and decide the case.

(4) Where no notice of opposition is given, or the person so giving notice of opposition does not appear, the comptroller shall determine whether and subject to what conditions, if any, the amendment ought to be allowed.

(5) The decision of the comptroller in either case shall be subject to an appeal to the law officer, who shall, if required, hear the person making the request to amend and, where notice of opposition has been given, the person giving that notice, if he is, in the opinion of the law officer, entitled to be heard in opposition to the request, and, where there is no opposition, the comptroller,

and may make an order determining whether and subject to what conditions (if any) the amendment ought to be allowed.

(6) No amendment shall be allowed that would make the specification, as amended, claim an invention substantially larger than or substantially different from the invention claimed by the specification as it stood before amendment.

(7) Leave to amend shall be conclusive as to the right of the party to make the amendment allowed, except in case of fraud; and the amendment shall be advertised in the prescribed manner, and shall in all courts and for all purposes be deemed to form part of the specification.

(8) This section shall not apply when and so long as any action for infringement or proceeding before the court for the revocation of a patent is pending.

Amendment of specification by the Court

22. In any action for infringement of a patent or proceedings before a court for the revocation of a patent the court may by order allow the patentee to amend his specification by way of disclaimer in such manner, and subject to such terms as to costs advertisement or otherwise, as the court may think fit:

Provided that no amendment shall be so allowed that would make the specification, as amended, claim an invention substantially larger than, or substantially different from, the invention claimed by the specification as it stood before the amendment, and where an application for such an order is made to the court notice of the application shall be given to the comptroller, and the comptroller shall have the right to appear and be heard, and shall appear if so directed by the court.

Restriction on recovery of damages

23. Where an amendment of a specification by way of disclaimer, correction, or explanation, has been allowed under this Act, no damages shall be given in any action in respect of the use of the invention before the disclaimer, correction, or explanation, unless the patentee establishes to the satisfaction of the court that his original claim was framed in good faith and with reasonable skill and knowledge.

Compulsory Licences and Revocation.

Compulsory licences and revocation

24.—(1) Any person interested may present a petition to the Board of Trade alleging that the reasonable requirements of the public with respect to a patented invention have not been satisfied, and praying for the grant of a compulsory licence, or, in the alternative, for the revocation of the patent.

(2) The Board of Trade shall consider the petition, and if the parties do not come to an arrangement between themselves the Board of Trade, if satisfied that a *primâ facie* case has been made out, shall refer the petition to the court, and, if the Board are not so satisfied, they may dismiss the petition.

(3) Where any such petition is referred by the Board of Trade to the court, and it is proved to the satisfaction of the court that the reasonable requirements of the public with reference to the patented invention have not been satisfied, the patentee may be ordered by the court to grant licences on such terms as the court may think just, or, if the court is of opinion that the reasonable requirements of the public will not be satisfied by the grant of licences, the patent may be revoked by order of the court:

Provided that an order of revocation shall not be made before

A.D. 1907

PART I
PATENTS

the expiration of three years from the date of the patent, or if the patentee gives satisfactory reasons for his default.

(4) On the hearing of any petition under this section the patentee and any person claiming an interest in the patent as exclusive licensee or otherwise, shall be made parties to the proceeding, and the law officer or such other counsel as he may appoint shall be entitled to appear and be heard.

(5) For the purposes of this section the reasonable requirements of the public shall not be deemed to have been satisfied—

(*a*) If by reason of the default of the patentee to manufacture to an adequate extent and supply on reasonable terms the patented article, or any parts thereof which are necessary for its efficient working, or to carry on the patented process to an adequate extent or to grant licences on reasonable terms, any existing trade or industry, or the establishment of any new trade or industry in the United Kingdom is unfairly prejudiced, or the demand for the patented article or the article produced by the patented process is not reasonably met; or

(*b*) if any trade or industry in the United Kingdom is unfairly prejudiced by the conditions attached by the patentee before or after the passing of this Act to the purchase, hire, or use of the patented article or to the using or working of the patented process.

(6) An order of the court directing the grant of any licence under this section shall, without prejudice to any other method of enforcement, operate as if it were embodied in a deed granting a licence and made between the parties to the proceeding.

Revocation of patent

25.—(1) Revocation of a patent may be obtained on petition to the court.

(2) Every ground on which—

(*a*) a patent might, immediately before the first day of January, one thousand eight hundred and eighty-four, have been repealed by *scire facias;* or

(*b*) a patent may be revoked under this Act either by the comptroller or as an alternative to the grant of a compulsory licence;

shall be available by way of defence to an action of infringement and shall also be a ground of revocation under this section.

(3) A petition for revocation of a patent may be presented—

(*a*) by the Attorney-General or any person authorized by him; or

(*b*) by any person alleging—

(i) that the patent was obtained in fraud of his rights, or of the rights of any person under or through whom he claims; or

(ii) that he, or any person under or through whom he claims, was the true inventor of any invention included in the claim of the patentee; or

(iii) that he, or any person under or through whom he claims an interest in any trade, business, or manufacture, had publicly manufactured, used, or sold, within this realm, before the date of the patent, anything claimed by the patentee as his invention.

26.—(1) Any person who would have been entitled to oppose the grant of a patent, or is the successor in interest of a person who was so entitled, may, within two years from the date of the patent, in the prescribed manner apply to the comptroller for an order revoking the patent on any one or more of the grounds on which the grant of the patent might have been opposed.

A.D. 1907

Part I Patents

Power of comptroller to revoke patents on certain grounds

Provided that when an action for infringement or proceedings for the revocation of the patent are pending in any court, an application under this section shall not be made except with the leave of the court.

(2) The comptroller shall give notice of the application to the patentee, and after hearing the parties, if desirous of being heard, may make an order revoking the patent or requiring the specification relating thereto to be amended by disclaimer, correction, or explanation, or dismissing the application; but the comptroller shall not make an order revoking the patent unless the circumstances are such as would have justified him in refusing to grant the patent had the proceedings been proceedings in an opposition to the grant of a patent.

(3) A patentee may at any time by giving notice in the prescribed manner to the comptroller offer to surrender his patent, and the comptroller may, if after giving notice of the offer and hearing all parties who desire to be heard he thinks fit, accept the offer, and thereupon make an order for the revocation of the patent.

(4) Any decision of the comptroller under this section shall be subject to appeal to the court.

Revocation of patents worked outside the United Kingdom

27.—(1) At any time not less than four years after the date of a patent and not less than one year after the passing of this Act, any person may apply to the comptroller for the revocation of the patent on the ground that the patented article or process is manufactured or carried on exclusively or mainly outside the United Kingdom.

(2) The comptroller shall consider the application, and, if after enquiry he is satisfied that the allegations contained therein are correct, then, subject to the provisions of this section, and unless the patentee proves that the patented article or process is manufactured or carried on to an adequate extent in the United Kingdom, or gives satisfactory reasons why the article or process is not so manufactured or carried on, the comptroller may make an order revoking the patent either—

(*a*) forthwith; or

(*b*) after such reasonable interval as may be specified in the order, unless in the meantime it is shown to his satisfaction that the patented article or process is manufactured or carried on within the United Kingdom to an adequate extent:

Provided that no such order shall be made which is at variance with any treaty, convention, arrangement, or engagement with any foreign country or British possession.

(3) If within the time limit in the order the patented article or process is not manufactured or carried on within the United Kingdom to an adequate extent, but the patentee gives satisfactory reasons why it is not so manufactured or carried on, the

comptroller may extend the period mentioned in the previous order for such period not exceeding twelve months as may be specified in the subsequent order.

(4) Any decision of the comptroller under this section shall be subject to appeal to the court, and on any such appeal the law officer or such other counsel as he may appoint shall be entitled to appear and be heard.

Register of Patents.

Register of patents

28.—(1) There shall be kept at the Patent Office a book called the register of patents, wherein shall be entered the names and addresses of grantees of patents, notifications of assignments and of transmissions of patents, of licences under patents, and of amendments, extensions, and revocations of patents, and such other matters affecting the validity or proprietorship of patents as may be prescribed.

(2) The register of patents existing at the commencement of this Act shall be incorporated with and form part of the register of patents under this Act.

(3) The register of patents shall be prima facie evidence of any matters by this Act directed or authorized to be inserted therein.

(4) Copies of deeds, licences, and any other documents affecting the proprietorship in any letters patent or in any licence thereunder, must be supplied to the comptroller in the prescribed manner for filing in the Patent Office.

Crown.

Patent to bind Crown

29. A patent shall have to all intents the like effect as against His Majesty the King as it has against a subject:

Provided that any Government department may, by themselves, their agents, contractors, or others, at any time after the application, use the invention for the services of the Crown on such terms as may, either before or after the use thereof, be agreed on, with the approval of the Treasury, between the department and the patentee, or, in default of agreement, as may be settled by the Treasury after hearing all parties interested.

Assignment to Secretary for War or the Admiralty of certain inventions

30.—(1) The inventor of any improvement in instruments or munitions of war may (either for or without valuable consideration) assign to the Secretary of State for War or the Admiralty on behalf of His Majesty all the benefit of the invention and of any patent obtained or to be obtained for the invention; and the Secretary of State or the Admiralty may be a party to the assignment.

(2) The assignment shall effectually vest the benefit of the invention and patent in the Secretary of State or the Admiralty on behalf of His Majesty, and all covenants and agreements therein contained for keeping the invention secret and otherwise shall be valid and effectual (notwithstanding any want of valuable consideration), and may be enforced accordingly by the Secretary of State or the Admiralty.

(3) Where any such assignment has been made, the Secretary of State or the Admiralty may at any time before the publication of the complete specification certify to the comptroller that, in the interest of the public service, the particulars of the

invention and of the manner in which it is to be performed should be kept secret.

(4) If the Secretary of State or the Admiralty so certify the application and specifications, with the drawings (if any), and any amendment of the complete specification, and any copies of such documents and drawings shall, instead of being left in the ordinary manner at the Patent Office, be delivered to the comptroller in a packet sealed by authority of the Secretary of State or the Admiralty.

(5) The packet shall, until the expiration of the term during which a patent for the invention may be in force, be kept sealed by the comptroller, and shall not be opened save under the authority of an order of the Secretary of State or the Admiralty or of the law officer.

(6) The sealed packet shall be delivered at any time during the continuance of the patent to any person authorized by the Secretary of State or the Admiralty to receive it, and shall if returned to the comptroller be again kept sealed by him.

(7) On the expiration of the term of the patent, the sealed packet shall be delivered to the Secretary of State or the Admiralty.

(8) Where the Secretary of State or the Admiralty certify as aforesaid, after an application for a patent has been left at the Patent Office, but before the publication of the complete specification, the application and specifications, with the drawings (if any), shall be forthwith placed in a packet sealed by authority of the comptroller, and the packet shall be subject to the foregoing provisions respecting a packet sealed by authority of the Secretary of State or the Admiralty.

(9) No proceeding by petition or otherwise shall lie for revocation of a patent granted for an invention in relation to which a certificate has been given by the Secretary of State or the Admiralty as aforesaid.

(10) No copy of any specification or other document or drawing, by this section required to be placed in a sealed packet, shall in any manner whatever be published or open to the inspection of the public, but, save as in this section otherwise directed, the provisions of this Act shall apply in respect of any such invention and patent as aforesaid.

(11) The Secretary of State or the Admiralty may at any time waive the benefit of this section with respect to any particular invention, and the specifications, documents, and drawings shall be thenceforth kept and dealt with in the ordinary way.

(12) The communication of any invention for any improvement in instruments or munitions of war to the Secretary of State or the Admiralty, or to any person or persons authorized by the Secretary of State or the Admiralty to investigate the same or the merits thereof, shall not, nor shall anything done for the purposes of the investigation, be deemed use or publication of such invention so as to prejudice the grant or validity of any patent for the same.

(13) Rules may be made under this Act, after consultation with the Secretary of State and the Admiralty, for the purpose of ensuring secrecy with respect to patents to which this section applies, and those rules may modify any of the provisions of

A.D. 1907

Part I
Patents

this Act in their application to such patents as aforesaid so far as may appear necessary for the purpose aforesaid.

Legal Proceedings.

Hearing with assessor

31.—(1) In an action or proceeding for infringement or revocation of a patent, the court may, if it think fit, and shall on the request of either of the parties to the proceeding, call in the aid of an assessor specially qualified, and try the case wholly or partially with his assistance; the action shall be tried without a jury unless the court otherwise directs.

(2) The Court of Appeal may, if they think fit, in any proceeding before them call in the aid of an assessor as aforesaid.

(3) The remuneration, if any, to be paid to an assessor under this section shall be determined by the court or the Court of Appeal, as the case may be, and be paid as part of the expenses of the execution of this Act.

Power to counterclaim for revocation in an action for infringement

32. A defendant in an action for infringement of a patent, if entitled to present a petition to the court for the revocation of the patent, may, without presenting such a petition, apply in accordance with the rules of the Supreme Court by way of counterclaim in the action for the revocation of the patent.

Exemption of innocent infringer from liability for damages

33. A patentee shall not be entitled to recover any damages in respect of any infringement of a patent granted after the commencement of this Act from any defendant who proves that at the date of the infringement he was not aware, nor had reasonable means of making himself aware, of the existence of the patent, and the marking of an article with the word "patent," "patented," or any word or words expressing or implying that a patent has been obtained for the article, stamped, engraved, impressed on, or otherwise applied to the article, shall not be deemed to constitute notice of the existence of the patent unless the word or words are accompanied by the year and number of the patent:

Provided that nothing in this section shall affect any proceedings for an injunction.

Order for inspection etc., in action

34. In an action for infringement of a patent, the court may on the application of either party make such order for an injunction inspection or account, and impose such terms and give such directions respecting the same and the proceedings thereon as the court may see fit.

Certificate of validity questioned and costs thereon

35. In an action for infringement of a patent, the court may certify that the validity of the patent came in question; and, if the court so certifies, then in any subsequent action for infringement the plaintiff in that action on obtaining a final order or judgment in his favour shall, unless the court trying the action otherwise directs, have his full costs, charges, and expenses as between solicitor and client.

Remedy in case of groundless threats of legal proceedings.

36. Where any person claiming to be the patentee of an invention, by circulars, advertisements, or otherwise, threatens any other person with any legal proceedings or liability in respect of any alleged infringement of the patent, any person aggrieved thereby may bring an action against him, and may obtain an injunction against the continuance of such threats, and may recover such damage (if any) as he has sustained thereby, if the alleged infringement to which the threats related was not in

fact an infringement of any legal rights of the person making such threats:

A.D. 1907

PART I PATENTS

Provided that this section shall not apply if the person making such threats with due diligence commences and prosecutes an action for infringement of his patent.

Miscellaneous.

Grant of patents to two or more persons

37. Where, after the commencement of this Act, a patent is granted to two or more persons jointly, they shall, unless otherwise specified in the patent, be treated for the purpose of the devolution of the legal interests therein as joint tenants, but, subject to any contract to the contrary, each of such persons shall be entitled to use the invention for his own profit without accounting to the others, but shall not be entitled to grant a licence without their consent, and, if any such person dies, his beneficial interest in the patent shall devolve on his personal representatives as part of his personal estate.

Avoidance of certain conditions attached to the sale, etc. of patented articles

38.—(1) It shall not be lawful in any contract made after the passing of this Act in relation to the sale or lease of, or licence to use or work, any article or process protected by a patent to insert a condition the effect of which will be—

(*a*) to prohibit or restrict the purchaser, lessee, or licensee from using any article or class of articles, whether patented or not, or any patented process, supplied or owned by any person other than the seller, lessor, or licensor or his nominees; or

(*b*) to require the purchaser, lessee, or licensee to acquire from the seller, lessor, or licensor, or his nominees, any article or class of articles not protected by the patent;

and any such condition shall be null and void, as being in restraint of trade and contrary to public policy:

Provided that this subsection shall not apply if—

(i) the seller, lessor, or licensor proves that at the time the contract was entered into the purchaser, lessee, or licensee had the option of purchasing the article or obtaining a lease or licence on reasonable terms, without such conditions as aforesaid; and

(ii) the contract entitles the purchaser, lessee, or licensee to relieve himself of his liability to observe any such condition on giving the other party three months notice in writing and on payment in compensation for such relief in the case of a purchase of such sum, or in the case of a lease or licence of such rent or royalty for the residue of the term of the contract, as may be fixed by an arbitrator appointed by the Board of Trade.

(2) Any contract relating to the lease of or licence to use or work any patented article or patented process, whether made before or after the passing of this Act, may at any time after the patent or all the patents by which the article or process was protected at the time of the making of the contract has or have ceased to be in force, and notwithstanding anything in the same or in any other contract to the contrary, be determined by either party on giving three months notice in writing to the other party;

A.D. 1907

PART I
PATENTS

but where any such notice is given determining any contract made before the passing of this Act, the party giving the notice shall be liable to pay such compensation as failing agreement may be awarded by an arbitrator appointed by the Board of Trade.

(3) Any contract made before the passing of this Act relating to the lease of or licence to use or work any patented article or process and containing any condition which, had the contract been made after the passing of this Act, would by virtue of this section have been null and void may, at any time before the contract is determinable under the last preceding subsection, and notwithstanding anything in the same or any other contract to the contrary, be determined by either party on giving three months notice in writing to the other party, but where any such notice is given the party giving the notice shall be liable to pay such compensation as, failing agreement, may be awarded by an arbitrator appointed by the Board of Trade.

(4) The insertion by the patentee in a contract made after the passing of this Act of any condition which by virtue of this section is null and void shall be available as a defence to an action for infringement of the patent to which the contract relates brought while that contract is in force.

(5) Nothing in this section shall—

(*a*) affect any condition in a contract whereby a person is prohibited from selling any goods other than those of a particular person; or

(*b*) be construed as validating any contract which would, apart from this section, be invalid; or

(*c*) affect any right of determining a contract or condition in a contract exerciseable independently of this section; or

(*d*) affect any condition in a contract for the lease of or licence to use a patented article, whereby the lessor or licensor reserves to himself or his nominees the right to supply such new parts of the patented article as may be required to put or keep it in repair.

Costs and security for costs

39.—(1) The comptroller shall, in proceedings relating to an opposition to the grant of a patent or to an application for the amendment of a specification or the revocation of a patent, have power by order to award to any party such costs as he may consider reasonable, and to direct how and by what parties they are to be paid, and any such order may be made a rule of the court.

(2) If a party giving notice of opposition to the grant of a patent or to the amendment of a specification, or applying to the comptroller for the revocation of a patent, or giving notice of appeal from any decision of the comptroller, neither resides nor carries on business in the United Kingdom or the Isle of Man, the comptroller, or, in case of appeal to the law officer, the law officer, may require such party to give security for costs of the proceedings or appeal, and in default of such security being given may treat the proceedings or appeal as abandoned.

Procedure on appeal to law officer

40. The law officer may examine witnesses on oath and administer oaths for that purpose, and may make rules regulating references and appeals to the law officer and the practice and procedure before him under this Part of this Act; and in any

proceeding before the law officer under this Part of this Act, the law officer may order costs to be paid by either party, and any such order may be made a rule of the court.

A.D. 1907

PART I
PATENTS

Provisions as to anticipation

41.—(1) An invention covered by any patent applied for on or after the first day of January one thousand nine hundred and five shall not be deemed to have been anticipated by reason only of its publication in a specification left pursuant to an application made in the United Kingdom not less than fifty years before the date of the application for the patent, or of its publication in a provisional specification of any date not followed by a complete specification.

(2) A patent shall not be held to be invalid by reason only of the invention in respect of which the patent was granted, or any part thereof, having been published prior to the date of the patent, if the patentee proves to the satisfaction of the court that the publication was made without his knowledge and consent, and that the matter published was derived or obtained from him, and, if he learnt of the publication before the date of his application for the patent, that he applied for and obtained protection for his invention with all reasonable diligence after learning of the publication.

Disconformity

42. A patent shall not be held to be invalid on the ground that the complete specification claims a further or different invention to that contained in the provisional, if the invention therein claimed, so far as it is not contained in the provisional, was novel at the date when the complete specification was put in, and the applicant was the first and true inventor thereof.

Patent on application of representative of deceased inventor

43.—(1) If the person claiming to be inventor of an invention dies without making an application for a patent for the invention, application may be made by, and a patent for the invention granted to, his legal representative.

(2) Every such application must contain a declaration by the legal representative that he believes him to be the true and first inventor of the invention.

Loss or destruction of patent

44. If a patent is lost or destroyed, or its non-production is accounted for to the satisfaction of the comptroller, the comptroller may at any time seal a duplicate thereof.

Provisions as to exhibitions

45.—(1) The exhibition of an invention at an industrial or international exhibition, certified as such by the Board of Trade, or the publication of any description of the invention during the period of the holding of the exhibition, or the use of the invention for the purpose of the exhibition in the place where the exhibition is held, or the use of the invention during the period of the holding of the exhibition by any person elsewhere, without the privity or consent of the inventor, shall not prejudice the right of the inventor to apply for and obtain a patent in respect of the invention or the validity of any patent granted on the application, provided that—

(*a*) the exhibitor, before exhibiting the invention, gives the comptroller the prescribed notice of his intention to do so; and

(*b*) the application for a patent is made before or within six months from the date of the opening of the exhibition.

(2) His Majesty may by Order in Council apply this section

A.D. 1907

PART I
PATENTS

to any exhibition mentioned in the Order in like manner as if it were an industrial or international exhibition certified as such by the Board of Trade, and any such Order may provide that the exhibitor shall be relieved from the condition of giving notice to the comptroller of his intention to exhibit, and shall be so relieved either absolutely or upon such terms and conditions as may be stated in the Order.

Publication of illustrated journal, indexes, etc.

46.—(1) The comptroller shall issue periodically an illustrated journal of patented inventions, as well as reports of patent cases decided by courts of law, and any other information that he may deem generally useful or important.

(2) Provision shall be made by the comptroller for keeping on sale copies of such journal, and also of all complete specifications of patents in force, with any accompanying drawings.

(3) The comptroller shall continue, in such form as he deems expedient, the indexes and abridgments of specifications hitherto published, and shall prepare and publish such other indexes, abridgments of specifications, catalogues, and other works relating to inventions, as he thinks fit.

Patent Museum

47.—(1) The control and management of the Patent Museum and its contents shall remain vested in the Board of Education, subject to such directors as His Majesty in Council may think fit to give.

(2) The Board of Education may at any time require a patentee to furnish them with a model of his invention on payment to the patentee of the cost of the manufacture of the model, the amount to be settled, in case of dispute, by the Board of Trade.

Foreign vessels in British waters

48.—(1) A patent shall not prevent the use of an invention for the purposes of the navigation of a foreign vessel within the jurisdiction of any of His Majesty's Courts in the United Kingdom or Isle of Man, or the use of an invention in a foreign vessel within that jurisdiction, provided it is not used therein for or in connexion with the manufacture or preparation of anything intended to be sold in or exported from the United Kingdom or Isle of Man.

(2) This section shall not extend to vessels of any foreign state of which the laws do not confer corresponding rights with respect to the use of inventions in British vessels while in the ports of that state, or in the waters within the jurisdiction of its courts.

A.D. 1907

PART II
DESIGNS

PART II.

DESIGNS.

Registration of Designs.

Application for registration of designs

49.—(1) The comptroller may, on the application made in the prescribed form and manner of any person claiming to be the proprietor of any new or original design not previously published in the United Kingdom, register the design under this Part of this Act.

(2) The same design may be registered in more than one class, and, in case of doubt as to the class in which a design ought to be registered, the comptroller may decide the question.

(3) The comptroller may, if he thinks fit, refuse to register any design presented to him for registration, but any person aggrieved by any such refusal may appeal to the Board of Trade, and the Board shall, after hearing the applicant and the comptroller, if so required, make an order determining whether, and subject to what conditions, if any, registration is to be permitted.

(4) An application which, owing to any default or neglect on the part of the applicant, has not been completed so as to enable registration to be effected within the prescribed time shall be deemed to be abandoned.

(5) A design when registered shall be registered as of the date of the application for registration.

Registration of designs in new classes

50. Where a design has been registered in one or more classes of goods the application of the proprietor of the design to register it in some one or more other classes shall not be refused, nor shall the registration thereof be invalidated—

(*a*) on the ground of the design not being a new and original design, by reason only that it was so previously registered; or

(*b*) on the ground of the design having been previously published in the United Kingdom, by reason only that it has been applied to goods of any class in which it was so previously registered.

Certificate of registration

51.—(1) The comptroller shall grant a certificate of registration to the proprietor of the design when registered.

(2) The comptroller may, in case of loss of the original certificate, or in any other case in which he deems it expedient, furnish one or more copies of the certificate.

Register of designs

52.—(1) There shall be kept at the Patent Office a book called the Register of Designs wherein shall be entered the names and addresses of proprietors of registered designs, notifications of assignments and of transmissions of registered designs, and such other matters as may be prescribed.

(2) The register of designs existing at the commencement of this Act shall be incorporated with and form part of the register of designs under this Act.

(3) The register of designs shall be prima facie evidence of any matters by this Act directed or authorized to be entered therein.

Copyright in Registered Designs.

Copyright on registration

53.—(1) When a design is registered, the registered proprietor of the design shall, subject to the provisions of this Act, have copyright in the design during five years from the date of registration.

(2) If within the prescribed time before the expiration of the said five years application for the extension of the period of copyright is made to the comptroller in the prescribed manner, the comptroller shall on payment of the prescribed fee extend the period of copyright for a second period of five years from the expiration of the original period of five years.

(3) If within the prescribed time before the expiration of such second period of five years application for the extension of the period of copyright is made to the comptroller in the prescribed

A.D. 1907

Part II
Designs

manner, the comptroller may, subject to any rules under this Act, on payment of the prescribed fee, extend the period of copyright for a third period of five years from the expiration of the second period of five years.

Requirements before delivery on sale

54.—(1) Before delivery on sale of any articles to which a registered design has been applied, the proprietor shall—

(*a*) (if exact representations or specimens were not furnished on the application for registration), furnish to the comptroller the prescribed number of exact representations or specimens of the design; and if he fails to do so the comptroller may erase his name from the register, and thereupon the copyright in the design shall cease; and

(*b*) cause each such article to be marked with the prescribed mark, or with the prescribed words or figures denoting that the design is registered; and if he fails to do so the proprietor shall not be entitled to recover any penalty or damages in respect of any infringement of his copyright in the design unless he shows that he took all proper steps to ensure the marking of the article, or unless he shows that the infringement took place after the person guilty thereof knew or had received notice of the existence of the copyright in the design.

(2) Where a representation is made to the Board of Trade by or on behalf of any trade or industry that in the interests of the trade or industry it is expedient to dispense with or modify as regards any class or description of articles any of the requirements of this section as to marking, the Board may, if they think fit, by rule under this Act dispense with or modify such requirements as regards any such class or description of articles to such extent and subject to such conditions as they think fit.

Effect of disclosure on copyright

55. The disclosure of a design by the proprietor to any other person, in such circumstances as would make it contrary to good faith for that other person to use or publish the design, and the disclosure of a design in breach of good faith by any person other than the proprietor of the design, and the acceptance of a first and confidential order for goods bearing a new or original textile design intended for registration, shall not be deemed to be a publication of the design sufficient to invalidate the copyright thereof if registration thereof is obtained subsequently to the disclosure or acceptance.

Inspection of registered designs

56.—(1) During the existence of copyright in a design, or such shorter period not being less than two years from the registration of the design as may be prescribed, the design shall not be open to inspection except by the proprietor or a person authorized in writing by him, or a person authorized by the comptroller or by the court, and furnishing such information as may enable the comptroller to identify the design, and shall not be open to the inspection of any person except in the presence of the comptroller, or of an officer acting under him, and on payment of the prescribed fee; and the person making the inspection shall not be entitled to take any copy of the design, or of any part thereof:

Provided that where registration of a design is refused on the ground of identity with a design already registered, the applicant for registration shall be entitled to inspect the design so registered.

(2) After the expiration of the copyright in a design, or such shorter period as aforesaid, the design shall be open to inspection, and copies thereof may be taken by any person on payment of the prescribed fee.

(3) Different periods may be prescribed under this section for different classes of goods.

Information as to existence of copyright

57. On the request of any person furnishing such information as may enable the comptroller to identify the design, and on payment of the prescribed fee, the comptroller shall inform such person whether the registration still exists in respect of the design, and if so, in respect of what classes of goods, and shall state the date of registration, and the name and address of the registered proprietor.

Cancellation of registration of designs used wholly or mainly abroad

58.—(1) At any time after the registration of a design any person may apply to the comptroller for the cancellation of the registration on the ground that the design is used for manufacture exclusively or mainly outside the United Kingdom, and where such an application is made the provisions of this Act with respect to the revocation of patents worked outside the United Kingdom (including those relating to costs) shall apply with the necessary modifications, except that there shall be no appeal from the decision of the comptroller.

(2) Such ground as aforesaid shall be available by way of a defence to an action for infringement of the copyright in the design.

Industrial and International Exhibitions.

Provisions as to exhibitions

59.—(1) The exhibition at an industrial or international exhibition certified as such by the Board of Trade, or the exhibition elsewhere during the period of the holding of the exhibition, without the privity or consent of the proprietor, of a design, or of any article to which a design is applied, or the publication, during the holding of any such exhibition, of a description of a design, shall not prevent the design from being registered, or invalidate the registration thereof: Provided that—

(*a*) The exhibitor, before exhibiting the design or article, or publishing a description of the design, gives the comptroller the prescribed notice of his intention to do so; and

(*b*) The application for registration is made before or within six months from the date of the opening of the exhibition.

(2) His Majesty may, by Order in Council, apply this section to any exhibition mentioned in the Order in like manner as if it were an industrial or international exhibition certified as such by the Board of Trade, and any such Order may provide that the exhibitor shall be relieved from the condition of giving notice to the comptroller of his intention to exhibit, and shall be so relieved either absolutely or upon such terms and conditions as may be stated in the Order.

A.D. 1907

PART II
DESIGNS

Legal Proceedings.

Piracy of registered design

60.—(1) During the existence of copyright in any design it shall not be lawful for any person—

(*a*) For the purposes of sale to apply or cause to be applied to any article in any class of goods in which the design is registered the design or any fraudulent or obvious imitation thereof, except with the licence or written consent of the registered proprietor, or to do anything with a view to enable the design to be so applied; or

(*b*) Knowing that the design or any fraudulent or obvious imitation thereof has been applied to any article without the consent of the registered proprietor to publish or expose or cause to be published or exposed for sale that article.

(2) If any person acts in contravention of this section he shall be liable for every contravention to pay to the registered proprietor of the design a sum not exceeding fifty pounds, recoverable as a simple contract debt, or if the proprietor elects to bring an action for the recovery of damages for such contravention, and for an injunction against the repetition thereof, he shall be liable to pay such damages as may be awarded and to be restrained by injunction accordingly:

Provided that the total sum recoverable as a simple contract debt in respect of any one design shall not exceed one hundred pounds.

Application of certain provisions of the Act as to patents to designs

61. The provisions of this Act with regard to certificates of the validity of a patent, and to the remedy in case of groundless threats of legal proceedings by a patentee shall apply in the case of registered designs in like manner as they apply in the case of patents, with the substitution of references to the copyright in a design for references to a patent, and of references to the proprietor of a design for references to the patentee, and of references to the design for references to the invention.

PART III.

GENERAL.

PART III
GENERAL

Patent Office and Proceedings thereat.

Patent Office. 5 Edw. VII, c. 15

62.—(1) The Treasury may continue to provide for the purposes of this Act and the Trade Marks Act, 1905, an office with all requisite buildings and conveniences, which shall be called, and is in this Act referred to as, the Patent Office.

(2) The Patent Office shall be under the immediate control of the comptroller, who shall act under the superintendence and direction of the Board of Trade.

(3) Any act or thing directed to be done by or to the comptroller may be done by or to any officer authorized by the Board of Trade.

(4) Rules under this Act may provide for the establishment of branch offices for designs at Manchester or elsewhere, and for any document or thing required by this Act to be sent to or done at the Patent Office being sent to or done at any branch office which may be established.

Officers and clerks

63.—(1) There shall continue to be a comptroller-general of patents, designs, and trade marks, and the Board of Trade may, subject to the approval of the Treasury, appoint the comptroller, and so many examiners and other officers and clerks, with such designations and duties as the Board of Trade think fit, and may remove any of those officers and clerks.

(2) The salaries of those officers and clerks shall be appointed by the Board of Trade, with the concurrence of the Treasury, and those salaries and the other expenses of the execution of this Act and the Trade Marks Act, 1905, shall continue to be paid out of money provided by Parliament.

Seal of Patent Office

64. Impressions of the seal of the Patent Office shall be judicially noticed and admitted in evidence.

Fees.

Fee

65. There shall be paid in respect of the grant of patents and the registration of designs, and applications therefor, and in respect of other matters with relation to patents and designs under this Act, such fees as may be, with the sanction of the Treasury, prescribed by the Board of Trade, so however that the fees prescribed in respect of the instruments and matters mentioned in the First Schedule to this Act shall not exceed those specified in that Schedule.

Provisions as to Registers and other Documents in Patent Office.

Trust not to be entered in registers

66. There shall not be entered in any register kept under this Act, or be receivable by the comptroller, any notice of any trust expressed, implied or constructive.

Inspection of and extracts from registers

67. Every register kept under this Act shall at all convenient times be open to the inspection of the public, subject to the provisions of this Act and to such regulations as may be prescribed; and certified copies, sealed with the seal of the Patent Office, of any entry in any such register shall be given to any person requiring the same on payment of the prescribed fee.

Privilege of reports of examiners

68. Reports of examiners made under this Act shall not in any case be published or be open to public inspection, and shall not be liable to production or inspection in any legal proceeding, unless the court or officer having power to order discovery in such legal proceeding certifies that such production or inspection is desirable in the interests of justice, and ought to be allowed.

Prohibition of publication of specification, drawings, etc., where application abandoned, etc.

69.—(1) Where an application for a patent has been abandoned, or become void, the specifications and drawings (if any) accompanying or left in connexion with such application, shall not, save as otherwise expressly provided by this Act, at any time be open to public inspection or be published by the comptroller.

(2) Where an application for a design has been abandoned or refused the application and any drawings, photographs, tracings, representations, or specimens left in connexion with the application shall not at any time be open to public inspection or be published by the comptroller.

Power for comptroller to correct clerical errors

70. The comptroller may, on request in writing accompanied by the prescribed fee,—

(*a*) correct any clerical error in or in connexion with an application for a patent or in any patent or any specification;

A.D. 1907

Part III
General

(b) cancel the registration of a design either wholly or in respect of any particular goods in connexion with which the design is registered;

(c) correct any clerical error in the representation of a design or in the name or address of the proprietor of any patent or design, or in any other matter which is entered upon the register of patents or the register of designs.

Entry of assignments and transmissions in registers

71.—(1) Where a person becomes entitled by assignment, transmission, or other operation of law to a patent, or to the copyright in a registered design, the comptroller shall, on request and on proof of title to his satisfaction, register him as the proprietor of a patent or design.

(2) Where any person becomes entitled as mortgagee, licensee, or otherwise to any interest in a patent or design, the comptroller shall, on request and on proof of title to his satisfaction, cause notice of the interest to be entered in the prescribed manner in the register of patents or designs, as the case may be.

(3) The person registered as the proprietor of a patent or design shall, subject to the provisions of this Act and to any rights appearing from the register to be vested in any other person, have power absolutely to assign, grant licences as to, or otherwise deal with, the patent or design and to give effectual receipts for any consideration for any such assignment, licence, or dealing: Provided that any equities in respect of the patent or design may be enforced in like manner as in respect of any other personal property.

Rectification of registers by Court

72.—(1) The court may, on the application in the prescribed manner of any person aggrieved by the non-insertion in or omission from the register of patents or designs of any entry or by any entry made in either such register without sufficient cause, or by any entry wrongly remaining on either such register, or by an error or defect in any entry in either such register, make such order for making, expunging, or varying such entry as it may think fit.

(2) The court may in any proceeding under this section decide any question that it may be necessary or expedient to decide in connexion with the rectification of a register.

(3) The prescribed notice of any application under this section shall be given to the comptroller, who shall have the right to appear and be heard thereon, and shall appear if so directed by the court.

(4) Any order of the court rectifying a register shall direct that notice of the rectification be served on the comptroller in the prescribed manner, who shall upon the receipt of such notice rectify the register accordingly.

Powers and Duties of Comptroller.

Exercise of discretionary power by comptroller

73. Where any discretionary power is by or under this Act given to the comptroller, he shall not exercise that power adversely to the applicant for a patent, or for amendment of a specification, or for registration of a design, without (if so required within the prescribed time by the applicant) giving the applicant an opportunity of being heard.

A.D. 1907

PART III
GENERAL

74. The comptroller may, in any case of doubt or difficulty arising in the administration of any of the provisions of this Act, apply to a law officer for directions in the matter.

Power of comptroller to take directions of law officers

75. The comptroller may refuse to grant a patent for an invention, or to register a design, of which the use would, in his opinion, be contrary to law or morality.

Refusal to grant patent, etc., in certain cases

76. The comptroller shall, before the first day of June in every year, cause a report respecting the execution by or under him of this Act to be laid before both Houses of Parliament, and therein shall include for the year to which the report relates all general rules made in that year under or for the purposes of this Act, and an account of all fees, salaries, and allowances, and other money received and paid under this Act.

Annual reports of comptroller

Evidence, Etc.

Evidence before comptroller

77.—(1) Subject to rules under this Act in any proceeding under this Act before the comptroller the evidence shall be given by statutory declaration in the absence of directions to the contrary; but in any case in which the comptroller thinks it right so to do, he may take evidence *vivâ voce* in lieu of or in addition to evidence by declaration or allow any declarant to be cross-examined on his declaration. Any such statutory declaration may in the case of appeal be used before the court in lieu of evidence by affidavit, but if so used shall have all the incidents and consequences of evidence by affidavit.

(2) In case any part of the evidence is taken *vivâ voce*, the comptroller shall, in respect of requiring the attendance of witnesses and taking evidence on oath, be in the same position in all respects as an official referee of the Supreme Court.

Certificate o comptroller to be evidence

78. A certificate purporting to be under the hand of the comptroller as to any entry, matter, or thing which he is authorized by this Act, or any general rules made thereunder, to make or do, shall be *primâ facie* evidence of the entry having been made, and of the contents thereof, and of the matter or thing having been done or left undone.

Evidence of documents in Patent Office

79. Printed or written copies or extracts, purporting to be certified by the comptroller and sealed with the seal of the Patent Office, of or from patents, specifications, and othor documents in the Patent Office, and of or from registers and other books kept there, shall be admitted in evidence in all courts in His Majesty's dominions, and in all proceedings, without further proof or production of the originals.

Transmission of certified printed copies of specifications, etc.

80.—(1) Copies of all specifications, drawings, and amendments left at the Patent Office after the commencement of this Act, printed for and sealed with the seal of the Patent Office, shall be transmitted to the Edinburgh Museum of Science and Art, and to the Enrolments Office of the Chancery Division in Ireland, and to the Rolls Office in the Isle of Man, within twenty-one days after they have been accepted or allowed at the Patent Office.

(2) Certified copies of or extracts from any such documents and of any documents so transmitted in pursuance of any enactment repealed by this Act shall be given to any person on payment of the prescribed fee; and any such copy or extract shall be admitted in evidence in all courts in Scotland and Ireland and

A.D. 1907

Part III
General

in the Isle of Man without further proof or production of the originals.

Applications and notices by post

81. Any application, notice, or other document authorized or required to be left, made, or given at the Patent Office or to the comptroller, or to any other person under this Act, may be sent by post.

Excluded days

82. Where the last day fixed by this Act for doing anything under this Act falls on any day specified in rules under this Act as an excluded day, the rules may provide for the thing being done on the next following day not being an excluded day.

Declaration by infant, lunatic, etc.

83.—(1) If any person is, by reason of infancy, lunacy, or other disability, incapable of making any declaration or doing anything required or permitted by or under this Act, the guardian or committee (if any) of the person subject to the disability, or, if there be none, any person appointed by any court possessing jurisdiction in respect of his property, may make such declaration or a declaration as nearly corresponding thereto as circumstances permit, and do such thing in the name and on behalf of the person subject to the disability.

(2) An appointment may be made by the court for the purposes of this section upon the petition of any person acting on behalf of the person subject to the disability or of any other person interested in the making of the declaration or the doing of the thing.

Register of Patent Agents.

Register of patent agents

84.—(1) A person shall not be entitled to describe himself as a patent agent, whether by advertisement, by description on his place of business, by any document issued by him, or otherwise, unless he is registered as a patent agent in pursuance of this Act or an Act repealed by this Act.

(2) Every person who proves to the satisfaction of the Board of Trade that prior to the twenty-fourth day of December, one thousand eight hundred and eighty-eight, he had been *bona fide* practising as a patent agent shall be entitled to be registered as a patent agent in pursuance of this Act.

(3) If any person knowingly describes himself as a patent agent in contravention of this section he shall be liable on conviction under the Summary Jurisdiction Acts to a fine not exceeding twenty pounds.

(4) In this section "patent agent" means exclusively an agent for obtaining patents in the United Kingdom.

Agents for patents

85.—(1) Rules under this Act may authorize the comptroller to refuse to recognize as agent in respect of any business under this Act any person whose name has been erased from the register of patent agents, or who is proved to the satisfaction of the Board of Trade, after being given an opportunity of being heard, to have been convicted of such an offence or to have been guilty of such misconduct as would have rendered him liable, if his name had been on the register of patent agents, to have his name erased therefrom, and may authorize the comptroller to refuse to recognize as agent in respect of any business under this Act any company which, if it had been an individual, the comptroller could refuse to recognize as such agent.

(2) Where a company or firm acts as agents, such rules as

aforesaid may authorize the comptroller to refuse to recognize the company or firm as agent if any person whom the comptroller could refuse to recognize as an agent acts as director or manager of the company or is a partner in the firm.

A.D. 1907

PART III
GENERAL

(3) The comptroller shall refuse to recognize as agent in respect of any business under this Act any person who neither resides nor has a place of business in the United Kingdom or the Isle of Man.

Powers, etc., of Board of Trade.

Power for Board of Trade to make general rules

86.—(1) The Board of Trade may make such general rules and do such things as they think expedient, subject to the provisions of this Act—

(*a*) For regulating the practice of registration under this Act:
(*b*) For classifying goods for the purposes of designs:
(*c*) For making or requiring duplicates of specifications, drawings, and other documents:
(*d*) For securing and regulating the publishing and selling of copies, at such prices and in such manner as the Board of Trade think fit, of specifications, drawings, and other documents:
(*e*) For securing and regulating the making, printing, publishing, and selling of indexes to, and abridgments of, specifications and other documents in the Patent Office; and providing for the inspection of indexes and abridgments and other documents:
(*f*) For regulating (with the approval of the Treasury) the presentation of copies of Patent Office publications to patentees and to public authorities, bodies, and institutions at home and abroad:
(*g*) For regulating the keeping of the register of patent agents under this Act:
(*h*) Generally for regulating the business of the Patent Office, and all things by this Act placed under the direction or control of the comptroller, or of the Board of Trade.

(2) General rules shall whilst in force be of the same effect as if they were contained in this Act.

(3) Any rules made in pursuance of this section shall be advertised twice in the official journal to be issued by the comptroller, and shall be laid before both Houses of Parliament as soon as practicable after they are made, and if either House of Parliament, within the next forty days after any rules have been so laid before that house, resolves that the rules or any of them ought to be annulled, the rules or those to which the resolution applies shall after the date of such resolution be of no effect, without prejudice to the validity of anything done in the meantime under the rules or to the making of any new rules.

Proceedings of the Board of Trade

87.—(1) All things required or authorized under this Act to be done by, to, or before the Board of Trade, may be done by, to, or before the President or a secretary or an assistant secretary of the Board.

(2) All documents purporting to be orders made by the Board of Trade and to be sealed with the seal of the Board, or to be signed by a secretary or assistant secretary of the Board, or by any

A.D. 1907

PART III
GENERAL

person authorized in that behalf by the President of the Board, shall be received in evidence, and shall be deemed to be such orders without further proof, unless the contrary is shown.

(3) A certificate, signed by the President of the Board of Trade, that any order made or act done is the order or act of the Board, shall be conclusive evidence of the fact so certified.

Provision as to Order in Council

88. An Order in Council under this Act shall, from a date to be mentioned for the purpose in the Order, take effect as if it had been contained in this Act; but may be revoked or varied by a subsequent Order.

Offences.

Offences

89.—(1) If any person makes or causes to be made a false entry in any register kept under this Act, or a writing falsely purporting to be a copy of an entry in any such register, or produces or tenders or causes to be produced or tendered in evidence any such writing, knowing the entry or writing to be false, he shall be guilty of a misdemeanor.

(2) If any person falsely represents that any article sold by him is a patented article, or falsely describes any design applied to any article sold by him as registered, he shall be liable for every offence, on conviction under the Summary Jurisdiction Acts, to a fine not exceeding five pounds.

(3) If any person sells an article having stamped, engraved, or impressed thereon or otherwise applied thereto the word "patent," "patented," "registered," or any other word expressing or implying that the article is patented or that the design applied thereto is registered, he shall be deemed for the purposes of this section to represent that the article is a patented article or that the design applied thereto is a registered design.

(4) Any person who, after the copyright in a design has expired, puts or causes to be put on any article to which the design has been applied the word "registered," or any word or words implying that there is a subsisting copyright in the design, shall be liable on conviction under the Summary Jurisdiction Acts, to a fine not exceeding five pounds.

(5) If any person uses on his place of business, or on any document issued by him, or otherwise, the words "Patent Office," or any other words suggesting that his place of business is officially connected with, or is, the Patent Office, he shall be liable on conviction under the Summary Jurisdiction Acts to a fine not exceeding twenty pounds.

Unauthorized assumption of Royal Arms

90.—(1) The grant of a patent under this Act shall not be deemed to authorize the patentee to use the Royal Arms or to place the Royal Arms on any patented article.

(2) If any person, without the authority of His Majesty, uses in connexion with any business, trade, calling, or profession the Royal Arms (or arms so nearly resembling them as to be calculated to deceive) in such manner as to be calculated to lead to the belief that he is duly authorized to use the Royal Arms, he shall be liable on conviction under the Summary Jurisdiction Acts to a fine not exceeding twenty pounds:

Provided that nothing in this section shall be construed as affecting the right, if any, of the proprietor of a trade mark containing such arms to continue to use such trade mark,

International and Colonial Arrangements.

A.D. 1907

PART III GENERAL

International and Colonial arrangement

91.—(1) If His Majesty is pleased to make any arrangement with the government of any foreign state for mutual protection of inventions, or designs, or trade marks, then any person who has applied for protection for any invention, design, or trade mark in that state shall be entitled to a patent for his invention or to registration of his design or trade mark under this Act or the Trade Marks Act, 1905, in priority to other applicants; and the patent or registration shall have the same date as the date of the application in the foreign state.

Provided that—

(*a*) The application is made, in the case of a patent within twelve months, and in the case of a design or trade mark within four months, from the application for protection in the foreign state; and

(*b*) Nothing in this section shall entitle the patentee or proprietor of the design or trade mark to recover damages for infringements happening prior to the actual date on which his complete specification is accepted, or his design or trade mark is registered, in this country.

(2) The patent granted for the invention or the registration of a design or trade mark shall not be invalidated—

(*a*) in the case of a patent, by reason only of the publication of a description of, or use of, the invention; or

(*b*) in the case of a design, by reason only of the exhibition or use of, or the publication of a description or representation of, the design; or

(*c*) in the case of a trade mark, by reason only of the use of the trade mark,

in the United Kingdom or the Isle of Man during the period specified in this section as that within which the application may be made.

(3) The application for the grant of a patent, or the registration of a design, or the registration of a trade mark under this section, must be made in the same manner as an ordinary application under this Act or the Trade Marks Act, 1905: Provided that—

(*a*) In the case of patents the application shall be accompanied by a complete specification, which, if it is not accepted within the twelve months from the application for protection in the foreign state, shall with the drawings (if any) be open to public inspection at the expiration of that period; and

(*b*) In the case of trade marks, any trade mark the registration of which has been duly applied for in the country of origin may be registered under the Trade Marks Act, 1905.

(4) The provisions of this section shall apply only in the case of those foreign states with respect to which His Majesty by Order in Council declares them to be applicable, and so long only in the case of each state as the Order in Council continues in force with respect to that state.

A.D. 1907

PART III
GENERAL

(5) Where it is made to appear to His Majesty that the legislature of any British possession has made satisfactory provision for the protection of inventions, designs, and trade marks, patented or registered in this country, it shall be lawful for His Majesty, by Order in Council, to apply the provisions of this section to that possession, with such variations or additions, if any, as may be stated in the Order.

Definitions.

Provisions as to "the Court"

92.—(1) In this Act, unless the context otherwise requires, "the Court" means, subject to the provisions as to Scotland, Ireland, and the Isle of Man, the High Court in England.

(2) Where by virtue of this Act a decision of the comptroller is subject to an appeal to the court, or a petition may be referred or presented to the court, the appeal shall, subject to and in accordance with rules of the Supreme Court, be made and the petition referred or presented to such judge of the High Court as the Lord Chancellor may select for the purpose, and the decision of that judge shall be final, except in the case of an appeal from a decision of the comptroller revoking a patent on any ground on which the grant of such patent might have been opposed.

Definitions

93. In this Act, unless the context otherwise requires,—

"Law officer" means the Attorney-General or Solicitor-General for England:

"Prescribed" means prescribed by general rules under this Act:

"British possession" does not include the Isle of Man or the Channel Islands:

"Patent" means letters patent for an invention:

"Patentee" means the person for the time being entitled to the benefit of a patent:

"Invention" means any manner of new manufacture the subject of letters patent and grant of privilege within section six of the Statute of Monopolies (that is, the Act of the twenty-first year of the reign of King James the First, chapter three, intituled "An Act concerning "monopolies and dispensations with penal laws and "the forfeiture thereof"), and includes an alleged invention:

"Inventor" and "applicant" shall, subject to the provisions of this Act, include the legal representative of a deceased inventor or applicant:

54 Geo. III, c. 56

"Design" means any design (not being a design for a sculpture or other thing within the protection of the Sculpture Copyright Act, 1814) applicable to any article, whether the design is applicable for the pattern, or for the shape or configuration, or for the ornament thereof, or for any two or more of such purposes, and by whatever means it is applicable, whether by printing, painting, embroidering, weaving, sewing, modelling, casting, embossing, engraving, staining, or any other means whatever, manual, mechanical, or chemical, separate or combined:

"Article" means (as respects designs) any article of manufacture and any substance artificial or natural, or partly artificial and partly natural:

"Copyright" means the exclusive right to apply a design to any article in any class in which the design is registered:

"Proprietor of a new and original design,"—

(*a*) Where the author of the design, for good consideration, executes the work for some other person, means the person for whom the design is so executed; and

(*b*) Where any person acquires the design or the right to apply the design to any article, either exclusively of any other person or otherwise, means, in the respect and to the extent in and to which the design or right has been so acquired, the person by whom the design or right is so acquired; and

(*c*) In any other case, means the author of the design; and where the property in, or the right to apply, the design has devolved from the original proprietor upon any other person, includes that other person.

Application to Scotland, Ireland, and the Isle of Man.

94. In the application of this Act to Scotland— Application to Scotland

(1) In any action for infringement of a patent in Scotland the provisions of this Act with respect to calling in the aid of an assessor shall apply, and the action shall be tried without a jury unless the court otherwise direct, but otherwise nothing shall affect the jurisdiction and forms of process of the courts in Scotland in such an action or in any action or proceeding respecting a patent hitherto competent to those courts; and for the purposes of the provisions so applied "court of appeal" shall mean any court to which such action is appealed:

(2) Any offence under this Act declared to be punishable on conviction under the Summary Jurisdiction Acts may be prosecuted in the sheriff court:

(3) Proceedings for revocation of a patent shall be in the form of an action of reduction at the instance of the Lord Advocate, or at the instance of a party having interest with his concurrence which concurrence may be given on just cause shown only, and service of all writs and summonses in that action shall be made according to the forms and practice existing at the commencement of this Act:

(4) The provisions of this Act conferring a special jurisdiction on the court as defined by this Act shall not, except so far as the jurisdiction extends, affect the jurisdiction of any court in Scotland in any proceedings relating to patents or to designs; and with reference to any such proceedings, the term "the Court" shall mean any Lord Ordinary of the Court of Session, and the term "Court of Appeal" shall mean either Division of that Court:

A.D. 1907

PART III
GENERAL

(5) Notwithstanding anything in this Act, the expression "the Court" shall, as respects petitions for compulsory licences or revocation which are referred by the Board of Trade to the Court, in Scotland, mean any Lord Ordinary of the Court of Session, and shall in reference to proceedings in Scotland for the extension of the term of a patent mean such Lord Ordinary:

(6) The expression "Rules of the Supreme Court" shall, except in section ninety-two of this Act, mean act of sederunt:

(7) If any rectification of a register under this Act is required in pursuance of any proceeding in a court, a copy of the order, decree, or other authority for the rectification, shall be served on the comptroller, and he shall rectify the register accordingly:

(8) The expression "injunction" means "interdict."

Application to Ireland

95. In the application of this Act to Ireland—

(1) All parties shall, notwithstanding anything in this Act, have in Ireland their remedies under or in respect of a patent as if the same had been granted to extend to Ireland only:

(2) The provisions of this Act conferring a special jurisdiction on the court, as defined by this Act, shall not, except so far as the jurisdiction extends, affect the jurisdiction of any court in Ireland in any proceedings relating to patents or to designs; and with reference to any such proceedings the term "the Court" means the High Court in Ireland:

(3) If any rectification of a register under this Act is required in pursuance of any proceeding in a court, a copy of the order, decree, or other authority for the rectification shall be served on the comptroller, and he shall rectify the register accordingly.

Isle of Man

96. This Act shall extend to the Isle of Man, subject to the following modifications—

(1) Nothing in this Act shall affect the jurisdiction of the courts in the Isle of Man in proceedings for infringement, or in any action or proceeding respecting a patent or design competent to those courts:

(2) The punishment for a misdemeanour under this Act in the Isle of Man shall be imprisonment for any term not exceeding two years, with or without hard labour, and with or without a fine not exceeding one hundred pounds, at the discretion of the court:

(3) Any offence under this Act committed in the Isle of Man which would in England be punishable on summary conviction may be prosecuted, and any fine in respect thereof recovered, at the instance of any person aggrieved, in the manner in which offences punishable on summary conviction may for the time being be prosecuted.

Repeal, Savings, and Short Title.

Saving for prerogative

97. Nothing in this Act shall take away, abridge, or prejudicially affect the prerogative of the Crown in relation to the

A.D. 1907

PART III
GENERAL

granting of any letters patent or to the withholding of a grant thereof.

Repeal and savings

98.—(1) The enactments mentioned in the Second Schedule to this Act are hereby repealed to the extent specified in the third column of that schedule—

(*a*) As respects the enactments mentioned in Part I of that schedule, as from the commencement of this Act;

(*b*) As respects the enactments mentioned in Part II of that schedule, as from the date when rules of the Supreme Court regulating the matters dealt with in those enactments come into operation;

(*c*) As respects the enactments mentioned in Part III of that schedule, as from the date when rules under this Act regulating the matters dealt with in those enactments come into operation;

and the enactments mentioned in Part II and Part III of that schedule shall, until so repealed, have effect as if they formed part of this Act;

Provided that this repeal shall not affect any convention, Order in Council, rule, or table of fees having effect under any enactment so repealed, but any such convention, Order in Council, rule, or table of fees, in force at the commencement of this Act shall continue in force, and may be repealed, altered or amended, as if it had been made under this Act.

(2) Except where otherwise expressly provided, this Act shall extend to all patents granted and all designs registered before the commencement of this Act, and to applications then pending, in substitution for such enactments as would have applied thereto if this Act had not been passed.

Short title and commencement

99 This Act may be cited as the Patents and Designs Act, 1907, and shall, save as otherwise expressly provided, come into operation on the first day of January one thousand nine hundred and eight.

SCHEDULES.

FIRST SCHEDULE.

FEES ON INSTRUMENTS FOR OBTAINING PATENTS AND RENEWAL.

(*a*) *Up to sealing.*

	£	s.	d.	£	s.	d.
On application for provisional protection	1	0	0			
On filing complete specification . .	3	0	0			
				4	0	0
or						
On filing complete specification with first application				4	0	0
On the sealing of the patent in respect of investigations as to anticipation				1	0	0
(*b*) *Further before end of four years from date of patent.*						
On certificate of renewal				50	0	0
(*c*) *Further before end of eight years from date of patent.*						
On certificate of renewal				100	0	0

A.D. 1907

PART III
GENERAL

Or in lieu of the fees of £50 and £100 the following annual fees :

Before the expiration of the—

	£	s.	d.
Fourth year from the date of the patent	10	0	0
Fifth ,, ,, ,,	10	0	0
Sixth ,, ,, ,,	10	0	0
Seventh ,, ,, ,,	10	0	0
Eighth ,, ,, ,,	15	0	0
Ninth ,, ,, ,,	15	0	0
Tenth ,, ,, ,,	20	0	0
Eleventh ,, ,, ,,	20	0	0
Twelfth ,, ,, ,,	20	0	0
Thirteenth ,, ,, ,,	20	0	0

A.D. 1907

Section 98

SECOND SCHEDULE.

ENACTMENTS REPEALED.

PART I.

Session and Chapter.	Short Title.	Extent of Repeal.
46 & 47 Vict., c. 57.	The Patents, Designs, and Trade Marks Act, 1883.	The whole Act, except subsections (5), (6), and (7) of section twenty-six, section twenty-nine, subsections (2) and (3) of section forty-seven, and section forty-eight.
48 & 49 Vict., c. 63.	The Patents, Designs, and Trade Marks (Amendment) Act, 1885.	The whole Act.
49 & 50 Vict., c. 37	The Patents Act, 1886.	The whole Act.
51 & 52 Vict., c. 50.	The Patents, Designs, and Trade Marks Act, 1888.	The whole Act.
1 Edw. VII, c. 18.	The Patents Act, 1901.	The whole Act.
7 Edw. VII, c. 34.	The Patents Act, 1902.	The whole Act.
7 Edw. VII, c. 28.	The Patents and Designs (Amendment) Act, 1907.	The whole Act.

PART II.

Session and Chapter.	Short Title.	Extent of Repeal.
46 & 47 Vict., c. 57.	The Patents, Designs, and Trade Marks Act, 1883.	Subsections (5), (6), and (7), of section twenty-six, and section twenty-nine.

PART III.

Session and Chapter.	Short Title.	Extent of Repeal.
46 & 47 Vict., c. 57.	The Patents, Designs, and Trade Marks Act, 1883.	Subsections (2) and (3) of section forty-seven and section forty-eight.

PATENTS AND DESIGNS ACT, 1919.

[9 & 10 Geo. V.]

Chapter 80.

A.D. 1919

An Act to amend the Patents and Designs Acts.

[23rd December, 1919.]

Be it enacted by the King's most Excellent Majesty, by and with the advice and consent of the Lords Spiritual and Temporal, and Commons, in this present Parliament assembled, and by the authority of the same, as follows—

Provisions for the prevention of abuse of monopoly rights. 7 Edw. VII, c. 29.

1. For section twenty-seven of the Patents and Designs Act, 1907 (hereinafter referred to as the principal Act), the following section shall be substituted—

" 27.—(1) Any person interested may at any time apply to the comptroller alleging in the case of any patent that there has been an abuse of the monopoly rights thereunder and asking for relief under this section.

(2) The monopoly rights under a patent shall be deemed to have been abused in any of the following circumstances—

(*a*) If at any time after the expiration of four years from the date of the patent, the patented invention (being one capable of being worked in the United Kingdom), is not being worked within the United Kingdom on a commercial scale, and no satisfactory reason can be given for such non-working:

Provided that, if an application is presented to the comptroller on this ground, and the comptroller is of opinion that the time which has elapsed since the date of the patent has by reason of the nature of the invention or for any other cause been insufficient to enable the invention to be worked within the United Kingdom on a commercial scale, the comptroller may adjourn the application for such period as will in his opinion be sufficient for that purpose:

(*b*) If the working of the invention within the United Kingdom on a commercial scale is being prevented or hindered by the importation from abroad of the patented article by the patentee or persons claiming under him, or by persons directly or indirectly purchasing from him, or by other persons against whom the patentee is not taking or has not taken any proceedings for infringement:

(*c*) If the demand for the patented article in the United Kingdom is not being met to an adequate extent and on reasonable terms:

(*d*) If, by reason of the refusal of the patentee to grant a licence or licences upon reasonable terms, the trade or industry of the United Kingdom or the trade of any person or class of persons trading in the United Kingdom, or the establishment of any new trade or industry in the United Kingdom, is prejudiced, and it is in the public interest that a licence or licences should be granted:

(*e*) If any trade or industry in the United Kingdom, or any person or class of persons engaged therein, is unfairly prejudiced by the conditions attached by the patentee, whether before or after the passing of this Act, to the purchase, hire, licence, or use of the patented article, or to the using or working of the patented process: A.D. 1919

Provided that, for the purpose of determining whether there has been any abuse of the monopoly rights under a patent, it shall be taken that patents for new inventions are granted not only to encourage invention but to secure that new inventions shall so far as possible be worked on a commercial scale in the United Kingdom without undue delay.

(3) On being satisfied that a case of abuse of the monopoly rights under a patent has been established, the comptroller may exercise any of the following powers as he may deem expedient in the circumstances—

(*a*) He may order the patent to be indorsed with the words 'licences of right' and thereupon the same rules shall apply as are provided in this Act in respect of patents so indorsed, and an exercise by the comptroller of this power shall entitle every existing licensee to apply to the comptroller for an order entitling him to surrender his licence in exchange for a licence to be settled by the comptroller in like manner as if the patent had been so indorsed at the request of the patentee, and the comptroller may make such order; and an order that a patent be so indorsed may be made notwithstanding that there may be an agreement subsisting which would have precluded the indorsement of the patent at the request of the patentee:

(*b*) He may order the grant to the applicant of a licence on such terms as the comptroller may think expedient, including a term precluding the licensee from importing into the United Kingdom any goods the importation of which, if made by persons other than the patentee or persons claiming under him, would be an infringement of the patent, and in such case the patentee and all licensees for the time being shall be deemed to have mutually covenanted against such importation. A licensee under this paragraph shall be entitled to call upon the patentee to take proceedings to prevent infringement of the patent, and if the patentee refuses, or neglects to do so within two months after being so called upon, the licensee may institute proceedings for infringement in his own name as though he were the patentee, making the patentee a defendant. A patentee so added as defendant shall not be liable for any costs unless he enters an appearance and takes part in the proceedings. Service on him may be effected by leaving the writ at his address for service given on the register:

In settling the terms of a licence under this paragraph the comptroller shall be guided as far as may be by the same considerations as are specified in section twenty-four of this Act for his guidance in settling licences under that section:

A.D. 1919

(c) If the comptroller is satisfied that the invention is not being worked on a commercial scale within the United Kingdom, and is such that it cannot be so worked without the expenditure of capital for the raising of which it will be necessary to rely on the patent monopoly, he may, unless the patentee or those claiming under him will undertake to find such capital, order the grant to the applicant, or any other person, or to the applicant and any other person or persons jointly, if able and willing to provide such capital, of an exclusive licence on such terms as the comptroller may think just, but subject as hereinafter provided:

(d) If the comptroller is satisfied that the objects of this section cannot be attained by the exercise of any of the foregoing powers, he may order the patent to be revoked, either forthwith or after such reasonable interval as may be specified in the order, unless in the meantime such conditions as may be prescribed in the order with a view to attaining the objects of this section are fulfilled, and the comptroller may, on reasonable cause shown in any case, by subsequent order extend the interval so specified:

Provided that the comptroller shall make no order for revocation which is at variance with any treaty, convention, arrangement, or engagement with any foreign country or British possession:

(e) If the comptroller is of opinion that the objects of this section will be best attained by making no order under the above provisions of this section, he may make an order refusing the application and dispose of any question as to costs thereon as he thinks just.

(4) In settling the terms of any such exclusive licence as i :provided in paragraph (c) of the last preceding subsection, due regard shall be had to the risks undertaken by the licensee in providing the capital and working the invention, but, subject thereto, the licence shall be so framed as—

(a) to secure to the patentee the maximum royalty compatible with the licensee working the invention within the United Kingdom on a commercial scale and at a reasonable profit;

(b) to guarantee to the patentee a minimum yearly sum by way of royalty, if and so far as it is reasonable so to do, having regard to the capital requisite for the proper working of the invention and all the circumstances of the case;

and, in addition to any other powers expressed in the licence or order, the licence and the order granting the licence shall be made revocable at the discretion of the comptroller if the licensee fails to expend the amount specified in the licence as being the amount which he is able and willing to provide for the purpose of working the invention on a commercial scale within the United Kingdom, or if he fails so to work the invention within the time specified in the order.

(5) In deciding to whom such an exclusive licence is to be granted the comptroller shall, unless good reason is shown to

the contrary, prefer an existing licensee to a person having no registered interest in the patent. A.D. 1919

(6) The order granting an exclusive licence under this section shall operate to take away from the patentee any right which he may have as patentee to work or use the invention and to revoke all existing licences, unless otherwise provided in the order, but on granting an exclusive licence the comptroller may, if he thinks it fair and equitable, make it a condition that the licensee shall give proper compensation to be fixed by the comptroller for any money or labour expended by the patentee or any existing licensee in developing or exploiting the invention.

(7) Every application presented to the comptroller under this section must set out fully the nature of the applicant's interest and the facts upon which the applicant bases his case and the relief which he seeks. The application must be accompanied by statutory declarations verifying the applicant's interest and the facts set out in the application.

(8) The comptroller shall consider the matters alleged in the application and declarations, and, if satisfied that the applicant has a *bona fide* interest and that a prima facie case for relief has been made out, he shall direct the applicant to serve copies of the application and declarations upon the patentee and upon any other persons appearing from the register to be interested in the patent, and shall advertise the application in the Illustrated Official Journal (Patents).

(9) If the patentee or any person is desirous of opposing the granting of any relief under this section, he shall, within such time as may be prescribed or within such extended time as the comptroller may on application further allow, deliver to the comptroller a counter statement verified by a statutory declaration fully setting out the grounds on which the application is to be opposed.

(10) The comptroller shall consider the counter statement and declarations in support thereof and may thereupon dismiss the application if satisfied that the allegations in the application have been adequately answered, unless any of the parties demands a hearing or unless the comptroller himself appoints a hearing. In any case the comptroller may require the attendance before him of any of the declarants to be cross-examined or further examined upon matters relevant to the issues raised in the application and counter statement, and he may, subject to due precautions against disclosure of information to rivals in trade, require the production before him of books and documents relating to the matter in issue.

(11) All orders of the comptroller under this section shall be subject to appeal to the Court, and on any such appeal the law officer or such other counsel as he may appoint shall be entitled to appear and be heard.

(12) In any case where the comptroller does not dismiss an application as hereinbefore provided, and

(*a*) if the parties interested consent, or

(*b*) if the proceedings require any prolonged examination of documents or any scientific or local investigation which cannot in the opinion of the comptroller conveniently be made before him;

A.D. 1919

the comptroller may at any time order the whole proceedings or any question or issue of fact arising thereunder to be referred to an arbitrator agreed on by the parties, or in default of agreement appointed by the comptroller, and, where the whole proceedings are so referred, the award of such arbitrator shall, if all the parties consent, be final, but otherwise shall be subject to the same appeal as the decision of the comptroller under this section, and, where a question or issue of fact is so referred, the arbitrator shall report his findings to the comptroller.

(13) For the purposes of this section, the expression 'patented article' includes articles made by a patented process."

Provision as to patents indorsed "licences of right"

2. For section twenty-four of the principal Act, the following section shall be substituted—

"24.—(1) At any time after the sealing of a patent the comptroller shall, if the patentee so requests, cause the patent to be indorsed with the words 'licences of right,' and a corresponding entry to be made in the register, and thereupon—

(*a*) any person shall at any time thereafter be entitled as of right to a licence under the patent upon such terms as, in default of agreement, may be settled by the comptroller on the application of either the patentee or the applicant:

Provided that any licence the terms of which are settled by agreement shall be deemed, unless otherwise expressly provided, to include the terms and conditions specified in paragraphs (*c*) and (*d*) of this subsection as if they had been imposed by the comptroller thereunder in like manner as if the terms had been settled by the comptroller:

(*b*) in settling the terms of any such licence the comptroller shall be guided by the following considerations—

(i) he shall, on the one hand, endeavour to secure the widest possible user of the invention in the United Kingdom consistent with the patentee deriving a reasonable advantage from his patent rights;

(ii) he shall, on the other hand, endeavour to secure to the patentee the maximum advantage consistent with the invention being worked by the licensee at a reasonable profit in the United Kingdom;

(iii) he shall also endeavour to secure equality of advantage among the several licensees, and for this purpose may, on due cause being shown, reduce the royalties or other payments accruing to the patentee under any licence previously granted:

Provided that, in considering the question of equality of advantage, the comptroller shall take into account any work done or outlay incurred by any previous licensee with a view to testing the commercial value of the invention or to securing the working thereof on a commercial scale in the United Kingdom:

(*c*) any such licence the terms of which are settled by the comptroller may be so framed as to preclude the licensee from importing into the United Kingdom any goods the importation of which, if made by persons other than the patentee or those claiming under him, would be an infringement of the patent, and in such a case the patentee and all licensees under the patent shall be deemed to have mutually covenanted against such importation: A.D. 1919

(*d*) every such licensee shall be entitled to call upon a patentee to take proceedings to prevent the infringement of the patent, and if the patentee refuses, or neglects to do so within two months after being so called upon, the licensee may institute proceedings for the infringement in his own name as though he were patentee, making the patentee a defendant. A patentee so added as defendant shall not be liable for any costs unless he enters an appearance and takes part in the proceedings. Service on him may be effected by leaving the writ at his address for service given on the register:

(*e*) if in any action for infringement of a patent so indorsed the infringing defendant is ready and willing to take a licence upon terms to be settled by the comptroller, no injunction against him shall be awarded, and the amount recoverable against him by way of damages (if any) shall not exceed double the amount which would have been recoverable against him as licensee if the licence had been dated prior to the earliest infringement:

Provided that this paragraph shall not apply where the infringement consists of the importation of infringing goods:

(*f*) the renewal fees payable by the patentee of a patent so indorsed shall, as from the date of the indorsement, be one moiety only of the fees which would otherwise have been payable.

(2) The comptroller shall, before acting on any request to indorse a patent made by the patentee under this section, advertise such request in the Illustrated Official Journal (Patents), and shall satisfy himself that the patentee is not precluded by contract from making such request, and for that purpose shall require from the patentee such evidence, by statutory declaration or otherwise, as he may deem necessary:

Provided that a patentee shall not be deemed to be so precluded by reason only of his having granted a licence under the patent where the licence does not limit his right to grant other licences.

(3) Any person, alleging that a request under this section has been made contrary to some contract in which he is interested, may apply to the comptroller within the prescribed time and in the prescribed manner, and the comptroller, if satisfied of the truth of such allegation, shall refuse to indorse the patent pursuant to the request or shall cause the indorsement, if already made, to be cancelled.

Any order under this subsection shall be subject to appeal to the court.

(4) All indorsements of patents under this section shall be entered on the register of patents and shall be published in the Illustrated Official Journal (Patents), and in such other manner as to the comptroller may seem desirable for the purpose of bringing the invention to the notice of manufacturers.

A.D. 1919

(5) If at any time it appears that in the case of a patent so indorsed there is no existing licence the comptroller may, if he thinks fit, on the application of the patentee and on payment by him of the unpaid moiety of all renewal fees which have become due since the indorsement, after due notice cancel the indorsement, and in that case the patentee's rights and liabilities shall be the same as if no such indorsement had been made."

Enforcement of order for grant of licence

3. After section twenty-seven of the principal Act, the following section shall be inserted—

"27A. Any order for the grant of a licence under this Act shall, without prejudice to any other method of enforcement, operate as if it were embodied in a deed granting a licence executed by the patentee and all other necessary parties."

Amendment of s. 11 of principal Act as to opposition to grant of patent

4. For paragraph (*b*) of subsection (1) of section eleven of the principal Act, which relates to the opposition to grants of patents, the following paragraphs shall be substituted—

"(*b*) that the invention has been published in any complete specification, or in any provisional specification followed by a complete specification, deposited pursuant to any application made in the United Kingdom within fifty years next before the date of the application for the patent the grant of which is being opposed, or has been made available to the public by publication in any document (other than a British specification) published in the United Kingdom prior to the application; or

(*bb*) that the invention has been claimed in any complete specification for a British patent which though not published at the date of the application for a patent the grant of which is opposed was deposited pursuant to an application for a patent which is or will be of prior date to such patent; or"

and after paragraph (*d*) of the same subsection the following paragraph shall be inserted—

"or (*e*) that in the case of an application under section ninety-one of this Act the specification describes or claims an invention other than that for which protection has been applied for in a foreign state or British possession and that such other invention forms the subject of an application made by the opponent in the interval between the leaving of the application in the foreign state or British possession and the leaving of the application in the United Kingdom."

Amendment of s. 12 of principal Act as to grant and sealing of patents

5. At the end of subsection (1) of section twelve of the principal Act, which relates to the grant and sealing of patents, the following proviso shall be added—

"Provided that where—

"(*a*) an applicant has agreed in writing to assign a patent when granted to another party or a joint applicant and refuses to proceed with the application; or

(*b*) disputes arise between joint applicants as to proceeding with an application;

the comptroller on proof of such agreement to his satisfaction, or if satisfied that one or more of such joint applicants ought to be allowed to proceed alone, may allow such other party or joint applicant to proceed with the application, and may grant a patent to him, so however that all parties interested shall be entitled to be heard before the comptroller, and an appeal shall lie from the decision of the comptroller under this proviso to the law officer." A.D. 1919

Term of patent

6.—(1) The term limiting the duration of patents shall be increased from fourteen to sixteen years, and accordingly in subsection (1) of section seventeen of the principal Act, for the word " fourteen " there shall be substituted the word " sixteen."

(2) Any patent the original term of which had not expired at the date of the commencement of this Act shall have effect as if the term mentioned therein was sixteen years instead of fourteen years, subject to the following conditions—

(*a*) any licence existing at that date which has been granted for the term of the patent shall be treated as having been granted for the term as so extended if the licensee so desires;

(*b*) if the patent would, apart from this section, have expired on or before the first day of January nineteen hundred and twenty, the patent shall, during the period of extension, be subject to all the provisions by this Act substituted for section twenty-four of the principal Act (except subsection (5) thereof) as if the patent had been endorsed " licences of right."

(3) Where any party to a contract with the patentee or any other person, entered into before the nineteenth day of November nineteen hundred and seventeen, is subjected to loss or liability by reason of the extension of the term of any patent under the provisions of this section, the court shall have power to determine in what manner and by which parties such loss or liability shall be borne.

Amendment of s. 18 of principal Act as to extension of term of patent

7.—(1) At the end of subsection (1) of section eighteen of the principal Act which relates to the extension of the term of a patent, the following proviso shall be inserted—

" Provided that the court may in its discretion extend such period within which such a petition may be presented."

(2) In subsection (5) of the same section, for the words " for a further term not exceeding seven years, or, in exceptional cases, fourteen years," there shall be substituted the words "for a further term not exceeding five years, or, in exceptional cases, ten years."

(3) At the end of the same section, the following subsection shall be added—

" (6) Where, by reason of hostilities between His Majesty and any foreign state, the patentee as such has suffered loss or damage (including loss of opportunity of dealing in or developing his invention owing to his having been engaged in work of national importance connected with such hostilities) an application under this section may be made by originating summons instead of by petition, and the court in considering its decision may have regard solely to the loss or damage so suffered by the patentee:

Provided that this subsection shall not apply if

A.D. 1919

the patentee is a subject of such foreign state as aforesaid, or is a company the business whereof is managed or controlled by such subjects or is carried on wholly or mainly for the benefit or on behalf of such subjects, notwithstanding that the company may be registered within His Majesty's Dominions."

Right of Crown to use patented inventions

8. For section twenty-nine of the principal Act, the following section shall be substituted—

"29.—(1) A patent shall have to all intents the like effect as against His Majesty the King as it has against a subject:

"Provided that any Government department may, by themselves or by such of their agents, contractors, or others as may be authorized in writing by them at any time after the application, make, use or exercise the invention for the services of the Crown on such terms as may, either before or after the use thereof, be agreed on, with the approval of the Treasury, between the department and the patentee, or, in default of agreement, as may be settled in the manner hereinafter provided. And the terms of any agreement or licence concluded between the inventor or patentee and any person other than a Government department, shall be inoperative so far as concerns the making, use or exercise of the invention for the service of the Crown:

"Provided further that, where an invention which is the subject of any patent has, before the date of the patent, been duly recorded in a document by, or tried by or on behalf of, any Government department (such invention not having been communicated directly or indirectly by the applicant for the patent or the patentee), any Government department, or such of their agents, contractors, or others, as may be authorized in writing by them, may make, use and exercise the invention so recorded or tried for the service of the Crown, free of any royalty or other payment to the patentee, notwithstanding the existence of the patent. If in the opinion of the department the disclosure to the applicant or the patentee, as the case may be, of the document recording the invention, or the evidence of the trial thereof, if required, would be detrimental to the public interest, it may be made confidentially to counsel on behalf of the applicant or patentee, or to any independent expert mutually agreed upon.

"(2) In case of any dispute as to the making, use or exercise of an invention under this section, or the terms therefor, or as to the existence or scope of any record or trial as aforesaid, the matter shall be referred to the court for decision, who shall have power to refer the whole matter or any question or issue of fact arising thereon to be tried before a special or official referee or an arbitrator upon such terms as it may direct. The court, referee, or arbitrator, as the case may be, may, with the consent of the parties, take into consideration the validity of the patent for the purposes only of the reference and for the determination of the issues between the applicant and such Government department. The court, referee, or arbitrator, further in settling the terms as aforesaid, shall be entitled to take into consideration any benefit or compensation which the patentee, or any other person interested in the patent, may have received directly or indirectly from the Crown or from any Government department in respect of such patent.

" (3) The right to use an invention for the services of the Crown under the provisions of this section or any provisions for which this section is substituted shall include, and shall be deemed always to have included, the power to sell any articles made in pursuance of such right which are no longer required for the services of the Crown. A.D. 1919

" (4) Nothing in this section shall affect the right of the Crown or of any person deriving title directly or indirectly from the Crown to sell or use any articles forfeited under the laws relating to the customs or excise."

Power of court to grant relief in respect of particular claims

9. After section thirty-two of the principal Act the following section shall be inserted—

" 32A. Notwithstanding anything to the contrary appearing in section twenty-three of this Act, if the court in any action for infringement of a patent finds that any one or more of the claims in the specification, in respect of which infringement is alleged, are valid, it shall, subject to its discretion as to costs and as to the date from which damages should be reckoned, and to such terms as to amendment as it may deem desirable, grant relief in respect of any of such claims which are infringed without regard to the invalidity of any other claim in the specification. In exercising such discretion, the court may take into consideration the conduct of the parties in inserting such invalid claims in the specification or permitting them to remain there."

Amendment of s. 34 of principal Act as to actions for infringement

10. In section thirty-four of the principal Act, which relates to actions for infringement of a patent, after the words, "infringement of a patent" there shall be inserted the words, "the plaintiff shall be entitled to relief by way of injunction and damages but not to an account of profits, but subject as aforesaid."

Chemical products and substances intended for food or medicine

11.—(1) After section thirty-eight of the principal Act, the following section shall be inserted—

" 38A.—(1) In the case of inventions relating to substances prepared or produced by chemical processes or intended for food or medicine, the specification shall not include claims for the substance itself, except when prepared or produced by the special methods or processes of manufacture described and claimed or by their obvious chemical equivalents: Provided that, in an action for infringement of a patent where the invention relates to the production of a new substance, any substance of the same chemical composition and constitution shall in the absence of proof to the contrary be deemed to have been produced by the patented process.

(2) In the case of any patent for an invention intended for or capable of being used for the preparation or production of food or medicine, the comptroller shall, unless he sees good reason to the contrary, grant to any person applying for the same, a licence limited to the use of the invention for the purposes of the preparation or production of food or medicine but not otherwise; and, in settling the terms of such licence and fixing the amount of royalty or other consideration payable, the comptroller shall have regard to the desirability of making the food or medicine available to the public at the lowest possible price consistent with giving

A.D. 1919

to the inventor due reward for the research leading to the invention.

Any decision of the comptroller under this subsection shall be subject to appeal to the court."

(2) This section shall apply only to patents applied for after the passing of this Act.

Costs and security for costs

12. Section thirty-nine of the principal Act, which relates to costs and security for costs, shall be repealed, and in lieu thereof the following section shall be inserted after section seventy-three—

"73A.—(1) The comptroller shall, in any proceedings before him under this Act, have power by order to award to any party such costs as he may consider reasonable, and to direct how and by what parties they are to be paid, and any such order may be made a rule of court.

(2) If any party giving notice of any opposition under this Act, or applying to the comptroller for the revocation of a patent, or giving notice of appeal from any decision of the comptroller under this Act, neither resides nor carries on business in the United Kingdom or the Isle of Man, the comptroller, or in case of appeal to the law officer or the court, the law officer or the court may require such party to give security for the costs of the proceedings or appeal, and in default of such security being given may proceed to treat the proceedings or appeal as abandoned."

Amendment of s. 41 (2) of principal Act as to anticipation

13.—(1) At the end of subsection (2) of section forty-one of the principal Act, the following proviso shall be added—

"Provided that the protection afforded by this subsection shall not extend to a patentee who has commercially worked his invention in the United Kingdom otherwise than for the purpose of reasonable trial of the invention prior to the application for the patent."

(2) This section shall not apply in the case of patents granted before the passing of this Act.

Cancellation of registration of designs

14. For section fifty-eight of the principal Act, which relates to the cancellation of the registration of designs, the following section shall be substituted—

"58.—(1) At any time after the registration of a design any person interested may apply to the comptroller for the cancellation of the registration of the design, on either of the following grounds—

(*a*) That the design has been published in the United Kingdom prior to the date of registration:

(*b*) That the design is applied by manufacture to any article in a foreign country, and is not so applied by manufacture in the United Kingdom to such an extent as is reasonable in the circumstances of the case:

Provided that, if the application be on the last-mentioned ground, and the comptroller is satisfied that the time which has elapsed from the date of registration has been insufficient for such application by manufacture in the United Kingdom, the comptroller may adjourn the application for such time as he may deem sufficient for that purpose; and that in lieu of cancellation the comptroller may order the grant of a compulsory licence on such terms as he may consider just. A.D. 1919

(2) An appeal shall lie from any order or the comptroller under this section to the court, and the comptroller may at any time refer any such application to the court for trial."

15. After section fifty-eight of the principal Act, the following section shall be inserted— Registration of designs to bind the Crown

" 58A. The registration of a design shall have to all intents the like effect as against His Majesty the King as it has against a subject:

" Provided that the provisions of section twenty-nine of this Act shall apply to registered designs as though those provisions were herein re-enacted and in terms made applicable to registered designs."

16. For section seventy-one of the principal Act the following section shall be substituted— Registration of assignments etc.

71.—(1) Where a person becomes entitled by assignment, transmission, or other operation of law to a patent or to the copyright in a registered design, he shall make application to the comptroller to register his title, and the comptroller shall, on receipt of such application and on proof of title to his satisfaction, register him as the proprietor of such patent or design and shall cause an entry to be made in the prescribed manner on the register of the assignment, transmission, or other instrument affecting the title.

(2) Where any person becomes entitled as mortgagee, licensee, or otherwise to any interest in a patent or design, he shall make application to the comptroller to register his title, and the comptroller shall, on receipt of such application and on proof of title to his satisfaction, cause notice of the interest to be entered in the prescribed manner in the register of patents or designs, as the case may be, with particulars of the instrument, if any, creating such interest.

(3) The person registered as the proprietor of a patent or design shall, subject to the provisions of the Act and to any rights appearing from the register to be vested in any other person, have power absolutely to assign, grant licences as to or otherwise deal with the patent or design, and to give effectual receipts for any consideration for any such assignment, licence or dealing:

Provided that any equities in respect of the patent or design may be enforced in like manner as in respect of any other personal property.

(4) Except in applications made under section seventy-two of this Act, a document or instrument in respect of which no entry has been made in the register in accordance with the provisions of subsections (1) and (2) aforesaid, shall not be admitted in evidence in any court in proof of the title to a patent or copyright in a design or to any interest therein unless the court otherwise directs.

17. At the end of section seventy-five of the principal Act, which relates to the powers of the comptroller to refuse to grant patents and to register designs, there shall be inserted the following words, " an appeal shall lie from the decision of the " comptroller under this section to the law officer." Amendment of s. 75 of principal Act as to refusal to grant patents, etc.

A.D. 1919

Registration of patent agents

18. For section eighty-four of the principal Act, which relates to the registration of patent agents, the following section shall be substituted—

" 84.—(1) No person shall practise, describe himself, or hold himself out, or permit himself to be described or held out, as a patent agent, unless—

(*a*) in the case of an individual, he is registered as a patent agent in the register of patent agents;
(*b*) in the case of a firm, every partner of the firm is so registered;
(*c*) in the case of a company which commenced to carry on business as a patent agent after the seventeenth day of November nineteen hundred and seventeen, every director and the manager (if any) of the company is so registered;
(*d*) in the case of a company which commenced to carry on business as a patent agent before that date, a manager or a director of the company is so registered:

Provided that in the last-mentioned case the name of such manager or director shall be mentioned as being a registered patent agent in all professional advertisements, circulars or letters in which the name of the company appears.

(2) Every individual not registered as a patent agent before the fifteenth day of July nineteen hundred and nineteen who proves to the satisfaction of the Board of Trade that prior to the first day of August nineteen hundred and seventeen he was *bona fide* practising as a patent agent, whether individually or as member of a firm, or as a manager or director of an incorporated company, shall be entitled to be registered as a patent agent if he makes an application for the purpose within such time as may be fixed by the Board of Trade, unless after giving an applicant an opportunity of being heard the Board of Trade are satisfied that he has whilst so practising been guilty of such misconduct as would have rendered him liable, if his name had been on the register of patent agents, to have his name erased therefrom.

(3) If any person contravenes the provisions of this section, he shall be liable on conviction under the Summary Jurisdiction Acts to a fine not exceeding twenty pounds, and in the case of a company every director, manager, secretary, or other officer of the company who is knowingly a party to the contravention shall be guilty of a like offence and liable to a like fine.

(4) For the purposes of this section, the expression " patent agent " means a person, firm, or company carrying on for gain in the United Kingdom the business of applying for or obtaining patents in the United Kingdom or elsewhere.

(5) Nothing in this section shall be taken to prohibit solicitors from taking such part as they have heretofore taken in any proceedings under this Act.

(6) No person not registered before the fifteenth day of July nineteen hundred and nineteen shall be registered as a patent agent unless he be a British subject."

Definitions

19. In section ninety-thrce of the principal Act, for the

definitions of " patentee " and " design " the following definitions shall respectively be substituted— A.D. 1919

" Patentee " means the person for the time being entered on the register as the grantee or proprietor of the patent ;

" Design " means only the features of shape, configuration, pattern, or ornament applied to any article by any industrial process or means, whether manual, mechanical, or chemical, separate or combined, which in the finished article appeal to and are judged solely by the eye ; but does not include any mode or principle of construction, or anything which is in substance a mere mechanical device.

In the same section the following definition shall be inserted—

" Working on a commercial scale " means the manufacture of the article or the carrying on of the process described and claimed in a specification for a patent in or by means of a definite and substantial establishment or organisation, and on a scale which is adequate and reasonable under all the circumstances.

Minor amendments of principal Act

20. The amendments specified in the second column of the Schedule to this Act, which relate to minor details, shall be made in the provisions of the principal Act specified in the first column of that schedule.

Construction, printing, and repeal

21.—(1) This Act shall, except where otherwise expressly provided, apply to patents granted and applications for and specifications relating to patents made and deposited, and designs registered, before as well as after the passing of this Act.

(2) Where by this Act any enactments or words are directed to be added to or omitted from the principal Act, or to be substituted for any other enactments or words in the principal Act, copies of the principal Act printed under the authority of His Majesty's Stationery Office after such direction takes effect may be printed with the enactments or words added or omitted, or substituted for other enactments or words as such direction requires, and with the sections, subsections, and paragraphs thereof numbered in accordance with such directions ; and the principal Act shall be construed as if it had at the time at which such direction takes effect been made with such addition, omission, or substitution.

(3) A reference in any Act of Parliament or other instrument to the principal Act shall, unless the context otherwise requires, be construed to refer to the principal Act as amended by this Act.

(4) The Patents and Designs Act, 1908, is hereby repealed.

Short title and commencement

22.—(1) This Act may be cited as the Patents and Designs Act, 1919, and the principal Act and this Act may be cited together as the Patents and Designs Acts, 1907 and 1919.

(2) The provisions by sections one and two of this Act substituted for sections twenty-seven and twenty-four of the principal Act shall not come into operation until such time, not being later than one year after the passing of this Act, as may be fixed by order of the Board of Trade, except so far as the provisions so substituted for the said section twenty-four are by subsection (2) of section six of this Act applied to the patents

A.D. 1919

therein mentioned; and the provisions of this Act relating to the terms on which an invention or registered design can be made, used or exercised by or on behalf of a Government department shall not come into operation until such time as may be fixed by order of the Board of Trade; save as aforesaid this Act shall come into operation on the passing thereof.

Section 20

SCHEDULE

Minor Amendments of Principal Act

Section Amended.	Nature of Amendment.
Section 5 .	In subsection (1) for the word "six" there shall be substituted the word "nine."
Section 6 .	In the proviso to subsection (3) for the words "treat the claim" there shall be substituted the words "allow an application"; and after the words "included in the complete specification" there shall be inserted the words "to be made and treated."
	In subsection (4) for the words "A refusal of the comptroller to accept a complete specification shall be subject to appeal" there shall be substituted the words "An appeal shall lie from the decision of the comptroller under this section."
	In subsection (5) for the word "twelve" there shall be substituted the word "fifteen."
Section 7 .	In subsection (4) the words "after hearing the applicant and" shall be omitted.
	Subsection (6) shall be omitted.
Section 8 .	For subsection (1) the following subsection shall be substituted— "(1) In addition to the investigation under the last preceding section, the examiner shall make an investigation for the purpose of ascertaining whether the invention claimed has been wholly or in part claimed in any specification published on or after the date of the application and deposited pursuant to a prior application.
	For the words in subsection (2) down to and including "deposited pursuant to a prior application" there shall be substituted the words "Where on such further investigation it appears that the invention claimed has been wholly or in part claimed in any such specification."
	Subsection (4) shall be omitted and after subsection (3) the following subsections shall be inserted— "(4) An appeal shall lie from the decision of the comptroller under this section to the law officer.

Section Amended.	Nature of Amendment.
	"(5) The investigations and reports required by this and the last preceding section shall not be held in any way to guarantee the validity of any patent and no liability shall be incurred by the Board of Trade or any officer thereof by reason of or in connection with any such investigation or report or any proceedings consequent thereon."
Section 12 .	In subsection (2) for the word "fifteen" in both places where it occurs there shall be substituted the word "eighteen." In paragraph (*b*) of the same subsection, after the words "as the law officer" there shall be inserted the words "or the comptroller as the case may be." In paragraph (*d*) of the same subsection for the words "in consequence of the neglect or failure of the applicant to pay any fee" there shall be substituted the words "for any reason."
Section 13 .	For the word "publication" there shall be substituted the word "acceptance."
Section 15 .	In subsection (2) for the words "on the ground of fraud" there shall be substituted the words "by the court on the ground that it has been obtained in fraud of the true and first inventor or where the grant has been refused by the comptroller under the provisions of paragraph (*a*) of subsection (1) of section eleven of this Act or revoked on the same ground under the provisions of section twenty-six of this Act." In the same subsection after the words "grant to him a patent" there shall be inserted the words "for the whole or any part of the invention," and after the words "patent so revoked" there shall be inserted the words "or as would have been borne by the patent if the grant thereof had not been refused."
Section 16 .	In subsection (2) for the words "and for the purpose of the provisions of this Act with respect to oppositions to the grant of patents" there shall be substituted the words "and in determining other questions under this Act."
Section 19 .	At the end of subsection (3) the following proviso shall be inserted— "Provided that, if the patent for the original invention is revoked, then the patent of addition shall, if the court or

A.D. 1919
Section 20

Section Amended.	Nature of Amendment.
	comptroller so orders, become an independent patent, and the fees payable, and the dates when they become payable shall be determined by its date, but its duration shall not exceed the unexpired term of the patent for the original invention."
Section 20 .	In subsection (5) the words " subject to an appeal to the court " shall be omitted, and after that subsection there shall be inserted the following subsection— " (6) An appeal shall lie from the decision of the comptroller under this section to the court."
Section 21 .	At the end of subsection (7) the following proviso shall be inserted— " Provided that the court shall be entitled in construing a specification as amended to refer to the specification as accepted and published."
Section 22 .	After the words " by way of disclaimer " there shall be inserted the words " correction or explanation."
Section 23 .	For the words " before the disclaimer correction or explanation," there shall be substituted the words " before the date of the decision allowing the amendment."
Section 25 .	In subsection (2) at the end of paragraph (*a*) the word " or " and paragraph (*b*) shall be omitted.
Section 26 .	In subsection (1) the words " in the prescribed manner " shall be omitted.
Section 31 .	In subsection (1) for the word " either " there shall be substituted the word " all."
Section 34 .	For the words " inspection or account " there shall be substituted the words " or inspection."
Section 35 .	For the words " validity of the patent " there shall be substituted the words " validity of any claim in the specification of the patent." After the words " subsequent action for infringement " there shall be inserted the words " of such claim," and after the words " solicitor and client " there shall be inserted the words " so far as that claim is concerned."
Section 36 .	For the words " to be the patentee of an invention " there shall be substituted the words " to have an interest in a patent." For the words " any legal rights of the person making such threats " there shall be substituted the words " the patent."

Section Amended.	Nature of Amendment.
	For the proviso there shall be substituted the following proviso— " Provided that this section shall not apply if an action for infringement of the patent is commenced and prosecuted with due diligence."
Section 38	After subsection (1) there shall be inserted the following paragraph— " In any action, application, or proceedings under this Act no person shall be estopped from applying for or obtaining relief by reason of any admission made by him as to the reasonableness of the terms offered to him under subsection (1) (i)."
Section 45 (1).	After the word " inventor " where it first occurs, there shall be inserted the words " or the reading of a paper by an inventor before a learned society or the publication of the paper in the society's transactions." In proviso (*a*) after the word " invention " there shall be inserted the words " or the person reading such paper or permitting such publication." At the end of proviso (*b*) there shall be inserted the words " or the reading or publication of such paper."
Section 49 (3).	For the words " Board of Trade " and " Board " respectively, there shall be substituted the word " Court " and after the words " any such refusal may " there shall be inserted the words " except where the refusal is given on a ground mentioned in section seventy-five of this Act."
Section 50 .	In paragraph (*a*) for the words " new and original " there shall be substituted the words " new or original " and at the end of the section there shall be inserted the following proviso— " Provided that such subsequent registration shall not extend the period of copyright in the design beyond that arising from the previous registration."
Section 68 .	At the end of the section there shall be inserted the following proviso— " Provided that, on application being made by any person in the prescribed form, the comptroller may disclose the result of a search made under section seven or eight of this Act on any particular application for the grant of a patent."
Section 77 .	In subsection (2) after the words " on oath "

A.D. 1919

Section 20

Section Amended.	Nature of Amendment.
	there shall be inserted the words "and discovery and production of documents."
Section 91 .	In subsection (5) for the word "and" there shall be substituted the word "or."
Section 92 .	In subsection (2) after the words "the appeal shall" there shall be inserted the words "except in the case of a petition for the revocation of a patent under section twenty-five of this Act, and"; and for the words "and the decision of that judge" to the end of the subsection there shall be substituted the words "an appeal shall not lie from any decision of such judge except in the case of an order revoking or confirming the revocation of a patent."
Section 93 .	For the words "Proprietor of a new and original design" there shall be substituted the words "Proprietor of a new or original design."
Section 94 .	For subsection (5) the following subsection shall be substituted— "(5) Notwithstanding anything in this Act, the expression 'the Court' shall in reference to proceedings in Scotland for the extension of the term of a patent mean any Lord Ordinary of the Court of Session."

APPENDIX IV

COPYRIGHT ACT, 1911.

[1 & 2 Geo. V, Ch. 46]

Chapter 46

An Act to amend and consolidate the Law relating to Copyright. [16th December, 1911.] A.D. 1911

Be it enacted by the King's most Excellent Majesty, by and with the advice and consent of the Lords Spiritual and Temporal, and Commons, in this present Parliament assembled, and by the authority of the same, as follows—

Part I.

Imperial Copyright.

Rights.

1.—(1) Subject to the provisions of this Act, copyright shall subsist throughout the parts of His Majesty's dominions to which this Act extends for the term herein-after mentioned in every original literary dramatic musical and artistic work, if— **Copyright**

(*a*) in the case of a published work, the work was first published within such parts of His Majesty's dominions as aforesaid: and

(*b*) in the case of an unpublished work, the author was at the date of the making of the work a British subject or resident within such parts of His Majesty's dominions as aforesaid;

but in no other works, except so far as the protection conferred by this Act is extended by Orders in Council thereunder relating to self-governing dominions to which this Act does not extend and to foreign countries.

(2) For the purposes of this Act, "copyright" means the sole right to produce or reproduce the work or any substantial part thereof in any material form whatsoever, to perform, or in the case of a lecture to deliver, the work or any substantial part thereof in public; if the work is unpublished, to publish the work or any substantial part thereof; and shall include the sole right,—

(*a*) to produce, reproduce, perform, or publish any translation of the work;

(*b*) in the case of a dramatic work, to convert it into a novel or other non-dramatic work;

(*c*) in the case of a novel or other non-dramatic work, or of an artistic work, to convert it into a dramatic work, by way of performance in public or otherwise;

(*d*) in the case of a literary, dramatic, or musical work, to make any record, perforated roll, cinematograph film, or other contrivance by means of which the work may be mechanically performed or delivered,

and to authorize any such acts as aforesaid.

16—(1790)

A.D. 1911

(3) For the purposes of this Act, publication, in relation to any work, means the issue of copies of the work to the public, and does not include the performance in public of a dramatic or musical work, the delivery in public of a lecture, the exhibition in public of an artistic work, or the construction of an architectural work of art, but, for the purposes of this provision, the issue of photographs and engravings of works of sculpture and architectural works of art shall not be deemed to be publication of such works.

Infringement of copyright

2.—(1) Copyright in a work shall be deemed to be infringed by any person who, without the consent of the owner of the copyright, does anything the sole right to do which is by this Act conferred on the owner of the copyright: Provided that the following acts shall not constitute an infringement of copyright:—

(i) Any fair dealing with any work for the purposes of private study, research, criticism, review, or newspaper summary:

(ii) Where the author of an artistic work is not the owner of the copyright therein, the use by the author of any mould, cast, sketch, plan, model, or study made by him for the purpose of the work, provided that he does not thereby repeat or imitate the main design of that work:

(iii) The making or publishing of paintings, drawings, engravings, or photographs of a work of sculpture or artistic craftsmanship, if permanently situate in a public place or building, or the making or publishing of paintings, drawings, engravings, or photographs (which are not in the nature of architectural drawings or plans) of any architectural work of art:

(iv) The publication in a collection, mainly composed of non-copyright matter, *bona fide* intended for the use of schools, and so described in the title and in any advertisements issued by the publisher, of short passages from published literary works not themselves published for the use of schools in which copyright subsists: Provided that not more than two of such passages from works by the same author are published by the same publisher within five years, and that the source from which such passages are taken is acknowledged:

(v) The publication in a newspaper of a report of a lecture delivered in public, unless the report is prohibited by conspicuous written or printed notice affixed before and maintained during the lecture at or about the main entrance of the building in which the lecture is given, and, except whilst the building is being used for public worship, in a position near the lecturer; but nothing in this paragraph shall affect the provisions in paragraph (i) as to newspaper summaries:

(vi) The reading or recitation in public by one person of any reasonable extract from any published work.

(2) Copyright in a work shall also be deemed to be infringed by any person who—

(*a*) sells or lets for hire, or by way of trade exposes or offers for sale or hire; or

A.D. 1911

(b) distributes either for the purposes of trade or to such an extent as to affect prejudicially the owner of the copyright; or
(c) by way of trade exhibits in public; or
(d) imports for sale or hire into any part of His Majesty's dominions to which this Act extends,

any work which to his knowledge infringes copyright or would infringe copyright if it had been made within the part of His Majesty's dominions in or into which the sale or hiring, exposure, offering for sale or hire, distribution, exhibition, or importation took place.

(3) Copyright in a work shall also be deemed to be infringed by any person who for his private profit permits a theatre or other place of entertainment to be used for the performance in public of the work without the consent of the owner of the copyright, unless he was not aware, and had no reasonable ground for suspecting, that the performance would be an infringement of copyright.

Term of copyright

3. The term for which copyright shall subsist shall, except as otherwise expressly provided by this Act, be the life of the author and a period of fifty years after his death:

Provided that at any time after the expiration of twenty-five years, or in the case of a work in which copyright subsists at the passing of this Act thirty years, from the death of the author of a published work, copyright in the work shall not be deemed to be infringed by the reproduction of the work for sale if the person reproducing the work proves that he has given the prescribed notice in writing of his intention to reproduce the work, and that he has paid in the prescribed manner to, or for the benefit of, the owner of the copyright royalties in respect of all copies of the work sold by him calculated at the rate of ten per cent. on the price at which he publishes the work; and, for the purposes of this proviso, the Board of Trade may make regulations prescribing the mode in which notices are to be given, and the particulars to be given in such notices, and the mode, time, and frequency of the payment of royalties, including (if they think fit) regulations requiring payment in advance or otherwise securing the payment of royalties.

Compulsory licences

4. If at any time after the death of the author of a literary, dramatic, or musical work which has been published or performed in public a complaint is made to the Judicial Committee of the Privy Council that the owner of the copyright in the work has refused to republish or to allow the republication of the work or has refused to allow the performance in public of the work, and that by reason of such refusal the work is withheld from the public, the owner of the copyright may be ordered to grant a licence to reproduce the work or perform the work in public, as the case may be, on such terms and subject to such conditions as the Judicial Committee may think fit.

Ownership of copyright, etc.

5.—(1) Subject to the provisions of this Act, the author of a work shall be the first owner of the copyright therein:

Provided that—

(a) where, in the case of an engraving, photograph, or portrait, the plate or other original was ordered by some other person and was made for valuable consideration in pursuance of that order, then, in the

A.D. 1911

absence of any agreement to the contrary, the person by whom such plate or other original was ordered shall be the first owner of the copyright; and

(b) where the author was in the employment of some other person under a contract of service or apprenticeship and the work was made in the course of his employment by that person, the person by whom the author was employed shall, in the absence of any agreement to the contrary, be the first owner of the copyright, but where the work is an article or other contribution to a newspaper, magazine, or similar periodical, there shall, in the absence of any agreement to the contrary, be deemed to be reserved to the author a right to restrain the publication of the work, otherwise than as part of a newspaper, magazine, or similar periodical.

(2) The owner of the copyright in any work may assign the right, either wholly or partially, and either generally or subject to limitations to the United Kingdom or any self-governing dominion or other part of His Majesty's dominions to which this Act extends, and either for the whole term of the copyright or for any part thereof, and may grant any interest in the right by licence, but no such assignment or grant shall be valid unless it is in writing signed by the owner of the right in respect of which the assignment or grant is made, or by his duly authorized agent:

Provided that, where the author of a work is the first owner of the copyright therein, no assignment of the copyright, and no grant of any interest therein, made by him (otherwise than by will) after the passing of this Act, shall be operative to vest in the assignee or grantee any rights with respect to the copyright in the work beyond the expiration of twenty-five years from the death of the author, and the reversionary interest in the copyright expectant on the termination of that period shall, on the death of the author, notwithstanding any agreement to the contrary, devolve on his legal personal representatives as part of his estate, and any agreement entered into by him as to the disposition of such reversionary interest shall be null and void, but nothing in this proviso shall be construed as applying to the assignment of the copyright in a collective work or a licence to publish a work or part of a work as part of a collective work.

(3) Where, under any partial assignment of copyright, the assignee becomes entitled to any right comprised in copyright, the assignee as respects the right so assigned, and the assignor as respects the rights not assigned, shall be treated for the purposes of this Act as the owner of the copyright, and the provisions of this Act shall have effect accordingly.

Civil Remedies.

Civil remedies for infringement of copyright

6.—(1) Where copyright in any work has been infringed, the owner of the copyright shall, except as otherwise provided by this Act, be entitled to all such remedies by way of injunction or interdict, damages, accounts, and otherwise, as are or may be conferred by law for the infringement of a right.

A.D. 1911

(2) The costs of all parties in any proceedings in respect of the infringement of copyright shall be in the absolute discretion of the Court.

(3) In any action for infringement of copyright in any work, the work shall be presumed to be a work in which copyright subsists and the plaintiff shall be presumed to be the owner of the copyright, unless the defendant puts in issue the existence of the copyright, or, as the case may be, the title of the plaintiff, and where any such question is in issue, then—

(*a*) if a name purporting to be that of the author of the work is printed or otherwise indicated thereon in the usual manner, the person whose name is so printed or indicated shall, unless the contrary is proved, be presumed to be the author of the work;

(*b*) if no name is so printed or indicated, or if the name so printed or indicated is not the author's true name or the name by which he is commonly known, and a name purporting to be that of the publisher or proprietor of the work is printed or otherwise indicated thereon in the usual manner, the person whose name is so printed or indicated shall, unless the contrary is proved, be presumed to be the owner of the copyright in the work for the purposes of proceedings in respect of the infringement of copyright therein.

Rights of owner against persons possessing or dealing with infringing copies, etc.

7. All infringing copies of any work in which copyright subsists, or of any substantial part thereof, and all plates used or intended to be used for the production of such infringing copies, shall be deemed to be the property of the owner of the copyright, who accordingly may take proceedings for the recovery of the possession thereof or in respect of the conversion thereof.

Exemption of innocent infringer from liability to pay damages, etc.

8. Where proceedings are taken in respect of the infringement of the copyright in any work and the defendant in his defence alleges that he was not aware of the existence of the copyright in the work, the plaintiff shall not be entitled to any remedy other than an injunction or interdict in respect of the infringement if the defendant proves that at the date of the infringement he was not aware and had no reasonable ground for suspecting that copyright subsisted in the work.

Restriction on remedies in the case of architecture.

9.—(1) Where the construction of a building or other structure which infringes or which, if completed, would infringe the copyright in some other work has been commenced, the owner of the copyright shall not be entitled to obtain an injunction or interdict to restrain the construction of such building or structure or to order its demolition.

(2) Such of the other provisions of this Act as provide that an infringing copy of a work shall be deemed to be the property of the owner of the copyright, or as impose summary penalties, shall not apply in any case to which this section applies.

Limitation of actions

10. An action in respect of infringement of copyright shall not be commenced after the expiration of three years next after the infringement.

Summary Remedies.

Penalties for dealing with infringing copies, etc.

11.—(1) If any person knowingly—

(*a*) makes for sale or hire any infringing copy of a work in which copyright subsists; or

A.D. 1911

(*b*) sells or lets for hire, or by way of trade exposes or offers for sale or hire any infringing copy of any such work; or

(*c*) distributes infringing copies of any such work either for the purposes of trade or to such an extent as to affect prejudicially the owner of the copyright; or

(*d*) by way of trade exhibits in public any infringing copy of any such work; or

(*e*) imports for sale or hire into the United Kingdom any infringing copy of any such work;

he shall be guilty of an offence under this Act and be liable on summary conviction to a fine not exceeding forty shillings for every copy dealt with in contravention of this section, but not exceeding fifty pounds in respect of the same transaction; or, in the case of a second or subsequent offence, either to such fine or to imprisonment with or without hard labour for a term not exceeding two months.

(2) If any person knowingly makes or has in his possession any plate for the purpose of making infringing copies of any work in which copyright subsists, or knowingly and for his private profit causes any such work to be performed in public without the consent of the owner of the copyright, he shall be guilty of an offence under this Act, and be liable on summary conviction to a fine not exceeding fifty pounds, or, in the case of a second or subsequent offence, either to such fine or to imprisonment with or without hard labour for a term not exceeding two months.

(3) The court before which any such proceedings are taken may, whether the alleged offender is convicted or not, order that all copies of the work or all plates in the possession of the alleged offender, which appear to it to be infringing copies or plates for the purpose of making infringing copies, be destroyed or delivered up to the owner of the copyright or otherwise dealt with as the court may think fit.

2 Edw. VII, c. 15
6 Edw. VII, c. 36

(4) Nothing in this section shall, as respects musical works, affect the provisions of the Musical (Summary Proceedings) Copyright Act, 1902, or the Musical Copyright Act, 1906.

Appeals to quarter sessions

12. Any person aggrieved by a summary conviction of an offence under the foregoing provisions of this Act may in England and Ireland appeal to a court of quarter sessions and in Scotland under and in terms of the Summary Jurisdiction (Scotland) Acts.

Extent of provisions as to summary remedies

13. The provisions of this Act with respect to summary remedies shall extend only to the United Kingdom.

Importation of Copies.

Importation of copies

14.—(1) Copies made out of the United Kingdom of any work in which copyright subsists which if made in the United Kingdom would infringe copyright, and as to which the owner of the copyright gives notice in writing by himself or his agent to the Commissioners of Customs and Excise, that he is desirous that such copies should not be imported into the United Kingdom, shall not be so imported, and shall, subject to the provisions of this section, be deemed to be included in the table of prohibitions and restrictions contained in section forty-two of the Customs Consolidation Act, 1876, and that section shall apply accordingly.

39 & 40 Vict., c. 36

(2) Before detaining any such copies or taking any further

proceedings with a view to the forfeiture thereof under the law relating to the Customs, the Commissioners of Customs and Excise may require the regulations under this section, whether as to information, conditions, or other matters, to be complied with, and may satisfy themselves in accordance with those regulations that the copies are such as are prohibited by this section to be imported.

(3) The Commissioners of Customs and Excise may make regulations, either general or special, respecting the detention and forfeiture of copies the importation of which is prohibited by this section, and the conditions, if any, to be fulfilled before such detention and forfeiture, and may, by such regulations, determine the information, notices, and security to be given, and the evidence requisite for any of the purposes of this section, and the mode of verification of such evidence.

(4) The regulations may apply to copies of all works the importation of copies of which is prohibited by this section, or different regulations may be made respecting different classes of such works.

(5) The regulations may provide for the informant reimbursing the Commissioners of Customs and Excise all expenses and damages incurred in respect of any detention made on his information, and of any proceedings consequent on such detention; and may provide for notices under any enactment repealed by this Act being treated as notices given under this section.

(6) The foregoing provisions of this section shall have effect as if they were part of the Customs Consolidation Act, 1876: Provided that, notwithstanding anything in that Act, the Isle of Man shall not be treated as part of the United Kingdom for the purposes of this section.

(7) This section shall, with the necessary modifications, apply to the importation into a British possession to which this Act extends of copies of works made out of that possession.

Delivery of Books to Libraries.

Delivery of copies to British Museum and other libraries

15.—(1) The publisher of every book published in the United Kingdom shall, within one month after the publication, deliver, at his own expense, a copy of the book to the trustees of the British Museum, who shall give a written receipt for it.

(2) He shall also, if written demand is made before the expiration of twelve months after publication, deliver within one month after receipt of that written demand or, if the demand was made before publication, within one month after publication, to some depot in London named in the demand a copy of the book for, or in accordance with the directions of, the authority having the control of each of the following libraries, namely: the Bodleian Library, Oxford, the University Library, Cambridge, the Library of the Faculty of Advocates at Edinburgh, and the Library of Trinity College, Dublin, and subject to the provisions of this section the National Library of Wales. In the case of an encyclopaedia, newspaper, review, magazine, or work published in a series of numbers or parts, the written demand may include all numbers or parts of the work which may be subsequently published.

(3) The copy delivered to the trustees of the British Museum

A.D. 1911

shall be a copy of the whole book with all maps and illustrations belonging thereto, finished and coloured in the same manner as the best copies of the book are published, and shall be bound, sewed, or stitched together, and on the best paper on which the book is printed.

(4) The copy delivered for the other authorities mentioned in this section shall be on the paper on which the largest number of copies of the book is printed for sale, and shall be in the like condition as the books prepared for sale.

(5) The books of which copies are to be delivered to the National Library of Wales shall not include books of such classes as may be specified in regulations to be made by the Board of Trade.

(6) If a publisher fails to comply with this section, he shall be liable on summary conviction to a fine not exceeding five pounds and the value of the book, and the fine shall be paid to the trustees or authority to whom the book ought to have been delivered.

(7) For the purposes of this section, the expression " book " includes every part or division of a book, pamphlet, sheet of letter-press, sheet of music, map, plan, chart or table separately published, but shall not include any second or subsequent edition of a book unless such edition contains additions or alterations either in the letterpress or in the maps, prints, or other engravings belonging thereto.

Special Provisions as to certain Works.

Works of joint authors

16.—(1) In the case of a work of joint authorship, copyright shall subsist during the life of the author who first dies and for a term of fifty years after his death, or during the life of the author who dies last, whichever period is the longer, and references in this Act to the period after the expiration of any specified number of years from the death of the author shall be construed as references to the period after the expiration of the like number of years from the death of the author who dies first or after the death of the author who dies last, whichever period may be the shorter, and in the provisions of this Act with respect to the grant of compulsory licences a reference to the date of the death of the author who dies last shall be substituted for the reference to the date of the death of the author.

(2) Where, in the case of a work of joint authorship, some one or more of the joint authors do not satisfy the conditions conferring copyright laid down by this Act, the work shall be treated for the purposes of this Act as if the other author or authors had been the sole author or authors thereof :

Provided that the term of the copyright shall be the same as it would have been if all the authors had satisfied such conditions as aforesaid.

(3) For the purposes of this Act, " a work of joint authorship " means a work produced by the collaboration of two or more authors in which the contribution of one author is not distinct from the contribution of the other author or authors.

(4) Where a married woman and her husband are joint authors of a work the interest of such married woman therein shall be her separate property.

A.D. 1911

Posthumous works

17.—(1) In the case of a literary dramatic or musical work, or an engraving, in which copyright subsists at the date of the death of the author or, in the case of a work of joint authorship, at or immediately before the date of the death of the author who dies last, but which has not been published, nor, in the case of a dramatic or musical work, been performed in public, nor, in the case of a lecture, been delivered in public, before that date, copyright shall subsist till publication, or performance or delivery in public, whichever may first happen, and for a term of fifty years thereafter, and the proviso to section three of this Act shall, in the case of such a work, apply as if the author had died at the date of such publication or performance or delivery in public as aforesaid.

(2) The ownership of an author's manuscript after his death, where such ownership has been acquired under a testamentary disposition made by the author and the manuscript is of a work which has not been published nor performed in public nor delivered in public, shall be primâ facie proof of the copyright being with the owner of the manuscript.

Provisions as to Government publications

18. Without prejudice to any rights or privileges of the Crown, where any work has, whether before or after the commencement of this Act, been prepared or published by or under the direction or control of His Majesty or any Government department, the copyright in the work shall, subject to any agreement with the author, belong to His Majesty, and in such case shall continue for a period of fifty years from the date of the first publication of the work.

Provisions as to mechanical instruments

19.—(1) Copyright shall subsist in records, perforated rolls, and other contrivances by means of which sounds may be mechanically reproduced, in like manner as if such contrivances were musical works, but the term of copyright shall be fifty years from the making of the original plate from which the contrivance was directly or indirectly derived, and the person who was the owner of such original plate at the time when such plate was made shall be deemed to be the author of the work, and, where such owner is a body corporate, the body corporate shall be deemed for the purposes of this Act to reside within the parts of His Majesty's dominions to which this Act extends if it has established a place of business within such parts.

(2) It shall not be deemed to be an infringement of copyright in any musical work for any person to make within the parts of His Majesty's dominions to which this Act extends records, perforated rolls, or other contrivances by means of which the work may be mechanically performed, if such person proves—

(*a*) that such contrivances have previously been made by, or with the consent or acquiescence of, the owner of the copyright in the work; and

(*b*) that he has given the prescribed notice of his intention to make the contrivances, and has paid in the prescribed manner to, or for the benefit of, the owner of the copyright in the work royalties in respect of all such contrivances sold by him, calculated at the rate herein-after mentioned :

A.D. 1911

Provided that—

(i) nothing in this provision shall authorize any alterations in, or omissions from, the work reproduced, unless contrivances reproducing the work subject to similar alterations and omissions have been previously made by, or with the consent or acquiescence of, the owner of the copyright, or unless such alterations or omissions are reasonably necessary for the adaptation of the work to the contrivances in question; and

(ii) for the purposes of this provision, a musical work shall be deemed to include any words so closely associated therewith as to form part of the same work, but shall not be deemed to include a contrivance by means of which sounds may be mechanically reproduced.

(3) The rate at which such royalties as aforesaid are to be calculated shall—

(*a*) in the case of contrivances sold within two years after the commencement of this Act by the person making the same, be two and one-half per cent.; and

(*b*) in the case of contrivances sold as aforesaid after the expiration of that period, five per cent.

on the ordinary retail selling price of the contrivance calculated in the prescribed manner, so however that the royalty payable in respect of a contrivance shall, in no case, be less than a half-penny for each separate musical work in which copyright subsists reproduced thereon, and, where the royalty calculated as aforesaid includes a fraction of a farthing, such fraction shall be reckoned as a farthing:

Provided that, if, at any time after the expiration of seven years from the commencement of this Act, it appears to the Board of Trade that such rate as aforesaid is no longer equitable, the Board of Trade may, after holding a public inquiry, make an order either decreasing or increasing that rate to such extent as under the circumstances may seem just, but any order so made shall be provisional only and shall not have any effect unless and until confirmed by Parliament; but, where an order revising the rate has been so made and confirmed, no further revision shall be made before the expiration of fourteen years from the date of the last revision.

(4) If any such contrivance is made reproducing two or more different works in which copyright subsists and the owners of the copyright therein are different persons, the sums payable by way of royalties under this section shall be apportioned amongst the several owners of the copyright in such proportions as, failing agreement, may be determined by arbitration.

(5) When any such contrivances by means of which a musical work may be mechanically performed have been made, then, for the purposes of this section, the owner of the copyright in the work shall, in relation to any person who makes the prescribed inquiries, be deemed to have given his consent to the making of such contrivances if he fails to reply to such inquiries within the prescribed time.

(6) For the purpose of this section, the Board of Trade may make regulations prescribing anything which under this section

is to be prescribed, and prescribing the mode in which notices are to be given and the particulars to be given in such notices, and the mode, time, and frequency of the payment of royalties, and any such regulations may, if the Board think fit, include regulations requiring payment in advance or otherwise securing the payment of royalties. A.D. 1911

(7) In the case of musical works published before the commencement of this Act, the foregoing provisions shall have effect, subject to the following modifications and additions:

(*a*) The conditions as to the previous making by, or with the consent or acquiescence of, the owner of the copyright in the work, and the restrictions as to alterations in or omissions from the work, shall not apply:

(*b*) The rate of two and one-half per cent. shall be substituted for the rate of five per cent. as the rate at which royalties are to be calculated, but no royalties shall be payable in respect of contrivances sold before the first day of July, nineteen hundred and thirteen, if contrivances reproducing the same work had been lawfully made, or placed on sale, within the parts of His Majesty's dominions to which this Act extends before the first day of July, nineteen hundred and ten:

(*c*) Notwithstanding any assignment made before the passing of this Act of the copyright in a musical work, any rights conferred by this Act in respect of the making, or authorizing the making, of contrivances by means of which the work may be mechanically performed shall belong to the author or his legal personal representatives and not to the assignee, and the royalties aforesaid shall be payable to, and for the benefit of, the author of the work or his legal personal representatives:

(*d*) The saving contained in this Act of the rights and interests arising from, or in connexion with, action taken before the commencement of this Act shall not be construed as authorizing any person who has made contrivances by means of which the work may be mechanically performed to sell any such contrivances, whether made before or after the passing of this Act, except on the terms and subject to the conditions laid down in this section:

(*e*) Where the work is a work on which copyright is conferred by an Order in Council relating to a foreign country, the copyright so conferred shall not, except to such extent as may be provided by the Order, include any rights with respect to the making of records, perforated rolls, or other contrivances by means of which the work may be mechanically performed.

(8) Notwithstanding anything in this Act, where a record, perforated roll, or other contrivance by means of which sounds may be mechanically reproduced has been made before the commencement of this Act, copyright shall, as from the commencement of this Act, subsist therein in like manner and for the like term as if this Act had been in force at the date of the making of the original plate from which the contrivance was directly or indirectly derived:

A.D. 1911

Provided that—

(i) the person who, at the commencement of this Act, is the owner of such original plate shall be the first owner of such copyright; and

(ii) nothing in this provision shall be construed as conferring copyright in any such contrivance if the making thereof would have infringed copyright in some other such contrivance, if this provision had been in force at the time of the making of the first-mentioned contrivance.

Provision as to political speeches

20. Notwithstanding anything in this Act, it shall not be an infringement of copyright in an address of a political nature delivered at a public meeting to publish a report thereof in a newspaper.

Provisions as to photographs

21. The term for which copyright shall subsist in photographs shall be fifty years from the making of the original negative from which the photograph was directly or indirectly derived, and the person who was owner of such negative at the time when such negative was made shall be deemed to be the author of the work, and, where such owner is a body corporate, the body corporate shall be deemed for the purposes of this Act to reside within the parts of His Majesty's dominions to which this Act extends if it has established a place of business within such parts.

Provisions as to designs registrable under 7 Edw. VII, c. 29

22.—(1) This Act shall not apply to designs capable of being registered under the Patents and Designs Act, 1907, except designs which, though capable of being so registered, are not used or intended to be used as models or patterns to be multiplied by any industrial process.

(2) General rules under section eighty-six of the Patents and Designs Act, 1907, may be made for determining the conditions under which a design shall be deemed to be used for such purposes as aforesaid.

Works of foreign authors first published in parts of His Majesty's dominions to which Act extends

23. If it appears to His Majesty that a foreign country does not give, or has not undertaken to give, adequate protection to the works of British authors, it shall be lawful for His Majesty by Order in Council to direct that such of the provisions of this Act as confer copyright on works first published within the parts of His Majesty's dominions to which this Act extends, shall not apply to works published after the date specified in the Order, the authors whereof are subjects or citizens of such foreign country, and are not resident in His Majesty's dominions, and thereupon those provisions shall not apply to such works.

Existing works

24.—(1) Where any person is immediately before the commencement of this Act entitled to any such right in any work as is specified in the first column of the First Schedule to this Act, or to any interest in such a right, he shall, as from that date, be entitled to the substituted right set forth in the second column of that schedule, or to the same interest in such a substituted right, and to no other right or interest, and such substituted right shall subsist for the term for which it would have subsisted if this Act had been in force at the date when the work was made and the work had been one entitled to copyright thereunder;

Provided that— A.D. 1911

(*a*) if the author of any work in which any such right as is specified in the first column of the First Schedule to this Act subsists at the commencement of this Act has, before that date, assigned the right or granted any interest therein for the whole term of the right, then at the date when, but for the passing of this Act, the right would have expired the substituted right conferred by this section shall, in the absence of express agreement, pass to the author of the work, and any interest therein created before the commencement of this Act and then subsisting shall determine; but the person who immediately before the date at which the right would so have expired was the owner of the right or interest shall be entitled at his option either—

(i) on giving such notice as herein-after mentioned, to an assignment of the right or the grant of a similar interest therein for the remainder of the term of the right for such consideration as, failing agreement, may be determined by arbitration; or

(ii) without any such assignment or grant, to continue to reproduce or perform the work in like manner as theretofore subject to the payment, if demanded by the author within three years after the date at which the right would have so expired, of such royalties to the author as, failing agreement, may be determined by arbitration, or, where the work is incorporated in a collective work and the owner of the right or interest is the proprietor of that collective work, without any such payment;

The notice above referred to must be given not more than one year nor less than six months before the date at which the right would have so expired, and must be sent by registered post to the author, or, if he cannot with reasonable diligence be found, advertised in the London Gazette and in two London newspapers:

(*b*) where any person has, before the twenty-sixth day of July nineteen hundred and ten, taken any action whereby he has incurred any expenditure or liability in connexion with the reproduction or performance of any work in a manner which at the time was lawful, or for the purpose of or with a view to the reproduction or performance of a work at a time when such reproduction or performance would, but for the passing of this Act, have been lawful, nothing in this section shall diminish or prejudice any rights or interest arising from or in connexion with such action which are subsisting and valuable at the said date, unless the person who by virtue of this section becomes entitled to restrain such reproduction or performance agrees to pay such

A.D. 1911

compensation as, failing agreement, may be determined by arbitration.

(2) For the purposes of this section, the expression "author" includes the legal personal representatives of a deceased author.

(3) Subject to the provisions of section nineteen subsections (7) and (8) and of section thirty-three of this Act, copyright shall not subsist in any work made before the commencement of this Act, otherwise than under, and in accordance with, the provisions of this section.

Application to British Possessions.

Application of Act to British dominions

25.—(1) This Act, except such of the provisions thereof as are expressly restricted to the United Kingdom, shall extend throughout His Majesty's dominions: Provided that it shall not extend to a self-governing dominion, unless declared by the Legislature of that dominion to be in force therein either without any modifications or additions, or with such modifications and additions relating exclusively to procedure and remedies, or necessary to adapt this Act to the circumstances of the dominion, as may be enacted by such Legislature.

(2) If the Secretary of State certifies by notice published in the London Gazette that any self-governing dominion has passed legislation under which works, the authors whereof were at the date of the making of the works British subjects resident elsewhere than in the dominion or (not being British subjects) were resident in the parts of His Majesty's dominions to which this Act extends, enjoy within the dominion rights substantially identical with those conferred by this Act, then, whilst such legislation continues in force, the dominion shall, for the purposes of the rights conferred by this Act, be treated as if it were a dominion to which this Act extends; and it shall be lawful for the Secretary of State to give such a certificate as aforesaid, notwithstanding that the remedies for enforcing the rights, or the restrictions on the importation of copies of works, manufactured in a foreign country, under the law of the dominion, differ from those under this Act.

Legislative powers of self-governing dominions

26.—(1) The Legislature of any self-governing dominion may, at any time, repeal all or any of the enactments relating to copyright passed by Parliament (including this Act) so far as they are operative within that dominion: Provided that no such repeal shall prejudicially affect any legal rights existing at the time of the repeal, and that, on this Act or any part thereof being so repealed by the Legislature of a self-governing dominion, that dominion shall cease to be a dominion to which this Act extends.

(2) In any self-governing dominion to which this Act does not extend, the enactments repealed by this Act shall, so far as they are operative in that dominion, continue in force until repealed by the Legislature of that dominion.

(3) Where His Majesty in Council is satisfied that the law of a self-governing dominion to which this Act does not extends provides adequate protection within the dominion for the works (whether published or unpublished) of authors who at the time of the making of the work were British subjects resident elsewhere than in that dominion, His Majesty in Council

may, for the purpose of giving reciprocal protection, direct that this Act, except such parts (if any) thereof as may be specified in the Order, and subject to any conditions contained therein, shall, within the parts of His Majesty's dominions to which this Act extends, apply to works the authors whereof were, at the time of the making of the work, resident within the first-mentioned dominion, and to works first published in that dominion; but, save as provided by such an Order, works the authors whereof were resident in a dominion to which this Act does not extend shall not, whether they are British subjects or not, be entitled to any protection under this Act except such protection as is by this Act conferred on works first published within the parts of His Majesty's dominions to which this Act extends: A.D. 1911

Provided that no such Order shall confer any rights within a self-governing dominion, but the Governor in Council of any self-governing dominion to which this Act extends, may, by Order, confer within that dominion the like rights as His Majesty in Council is, under the foregoing provisions of this subsection, authorized to confer within other parts of His Majesty's dominions.

For the purposes of this subsection, the expression "a "dominion to which this Act extends" includes a dominion which is for the purposes of this Act to be treated as if it were a dominion to which this Act extends.

Power of Legislatures of British possessions to pass supplemental legislation

27. The Legislature of any British possession to which this Act extends may modify or add to any of the provisions of this Act in its application to the possession, but, except so far as such modifications and additions relate to procedure and remedies, they shall apply only to works the authors whereof were, at the time of the making of the work, resident in the possession, and to works first published in the possession.

Application to protectorates

28. His Majesty may, by Order in Council, extend this Act to any territories under his protection and to Cyprus, and, on the making of any such Order, this Act shall, subject to the provisions of the Order, have effect as if the territories to which it applies or Cyprus were part of His Majesty's dominions to which this Act extends.

PART II.

INTERNATIONAL COPYRIGHT.

Power to extend Act to foreign works

29.—(1) His Majesty may, by Order in Council, direct that this Act (except such parts, if any, thereof as may be specified in the Order) shall apply—

(*a*) to works first published in a foreign country to which the Order relates, in like manner as if they were first published within the parts of His Majesty's dominions to which this Act extends;

(*b*) to literary, dramatic, musical, and artistic works, or any class thereof, the authors whereof were at the time of the making of the work subjects or citizens of a foreign country to which the order relates, in like manner as if the authors were British subjects;

(*c*) in respect of residence in a foreign country to which the Order relates, in like manner as if such residence were residence in the parts of His Majesty's dominions to which this Act extends;

A.D. 1911

and thereupon, subject to the provisions of this Part of this Act and of the Order, this Act shall apply accordingly:

Provided that—

(i) before making an Order in Council under this section in respect of any foreign country (other than a country with which His Majesty has entered into a convention relating to copyright), His Majesty shall be satisfied that that foreign country has made, or has undertaken to make, such provisions, if any, as it appears to His Majesty expedient to require for the protection of works entitled to copyright under the provisions of Part I. of this Act;

(ii) the Order in Council may provide that the term of copyright within such parts of His Majesty's dominions as aforesaid shall not exceed that conferred by the law of the country to which the Order relates;

(iii) the provisions of this Act as to the delivery of copies of books shall not apply to works first published in such country, except so far as is provided by the Order;

(iv) the Order in Council may provide that the enjoyment of the rights conferred by this Act shall be subject to the accomplishment of such conditions and formalities (if any) as may be prescribed by the Order;

(v) in applying the provision of this Act as to ownership of copyright, the Order in Council may make such modifications as appear necessary having regard to the law of the foreign country;

(vi) in applying the provisions of this Act as to existing works, the Order in Council may make such modifications as appear necessary, and may provide that nothing in those provisions as so applied shall be construed as reviving any right of preventing the production or importation of any translation in any case where the right has ceased by virtue of section five of the International Copyright Act, 1886.

49 & 50 Vict., c. 33

(2) An Order in Council under this section may extend to all the several countries named or described therein.

Application of Part II. to British possessions

30.—(1) An Order in Council under this Part of this Act shall apply to all His Majesty's dominions to which this Act extends except self-governing dominions and any other possession specified in the order with respect to which it appears to His Majesty expedient that the Order should not apply.

(2) The Governor in Council of any self-governing dominion to which this Act extends may, as respects that dominion, make the like orders as under this Part of this Act His Majesty in Council is authorized to make with respect to His Majesty's dominions other than self-governing dominions, and the provisions of this Part of this Act shall, with the necessary modifications, apply accordingly.

(3) Where it appears to His Majesty expedient to except from the provisions of any order any part of his dominions not

being a self-governing dominion, it shall be lawful for His Majesty by the same or any other Order in Council to declare that such order and this Part of this Act shall not, and the same shall not, apply to such part, except so far as is necessary for preventing any prejudice to any rights acquired previously to the date of such Order.

A.D. 1911

Part III.

Supplemental Provisions.

Abrogation of common law rights

31. No person shall be entitled to copyright or any similar right in any literary, dramatic, musical, or artistic work, whether published or unpublished, otherwise than under and in accordance with the provisions of this Act, or of any other statutory enactment for the time being in force, but nothing in this section shall be construed as abrogating any right or jurisdiction to restrain a breach of trust or confidence.

Provisions as to Orders in Council

32.—(1) His Majesty in Council may make Orders for altering, revoking, or varying any Order in Council made under this Act, or under any enactments repealed by this Act, but any Order made under this section shall not affect prejudicially any rights or interests acquired or accrued at the date when the Order comes into operation, and shall provide for the protection of such rights and interests.

(2) Every Order in Council made under this Act shall be published in the London Gazette and shall be laid before both Houses of Parliament as soon as may be after it is made, and shall have effect as if enacted in this Act.

Saving of university copyright. 15 Geo. III, c. 53

33. Nothing in this Act shall deprive any of the universities and colleges mentioned in the Copyright Act, 1775, of any copyright they already possess under that Act, but the remedies and penalties for infringement of any such copyright shall be under this Act and not under that Act.

Saving of compensation to certain libraries

34. There shall continue to be charged on, and paid out of, the Consolidated Fund of the United Kingdom such annual compensation as was immediately before the commencement of this Act payable in pursuance of any Act as compensation to a library for the loss of the right to receive gratuitous copies of books:

Provided that this compensation shall not be paid to a library in any year, unless the Treasury are satisfied that the compensation for the previous year has been applied in the purchase of books for the use of and to be preserved in the library.

Interpretation

35.—(1) In this Act, unless the context otherwise requires,—

"Literary work" includes maps, charts, plans, tables, and compilations;

"Dramatic work" includes any piece for recitation, choreographic work or entertainment in dumb show, the scenic arrangement or acting form of which is fixed in writing or otherwise, and any cinematograph production where the arrangement or acting form or the combination of incidents represented give the work an original character;

"Artistic work" includes works of painting, drawing, sculpture and artistic craftsmanship, and architectural works of art and engravings and photographs;

A.D. 1911

"Work of sculpture" includes casts and models;

"Architectural work of Art" means any building or structure having an artistic character or design, in respect of such character or design, or any model for such building or structure, provided that the protection afforded by this Act shall be confined to the artistic character and design, and shall not extend to processes or methods of construction;

"Engravings" include etchings, lithographs, wood-cuts, prints, and other similar works, not being photographs;

"Photograph" includes photo-lithograph and any work produced by any process analogous to photography;

"Cinematograph" includes any work produced by any process analogous to cinematography;

"Collective work" means—

(*a*) an encyclopaedia, dictionary, year book, or similar work;

(*b*) a newspaper, review, magazine, or similar periodical; and

(*c*) any work written in distinct parts by different authors, or in which works or parts of works of different authors are incorporated;

"Infringing," when applied to a copy of a work in which copyright subsists, means any copy, including any colourable imitation, made, or imported in contravention of the provisions of this Act;

"Performance" means any acoustic representation of a work and any visual representation of any dramatic action in a work, including such a representation made by means of any mechanical instrument;

"Delivery," in relation to a lecture, includes delivery by means of any mechanical instrument;

"Plate" includes any stereotype or other plate, stone, block, mould, matrix, transfer, or negative used or intended to be used for printing or reproducing copies of any work, and any matrix or other appliances by which records, perforated rolls or other contrivances for the acoustic representation of the work are or are intended to be made;

"Lecture" includes address, speech, and sermon;

"Self-governing dominion" means the Dominion of Canada, the Commonwealth of Australia, the Dominion of New Zealand, the Union of South Africa, and Newfoundland.

(2) For the purposes of this Act (other than those relating to infringements of copyright), a work shall not be deemed to be published or performed in public, and a lecture shall not be deemed to be delivered in public, if published, performed in public, or delivered in public, without the consent or acquiescence of the author, his executors administrators or assigns.

(3) For the purposes of this Act, a work shall be deemed to be first published within the parts of His Majesty's dominions to which this Act extends, notwithstanding that it has been published simultaneously in some other place, unless the publication in such parts of His Majesty's dominions as aforesaid is

colourable only and is not intended to satisfy the reasonable requirements of the public, and a work shall be deemed to be published simultaneously in two places if the time between the publication in one such place and the publication in the other place does not exceed fourteen days, or such longer period as may, for the time being, be fixed by Order in Council. A.D. 1911

(4) Where, in the case of an unpublished work, the making of a work has extended over a considerable period, the conditions of this Act conferring copyright shall be deemed to have been complied with, if the author was, during any substantial part of that period, a British subject or a resident within the parts of His Majesty's dominions to which this Act extends.

(5) For the purposes of the provisions of this Act as to residence, an author of a work shall be deemed to be a resident in the parts of His Majesty's dominions to which this Act extends if he is domiciled within any such part.

Repeal

36. Subject to the provisions of this Act, the enactments mentioned in the Second Schedule to this Act are hereby repealed to the extent specified in the third column of that schedule:

Provided that this repeal shall not take effect in any part of His Majesty's dominions until this Act comes into operation in that part.

Short title and commencement

37.—(1) This Act may be cited as the Copyright Act, 1911.

(2) This Act shall come into operation—

(*a*) in the United Kingdom, on the first day of July nineteen hundred and twelve or such earlier date as may be fixed by Order in Council;

(*b*) in a self-governing dominion to which this Act extends, at such date as may be fixed by the Legislature of that dominion;

(*c*) in the Channel Islands, at such date as may be fixed by the States of those islands respectively;

(*b*) in any other British possession to which this Act extends, on the proclamation thereof within the possession by the Governor.

A.D. 1911

Section 24

SCHEDULES.

First Schedule.

Existing Rights.

Existing Right.	Substituted Right.
(a) In the case of Works other than Dramatic and Musical Works.	
Copyright.	Copyright as defined by this Act.*
(b) In the case of Musical and Dramatic Works.	
Both copying and performing right	Copyright as defined by this Act.*
Copyright, but not performing right	Copyright as defined by this Act, except the sole right to perform the work or any substantial part thereof in public.
Performing right, but not copyright	The sole right to perform the work in public, but none of the other rights comprised in copyright as defined by this Act.

For the purposes of this Schedule the following expressions, where used in the first column thereof, have the following meanings:—

" Copyright," in the case of a work which according to the law in force immediately before the commencement of this Act has not been published before that date and statutory copyright wherein depends on publication, includes the right at common law (if any) to restrain publication or other dealing with the work;

" Performing right," in the case of a work which has not been performed in public before the commencement of this Act, includes the right at common law (if any) to restrain the performance thereof in public.

* In the case of an essay, article, or portion forming part of and first published in a review, magazine, or other periodical or work of a like nature, the right shall be subject to any right of publishing the essay, article, or portion in a separate form to which the author is entitled at the commencement of this Act, or would, if this Act had not been passed, have become entitled under section eighteen of the Copyright Act, 1842.

Second Schedule

A.D. 1911

Section 36

Enactments Repealed.

Session and Chapter.	Short Title.	Extent of Repeal.
8 Geo.2. c. 13	The Engraving Copyright Act, 1734.	The whole Act.
7 Geo.3. c. 38	The Engraving Copyright Act, 1767.	The whole Act.
15 Geo. 3 c. 53.	The Copyright Act, 1775	The whole Act.
17 Geo. 3. c. 57.	The Prints Copyright Act, 1777.	The whole Act.
54 Geo. 3. c. 56.	The Sculpture Copyright Act, 1814.	The whole Act.
3 & 4 Will. 4. c. 15.	The Dramatic Copyright Act, 1833.	The whole Act.
5 & 6 Will. 4. c. 65.	The Lectures Copyright Act, 1835.	The whole Act.
6 & 7 Will. 4. c. 59.	The Prints and Engravings Copyright (Ireland) Act, 1836.	The whole Act.
6 & 7 Will. 4. c. 110.	The Copyright Act, 1836	The whole Act.
5 & 6 Vict., c. 45.	The Copyright Act, 1842	The whole Act.
7 & 8 Vict., c. 12.	The International Copyright Act, 1844.	The whole Act.
10 & 11 Vict., c. 95.	The Colonial Copyright Act, 1847.	The whole Act.
15 & 16 Vict., c. 12.	The International Copyright Act, 1852.	The whole Act.
25 & 26 Vict., c. 68.	The Fine Arts Copyright Act, 1862.	Sections one to six. In section eight the words " and pursuant to any " Act for the protec- " tion of copyright en- " gravings," and "and " in any such Act as " aforesaid." Sections nine to twelve.
38 & 39 Vict., c. 12.	The International Copyright Act, 1875.	The whole Act.
39 & 40 Vict., c. 36.	The Customs Consolidation Act, 1876.	Sections forty-two, from " Books wherein " to " such copyright will expire." Sections forty four, forty-five, and one hundred and fifty-two.

A.D. 1911

Section 36

Session and Chapter.	Short Title.	Extent of Repeal.
45 & 46 Vict., c. 40.	The Copyright (Musical Compositions) Act, 1882.	The whole Act.
49 & 50 Vict., c. 33.	The International Copyright Act, 1886.	The whole Act.
51 & 52 Vict., c. 17.	The Copyright (Musical Compositions) Act, 1888.	The whole Act.
52 & 53 Vict., c. 42.	The Revenue Act, 1889	Section one, from "Books first published" to "as provided in that section."
6 Edw. 7. c. 36.	The Musical Copyright Act, 1906.	In section three the words "and which has "been registered in "accordance with the "provisions of the "Copyright Act, 1842, "or of the International Copyright Act, "1844, which registration may be effected notwithstanding "anything in the International Copyright Act, 1886."

INDEX

NOTE.—An index to a book should be something more than a mere list of the subjects discussed in the book. An index should be a good key to the contents, and should also be useful as a digest of the contents. Furthermore an index should be worth inspecting for ideas which it may suggest to an Inquirer.

ABILITY required, 21, 75, 127; may deteriorate, 56
Absence of any accepted basis of valuing, 106
Accountant's practice, 37
Accounting value of goodwill no guide to present value, 45, 91; permanent value fallacy, 77; treatment in accounts, 77–92
Accounts, only purchased goodwill is recorded in, 23; treatment in accounts of purchased goodwill, 77–92
Administration expenses, prodigal increase in, 75
Advertising, 33, 57
Agent's connection, 38
Alert purchaser, 25, 35, 72
Alienation of commercial goodwill for debt, 15
Amalgamations, danger of, 56
Amazing stories of success, 121
Analysis of British national capital, 132–137
Ancient use of the term "goodwill," 1
Annual drawings, 86, 92
—— provision to write off cost of goodwill needed, 25, 77–92
annuity value as a guide to value of goodwill, 20
10% three years' constant, 27
method of computing value, 28
20% three years' constant, 28
20% three years' diminishing, 29
difference in value is small between 20 years and 100 years' 10% annuity, 56
ditto ditto 20% annuity, 57
price varies with term of years and rate of interest, 80

Annual (*contd.*)—
difference between annuity and lease, 95
tables, 144–156
Anticipation, value of goodwill based on, v, 55, 61, 101
Appendices, 143–250
Appropriating profits in advance, 79
Architect's practice, 37
"As going-concern" valuations, 104
Author's work, 101
Average capital, 50

BALANCE sheet of limited company, 58
difficulty of judging value of shares from, 62
purchased goodwill as permanent asset, 78
suggested note of present value of goodwill, 91
values, 59, 78, 91
Banking connection, 32
Bankruptcy, trustee in, 15
Bargain should be adhered to, 86
Barrister's practice, 37
Barter, 127, 139
Baseless rumours, 62
Bases of plant valuation: three, [108
Basis
of value of goodwill, 19, 22, 104
of national capital valuations, 125
Bear operations in shares, 58
Bonus shares, 119, 121
Book debts, value of, 25, 62
—— value of goodwill no guide to present value, 45
British national capital, 127–142
—— —— debt (*see* National debt)

Brock & Co. *v.* Pain, 11
Buildings—
value of, 25, 62
as capital, 125
Bulk of value of goodwill not recorded in accounts, 23
Bull operations in shares, 58
Business connection, goodwill includes, v
——, definition of, 3
—— organizer's work, 101

Canvassing old customers, 17
Capital—
in permanent form should not be issued for goodwill, vii, 44, 82
when small, 33
in professional practices, 39
further capital needed by company, 63
invested or risked, 122
definition of, 125
Capitalization of income-tax statistics, 127
Certificates of value, 105
Change of public taste or custom, 34, 56, 71, 117
Changing conditions, 26, 34, 56, 71
Character of British national capital, 132
Cinema company prospectus, 115
Circular or prospectus, 119
Classes of enterprise, distinctions between, 35
Colonial government securities, 126, 137
Common law, goodwill protected by, v, 2
Commercial goodwill (*see* Goodwill)
Commodity, character of money, 110, 127
Common stock, 119
Company prospectus pitfalls, 104–124
Comparison—
value of 20 years and of 100 years 10% annuity, 56
ditto ditto 20% annuity, 57
life of business with life of man, 71
goodwill purchased with goodwill created, 78
annuity and lease 95
Competing business 5, 14, 15, 21, 56, 71
Competitor, 14, 21, 26, 71
Concession outside United Kingdom, 102
Connection of customers, 2
without exchangeable value may be highly prized, 22
Consideration for purchased goodwill redeemable form of security, 92
Contractor's connection, 38
Co-operation of capital and human effort, 139
Copyright—
goodwill includes, v
Copyright Act, 1911, vi, 2, 12, 229–247
alienation for debt, 15
without exchangeable value may be highly prized, 22
Cost of production, advertising, and selling, 57
Creation of goodwill, 23, 78, 101
Creditors as a set off against debtors, 126
Criticism of usual form of definition of goodwill, 2
Crown, rights of, to use invention, 9
Crutwell *v.* Lye, earliest reported decision on goodwill, 2
Cumulative preferred stock, 119
Currency inflation, 110, 126

Danger of great amalgamations, 56
Death of partner, 38, 40, 50
Debentures for purchased goodwill, 82, 86
and participating preference shares, 116
Debts, 25, 62, 126
Decay, signs of, 71
Decreasing profits and purchased goodwill, 77
Deferred debentures for purchased goodwill, 82, 86, 92
—— payment for goodwill, 43
—— shares, 104, 112–124
Definitions—
goodwill, vii, 2
Lord Eldon's, of goodwill, 2
trade, 3
business, 3

Definitions (*contd.*)—
monopoly, 5
invention, 7
trade name, 9
trade mark, 10
Lord Macnaughton's and others, of goodwill, 13, 14
Super-profit, 19
economic expenditure, 20
private undertaking, 37
public company, 55
normal development, 68
capital existing, 125
present exchangeable value, 126
Degree of risk, rate of interest depends on, 21
Demand of public may slacken or cease, 26
Dentist's practice, 37
Depreciation—
and wasting assets, 110, 131
of investments, 51
of plant, measurement of, 109
Descriptive circular or prospectus, 119
Designs—
goodwill includes, v
registration of, 9
Deterioration of directing ability 56
Diminishing accounting value of purchased goodwill, 26, 33, 39, 40, 77
Directing ability, 68
may deteriorate, 56
Directors accepting office without sufficient thought, 20
Disadvantages of old method of valuing goodwill, 53
Discriminating investor, 25, 35, 72
Dissolution of partnership, 17, 38, 39, 40
Dockyards as capital, 126
Doctor's practice, 33, 37
Drawings, annual, 86, 92

Earlier existing goodwill, cost should be gradually written off, 77
East India merchants' and agents' business, 41
Economic expenditure, meaning of, 20
—— meaning of the term "goodwill," v
—— unit of size in industry, 57
Efficient life of plant, 106
Effort (past) in seeking profit, v, 2, 19, 33
Eldon, Lord, definition of goodwill, 2
Eminent practitioner, 38
Enterprising management, 75
Established connection, where super-profit arises out of, 32, 55, 63
Estate duty statistics, 141
Exceptions to rule governing exchangeable value of goodwill, 21
Excess profits duty, 51
Exchangeable materials and commodities represent existing capital, 126, 139
Exchangeable value—
goodwill may or may not have, v, 19
in terms of gold standard, 111
Executors of deceased partner, 40, 50
Existing business, 2
Expired capital outlay, 19, 58, 62, 77
and income tax, 93, 131

Factories, etc., 104
—— as capital, 125
Factors to be regarded in valuing goodwill, 24
Fall in annual profits, 56, 70
Farmers' capital, 133
Fashion, change of, 34, 56
Floating assets of limited company, 58, 62
Fluctuating—
profits, 71, 89
interest, 92
cost of material and labour, 106
Forced sale of goodwill, 38, 52
Foreign government securities, 126, 137
—— vendor, 103
Founders' shares, 112
Freedom of trade, 3
Freehold land, 105

Fully-paid shares, 111
Furniture as capital, 126, 128, 134
Future income tax, 36, 40, 41, 47, 51, 52, 53, 66, 103
Future probabilities—
  value of goodwill depends upon, 20
  may deteriorate though profits increase, 55, 77
Future production, 137
—— super-profit, 19, 55, 91, 103

GAMBLING instinct, 57
Gilt-edged securities, normal interest sometimes 5 per cent., 24
Going-concern profits, basis value, 109
—— value, 104–107
Gold standard of value, 110, 126, 139
Good reputation, a form of goodwill, 1
Goodwill—
  is legal property, v, 1
  is generally assumed to possess exchangeable value, v
  acquired either by industry or by purchase, vi
  legal meaning is restricted, vi
  old definition of, 2
  new definition of, vii, 2
  value is present value of future super-profit, vii, 19, 25
  permanent share capital issued for, is wrong, vii, 44
  value of goodwill included in plant valuations, viii, 106
  early obscurity of, 1
  ancient use of the term, 1
  Lord Eldon's definition of, 2
  Lord Macnaughton's and others' definitions 13, 14
  personal and local, 14
  attached to premises, 14
  position of vendor of, 14
  alienation for debt, 15
  dissolution of partnership, 17
  wild estimates of value, 19
  without exchangeable value may be highly prized, 22
  super-profit theory of value, 22
Goodwill (*contd.*)—
  only purchased goodwill is recorded in accounts, 23
  factors in valuing, 24
  effect of interest on value, 29, 31
  varying conditions out of which value may arise, 31
  diminishing by equal sums, 33
  most valuable kinds, 34
  income-tax factor, 36, 93
  private undertakings, 37–54
  professional practice, 39
  deferred payment for, 43
  public companies, 55–76
  what part of premium on shares due to ? 59
  treatment in accounts, 77–92
  company-prospectus pitfalls, 112–124
  included in valuations of national capital, 125–142
Governing directors, 51
Government property as capital, 126, 134
Great amalgamations, 56, 68
Growing crops, 133
Guilds of traders abolished in 1835, 4

" HEADS I win, tails you lose," 123
Hidden reserve, 61
History of goodwill, 1–18
—— industrial plant, 110
Houses, value of, in the United Kingdom, 133
Human effort, unit, 127
—— life period compared with super-profit period, 80

ILLUSTRATIONS, vii
  10% three years' constant annuity, 27
  20% three years' constant annuity, 28
  20% three years' diminishing annuity, 29
  effect of interest on value of goodwill, 29, 31
  effect of income tax factor, 36
  retirement of partner, 39
  death of partner, 40
  partnership converted into limited liability company, 42

Illustrations (*contd.*)—
deferred payment for goodwill, 43
private limited company, death of one of two shareholders, 50
market quotation of shares at a premium, 58
issue of shares at a premium, 63
tests of stock exchange values, 69–76
writing off cost of purchased goodwill, 84–90
difference between annuity and lease, 95
goodwill included in plant valuation, 107
of manufacturing company prospectus, 112, 118
of cinema and café company prospectus, 115
Imitators attracted by superprofit, 26
Impersonal connection, 38
Importers and exporters of chemicals, 50
Income tax, 36, 40, 41, 47, 51, 52, 53, 66, 74
and purchased goodwill, 93–103
wrongly assessed on whole amount of annuity, 99
statistics, 127
Increase in administration expenses, 75
Increasing profits and purchased goodwill, 77
Indian government securities, 126, 137
Industrial enterprise, normal interest 10%, 24
—— organizer's work, 101
—— plant, 94, 104–110
Industry or production, capital employed in, 125, 136
Inflated income-tax statistics, 141–2
Inflation of currency, 110, 126
pre-war absence of, 139
Inherently wasting assets, 93, 104–110
Insurance company, value of shares, 73
—— connection, 32
Interest—
factor limits period of value of goodwill, 56, 80
normal rate of, 19
effect of, on value of goodwill, 29, 31
in professions less than in trades, 33
10% in trades, 34, 56–81
20% in speculative ventures, 35, 57, 81
and income-tax statistics, 131
Invention, meaning of, 7
Inventories of plant, 107
Inventory method of valuing national capital, 141
Inventor's work, 101
Investments—
depreciation of, 51
annuity and lease compared, 95

JOINT-stock enterprise, need of sounder finance, 90, 92

LABOUR, fluctuating cost of, 106
Land, 61, 105, 125
income-tax on annual value, 94
value of, in the United Kingdom, 133
Large undertakings, 56
Laws of England, vii
Leake's Register of Industrial Plant, 109
Leaseholds, 62
income tax on annual value, 94
compared with annuity, 95
Legal goodwill, vi, 2, 13, 15
—— meaning of goodwill, 2, 13
—— property, goodwill is, v
Leisure or consumption, capital employed for, 125, 136
Letters patent, 6
Life annuities, 94
Limitations to method of valuing national capital, 129
Limited participation preference shares, 111
Limit in years, 32, 34, 55, 56
Local goodwill, 14
—— loans, 126, 134
—— property as capital, 126, 134

Location of British national capital, 132
Long-distance estimates, 59
Losses, treatment of, in income tax statistics, 130
Lumping together values is unsatisfactory, 106

MAGNA Charta, 3
Management, remuneration for, 19
Manufacture, cost of, 57
Manufactured goods as capital, 125
Manufacturer's connection, 38
Manufacturing company prospectus, 112, 118
Market quotation of shares, 58, 91
Material or commodity—
all inherently wasting assets consist of, 94, 98
fluctuating cost of, 106
represents existing capital, 125
Mathematical interest tables, 41
Maturity of a business, 71
Measurement—
of value of goodwill, 80
of value of plant, 109
Medical practice, 33, 37
Merchant's connection, 38
Merchant Shipping Act, 1894, 4
Mills, factories, etc., 104
as capital, 125
Mines as capital, 125
Minimum wage of money, 24
Money—
can always obtain normal interest, 23
is a commodity, 95, 110
as capital, 126, 134, 137
Money, Sir L. Chiozza, 129, 134
Monopolies—
goodwill includes, v
Crown cannot generally grant, 3
definition, 5
Municipal Corporations Act, 1835, 4

NATIONAL capital valuations—
include value of goodwill, viii, 125–142
difficulties of future, 141
National debt, 126, 134, 141
—— telephone arbitration, 106
Natural raw materials, 94
Nature of goodwill, 1
New inventions, 26, 33, 35, 55
—— partners, 41
—— profit-seeking undertaking, 32, 35, 55
—— shares at a premium, 63
No common agreement on accounting treatment of purchased goodwill, 77
Nominal value shares, 104
"No par value" shares, 104, 118
Normal development, 68
Normal rate of interest, 19, 140
10% in trade not excessive, 34
20% in speculative ventures, 35
"Nothing is paid for goodwill," 105
Number of years' purchase, limit of, 34

OLD customers, 2
canvassing, 17
Old Metal Dealers Act, 1861, 4
—— writers, 1
Omissions from prospectus, 122
Optimistic statements in prospectus, 121
Ordinary business aptitude, 33, 34
—— shares, 59, 64, 77
issued fully paid, 111
Organizing ability, 57
Origin of goodwill, 1
Owners' services, 80

PARTICIPATING preference shares, 65
ranking between debentures and deferred shares, 115
Partnership—
converted into limited liability company, 41
dissolution of, 17, 38, 39
death of partner, 40
plan for writing off purchased goodwill, 89
Partners' services, 39
Past profits as guide to the future, 20, 91

Patents—
goodwill includes, v
meaning of the word, 7
alienation for debt, 15
wild estimates of value, 19
without exchangeable value may be highly prized, 22
new undertakings, 33, 55
Patents and Designs Act, 1907, vi, 2, 6, 175–209
Patents and Designs Act, 1919, vi, 2, 6, 210–228
Payment for purchased goodwill, 77
Period over which value of goodwill has arisen, 78
Permanent share capital, issued for goodwill is wrong, vii, 82
Perpetuity—
super-profit is not, 26, 34, 45, 55
with interest at 10%, 95% of present value expires in thirty-one years, 81
Personal goodwill, 14
Personal skill—
where super-profit dependent on, 32, 37, 39
where super-profit not dependent on, 68
Personal view of valuer, 106
Phenomenal developments, stories of, 121
Pitfalls for the investor, 104–124
Place-name as trade mark, 10, 11
Plant and machinery, value of, 25, 62
Plant valuations—
include sometimes value of goodwill, viii
three distinct bases, 108
Popular tastes, habits and customs, 32, 34
Preference shares, 59, 64
limited participation, 111
ranking between debentures and deferred shares, 115
Preliminary expenses, 51
Premium—
for purchase of lease compared with value of goodwill, 23
share quotations at a, 58
shares issued at a, 63
on shares may be distributed as dividend, 66
Premium (*contd.*)—
on shares not assessable to income tax, 66
rule for ascertaining value of goodwill involved, 66
Present exchangeable value, 126
—— goodwill worth next to nothing twenty years ago, 78
Price paid for purchased goodwill, 79
Private dwellings as capital, 126, 133
Private undertakings and goodwill, 37–54
valuing goodwill of, 38
private limited company, death of one of two partners, 50
plan for writing off purchased goodwill, 89
Probability of new inventions, 57
Produce broker's connection, 38
Production, cost of, 57
future, 137
Professional practices, 37, 39
Profit-seeking undertakings—
varying conditions of, 31
of world-renown, 34
Profits—
over-stated, 62
decreasing, 56, 70, 77
greater accuracy needed in computing, 110
estimates of, 112–124
taken by vendors, 111–124
Property—
goodwill is legal, v
not yielding income, 128
Proprietor's services, 80
Prospectus—
wild estimates contained in, 20, 57
caution needed, 104
of manufacturing company, 112, 118
of cinema and café company, [115
Public buildings as capital, 126
—— companies and goodwill, 55–76
—— company prospectus pitfalls, 104–124
—— Health Acts Amendment Act, 1907, 4
—— taste or custom, change of, 32, 34

Publisher's connection, 38
Purchased goodwill—
only, recorded in accounts, 23
treatment in accounts, 77–92
compared with created goodwill, 78
permanent share capital for, wrong, 82
and income tax, 93–103, 140
Purchaser of goodwill, deferred position of, 25

Qualified practitioner, 21

Railways as capital, 125
Ratio of administration expenses, 75
Raw materials, 94
Reasoning faculties in valuing goodwill, 80, 91
Record in accounts of purchased goodwill, 77–92
Redeemable securities for purchased goodwill, 82, 86, 92
Redemption of stock, 118, 120
Redistribution of wealth, 141
Register of wasting assets, 107, 109
Remuneration for management, 19
Repayment of share capital illegal, 82
Reserves, 60, 64, 69, 78
hidden, 61
overstated, 62
investment, 74
Residual value, 106
Restraint of trade by custom, by statute, 4
by agreement, 5
Retailer's connection, 38
Retail stores connection, 32
value of shares, 69
Retirement of partner, 38, 39
Rights—
goodwill consists wholly of, v, 2
growing out of past effort, vi, 2
of Crown, 9
without exchangeable value may be highly prized, 22
purchase of rights to future profits, 93
of different classes of shares, 104
Risk—
rate of interest depends on degree of, 21, 81
in professions less than in trades, 33
Rival businesses, 56
Rough-and-ready estimates of value of goodwill, 19, 79
Rule-of-thumb price-fixing, 80

"Safe as the Bank of England," 70
Sale of business implies sale of legal goodwill, 15
—— of goodwill to remaining partner, 39
Schemes for writing off purchased goodwill, 82–90
Selling, cost of, 57
Shaft sinking, 94
Share capital—
permanent form for goodwill is wrong, vii, 82
repayment illegal, 82
Shareholders—
resent writing off purchased goodwill, 78
more information needed by, 90
Shares issued at a premium, 63
Share-market manipulation, 62
Shares issued fully paid, 111
Share values, 53, 58, 91
Shipbroker's connection, 38
Shipping as capital, 125
Signs of decay, 71
Sinking fund, 118, 120–123
Skill, special, sometimes needed in profit-seeking, 21, 37
Small businesses, 38
Solicitor's practice, 33, 37
Sound finance, 50, 86
need for adoption of rules, 90
Spasmodic writing off unsatisfactory, 77
Special knowledge and qualifications sometimes needed in profit-seeking, 21, 33
Speculative property, 25, 34, 81
Stamp, C. B. E., D.Sc., Sir J., 125, 129, 131, 135, 139
Standard gold, 127
Statistics of income tax, 127–131
Statute law, commercial goodwill protected by, v
—— of monopolies, 6

Statutory profits, 129
Stimulus to good work provided by sound finance, 50
Stock-broker's connection, 38
Stock Exchange values tested—
  great retail business, 69
  insurance company, 73
Stock-in-trade, value of, 25, 62
Stock subscription agreement, 119
Super-profit, vii, 19
  theory of value, 22
  can never exist permanently, 26, 81
  varying conditions out of which may arise, 31
  most valuable kind, 34
  income-tax factor, 36
  period uncertain but limited, 80
Supply and demand, 127
Supposed reserve may be a myth, 62
Surgeon's practice, 37
Surname as trade mark, 12
Surveyor's practice, 37
Surviving value, 38

TABLES—
  illustrating rule as to value of goodwill when shares issued at a premium, 67
  showing number of years required to write off cost of goodwill, 83
  showing vendor's share of future super-profit, 85
  showing difference between annuity and lease, 96
  summary of constant and diminishing annuities, 145
  constant annuity at rates 12½% to 20%, 146–7
  diminishing annuity at rates 4% to 20%, 148–156
Taste, change of, 34, 56
Temporary character of super-profit, 26
Term of patent, 7
Test—
  against old method of valuing goodwill, 52
  of Stock Exchange values of great retail business, 69
  of Stock Exchange values of insurance company, 73
" Then-value " of plant, 25, 105–107
Theory of future super-profit, 22
Trade—
  definition of, 3
  normal interest 10%, 34, 56, 81
Trade marks—
  goodwill includes, v
  definition of, 10
  place name as, 11
  surname as, 12
  alienation for debt, 15
  without exchangeable value may be highly prized, 22
  most valuable connection, 34, 55, 68
  Trade Marks Act, 1905, v, 2, 10
  text of Act, 157–174
Trade name—
  definition of, 9
  as trade mark, 10
  alienation for debt, 15
  without exchangeable value may be highly prized, 22
  most valuable connection, 34, 55, 68
Tramways arbitration, 106
Transfer—
  of legal goodwill, 15
  of rights to future profits, 100
Treatment in accounts of purchased goodwill, 77–92
Trustee in bankruptcy, 15

UNCALLED capital, 74
Undistributed profits, 58, 64
Unexpired capital outlay, 106
Unexplored sources of super-profit, 34, 57
Unit of human effort, 127
United Kingdom —
  vendor of goodwill outside, 102
  capital inside and outside, 125
Unknown factors in new undertaking, 57
Use of name of old firm, 16

VALUATION of plant—
should disregard volume of profit arising, 107
three distinct bases, 108
Value—
basis of valuing, 104, 106
British national capital, 127–142
value of goodwill, 19
is fair present value of future super-profit, 25
effect of interest upon, 29, 31
varying conditions out of which value may arise, 31
income tax factor, 36
of private undertakings, 37–54
of professional practice, 39
deferred payment for, 43
private limited company, death of one of two shareholders, 50
of public companies, 55–76
rule for ascertaining value of goodwill involved when shares issued at a premium, 66
tests of Stock Exchange values, 69–76
treatment in accounts, 77–92
included in valuations of plant, 106
and valuations of national capital, 125–142
Valuer's certificates, 105
Varying conditions out of which super-profit arises, 31
Vast extent of goodwill, 1, 23
Vendor of goodwill, 14
wild estimates of value, 19
secured position of, 25
personal services of, 38
outside United Kingdom, 102
Vendor's shares, 111–124
Voting rights, 120

WAGE of money, 24
Wasting assets, 19, 25, 58, 59
two distinct classes, 93
and income-tax statistics, 131
Wealth, redistribution of, 141
Wearing apparel as capital, 134
Wild estimates of value of patents, 19, 57
Willing seller and buyer, 38
Working proprietors, 37
Works of art as capital, 134
World-wide connection, 68, 70
Written off—
cost of purchased goodwill should be, vii, 77
schemes for gradual writing off of cost of goodwill, viii, 77–92
writing off resented by shareholders, 78

YEARS' purchase, limit of number, 34, 55, 56, 80

Printed by Sir Isaac Pitman & Sons, Ltd., Bath, England
W—(1790)

DIMENSIONS OF ACCOUNTING THEORY AND PRACTICE

An Arno Press Collection

The American Association of University Instructors in Accounting. **Papers and Proceedings of the American Association of University Instructors in Accounting.** 1916-1925

Baily, Francis. **The Doctrine of Interest and Annuities.** 1808

Beckett, Thomas. **The Accountant's Assistant.** 1901

Blough, Carman G. **Practical Applications of Accounting Standards.** 1957

Bray, F[rank] Sewell. **Precision and Design in Accountancy.** 1947

Brief, Richard P., editor. **Dicksee's Contribution to Accounting Theory and Practice.** 1980

Brinton, Willard C. **Graphic Methods For Presenting Facts.** 1914

Brooks, Collin, editor. **The Royal Mail Case.** 1933

Burns, Thomas J. and Edward N. Coffman, editors. **Ohio State Institute of Accounting Conferences: Collected Papers, 1938-1963.** 1980

By a Chartered Accountant and William A. Vawter Foundation on Business Ethics. **The Etiquette of the Accountancy Profession and The Ethical Problems of Modern Accountancy.** 1927/1933

Carey, John L. **Professional Ethics of Public Accounting.** 1946

Cerboni, Giuseppe. **Primi Saggi Di Logismografia Presentati All' XI Congresso Degli Scienziati Italiani In Roma.** 1873

Cleveland, Frederick A. **Chapters on Municipal Administration and Accounting.** 1909

Cocke, Sir Hugh. **A Summary of the Principal Legal Decisions Affecting Auditors.** 1946

Cotter, Arundel. **Fool's Profits.** 1940

Courcelle-Seneuil, J.G. **Traité Élémentaire de Comptabilité.** 1869

Daniels, Mortimer B. **Corporation Financial Statements.** 1934

DeMond, C.W. **Price, Waterhouse & Company in America.** 1951

Devine, Carl Thomas. **Inventory Valuation and Periodic Income.** 1942

Dicksee, Lawrence Robert. **Business Methods and the War** with **The Fundamentals of Manufacturing Costs;** and **Published Balance Sheets and Window Dressing.** 1916/1927, 1928

Dicksee, Lawrence Robert. **Business Organisation.** 1910

Dicksee, Lawrence Robert and Editor of the Accountant's Library. **Fraudulent Accounting** and **Fraud in Accounts.** 1909/1924, 1925

Edwards, J.R., editor. **British Company Legislation and Company Accounts, 1844-1976.** 1980

Ficker, Nicholas Thiel. **Shop Expense.** 1917

Goldberg, Louis. **An Inquiry Into the Nature of Accounting.** 1965

Green, David, Jr. **Accounting for Corporate Retained Earnings.** 1980

Greene, Catharine De Motte. **The Dynamic Balance Sheet.** 1980

Hain, Hans Peter. **Uniformity and Diversity.** 1980

Hawawini, Gabriel A., and Ashok Vora, editors. **The History of Interest Approximations.** 1980

Hepworth, Samuel Richard. **Reporting Foreign Operations.** 1956

The Herwood Library of Accountancy. 1938

The Institute of Chartered Accountants in England and Wales *Library Catalogue, 1913.* 1913

The Institute of Chartered Accountants in England and Wales **Library Catalogue, 1937.** 1937

Het Internationaal Accountantscongres, Amsterdam 1926. 1927

Johnson, H. Thomas, editor. **System and Profits: Early Management Accounting at DuPont and General Motors.** 1980

King, George. **The Theory of Finance.** 1882

Langenderfer, Harold Q. **The Federal Income Tax: 1861-1872.** 1980

Leake, P.D. **Commercial Goodwill.** 1921

Leautey, Eugene and Adolfe Guilbaut. **La Science Des Comptes Mise A La Portée De Tous.** 1889

Levy, Saul. **Accountants' Legal Responsibility.** 1954

Lubell, Myron Samuel. **The Significance of Organizational Conflict on the Legislative Evolution of the Accounting Profession in the United States.** 1980

Marchi, Francesco. **I Cinquecontisti.** 1867

Merino, Barbara, editor. **Business Income and Price Levels.** 1980

Norris, Harry. **Accounting Theory.** 1946

O'Neill, Michael T., editor. **A.P. Richardson: The Ethics of a Humanist.** 1980

Parker, R.H., editor. **Bibliographies for Accounting Historians.** 1980

Parker, R.H., editor. **British Accountants: A Biographical Sourcebook.** 1980

Perera, M.H.B. **Accounting for State Industrial and Commercial Enterprises in a Developing Country.** 1980

Previts, Gary John. **A Critical Evaluation of Comparative Financial Accounting Thought in America 1900 to 1920.** 1980

Rich, Wiley Daniel. **Legal Responsibilities and Rights of Public Accountants.** 1935

Richardson, A[lphyon] P[erry], editor. **The Influence of Accountants' Certificates on Commercial Credit.** 1913

Roberts, Alfred R., editor. **Selected Papers of Earle C. King.** 1980

Saliers, Earl A. **Principles of Depreciation.** 1915

Schiff, Michael, editor. **The Hayden Stone Accounting Forums 1962-1967.** 1980

Schmalenbach, Eugen. **Dynamic Accounting.** 1959

Scovell, Clinton H. **Cost Accounting and Burden Application.** 1916

Sprague, T[homas] B[ond]. **A Treatis on Life Insurance Accounts** and **A Treatise on Insurance Companies' Accounts** 1874/1911

Stacey, Nicholas A.H., **English Accountancy 1800-1954.** 1954

Stamp, Edward, G.W. Dean, and P.W. Wolnizer, editors. **Notable Financial Causes Célèbres.** 1980

Staubus, George J. **An Accounting Concept of Revenue.** 1980

Taylor, R. Emmett. **No Royal Road.** 1942

Todhunter, Ralph. **Institute of Actuaries' Text-Book of the Principles of Interest, Life Annuities, and Assurances, and Their Practical Application.** 1901

Wells, Murry C., editor. **Controversies on the Theory of the Firm, Overhead Allocation and Transfer Pricing.** 1980

Wildman, John R. and Weldon Powell. **Capital Stock Without Par Value.** 1928